Constraining Public Libraries

The World Trade Organization's General Agreement on Trade in Services

Samuel E. Trosow
Kirsti Nilsen

THE SCARECROW PRESS, INC.
Lanham, Maryland • Toronto • Oxford
2006

SCARECROW PRESS, INC.

Published in the United States of America
by Scarecrow Press, Inc.
A wholly owned subsidiary of
The Rowman & Littlefield Publishing Group, Inc.
4501 Forbes Boulevard, Suite 200, Lanham, Maryland 20706
www.scarecrowpress.com

PO Box 317
Oxford
OX2 9RU, UK

British Library Cataloguing in Publication Information Available

Library of Congress Cataloging-in-Publication Data

Trosow, Samuel E.
Constraining public libraries : the World Trade Organization's General Agreement on Trade in Services / Samuel E. Trosow and Kristi Nilsen.
p. cm.
Includes bibliographical references and index.
ISBN-13: 978-0-8108-5237-2 (pbk. : alk. paper)
ISBN-10: 0-8108-5237-3 (pbk. : alk. paper)
1. Public libraries—Government policy. 2. Information services—Government policy. 3. Public libraries—Finance. 4. Information services—Finance. 5. General Agreement on Trade in Services (1994). 6. Service industries—Government policy. 7. International trade. 8. Information policy—Economic aspects. I. Nilsen, Kirsti, 1938– II. Title.
Z678.T76 2006
027.4—dc22 2006003653

∞™ The paper used in this publication meets the minimum requirements of American National Standard for Information Sciences—Permanence of Paper for Printed Library Materials, ANSI/NISO Z39.48-1992.
Manufactured in the United States of America.

Contents

Foreword

"What has the World Trade Organization (WTO) got to do with libraries?" I first had that question put to me at a Canadian Government NGO briefing during the 1999 WTO Ministerial in Seattle. Not a surprising question, perhaps, as a first reaction to the presence of library association representatives amid hundreds of lobbyists for agricultural and natural-resource interests. And of course there were the thousands on the streets protesting the impact of WTO decisions on the environment, the economies of developing countries, the security of union jobs in developed countries, the spread of sweatshops. It was little wonder that libraries were not a topic on people's minds when any mention of intellectual property was invariably a preamble to a discussion on drug patents.

Seven years later there is increasing awareness within the international library community that trade treaties do have the potential to impede, perhaps undermine, the operations of public-sector libraries. But there is still a lot of uncertainty given the complexities and proliferation of bilateral, regional, and international agreements, which may or may not have implications for our institutions. By focusing on public libraries and the General Agreement on Trade in Services (GATS) in particular, *Constraining Public Libraries* provides a concise and clear analysis of how the annex on services to the WTO agreement could harm the financial and regulatory underpinnings of the public library.

Nilsen and Trosow do an excellent job of providing an international context for major decisions that confront many library boards and their communities. The potential implications of user fees, outsourcing, and corporate sponsorship in light of GATS are troubling and should be carefully considered by any library contemplating changes in these areas.

Assessing the implications of trade treaties involves much ambiguity and uncertainty. Assertions about protections for public-sector agencies such as not-for-profit libraries are often untested. Indeed, that is extolled by some as a good thing in that binding panel rulings on the supposed exemptions for the broad public sector may interpret them very narrowly. While there cannot be certainty when considering how GATS will ultimately impinge upon public libraries, this book pinpoints potential problem areas.

The question "What has this got to do with libraries?" is still too often asked by trade officials, librarians, and trustees. Kirsti Nilsen and Sam Trosow's *Constraining Public Libraries* provides many of the answers. It will be a valuable tool in informing the dialogue within public libraries on the WTO in general, and GATS in particular, and providing the foundation for effective advocacy at the domestic and international levels to ensure that public libraries continue to play a central role in their communities for generations to come.

Paul Whitney
City Librarian
Vancouver Public Library

Preface

Although this is a coauthored book, it is not a work of joint authorship. Our approach has been to divide the subject matter of the book between us. Although we read, commented on, and approved each other's contributions, we were each ultimately responsible for our separate chapters. Samuel E. Trosow is the author of chapters 1, 2, 3, and 7, and Kirsti Nilsen is the author of chapters 4, 5, 6, and 8.

We are grateful for the outstanding research and editorial assistance provided by Sabina Iseli-Otto, an MLIS candidate at The University of Western Ontario. We appreciate as well the comments of anonymous readers. This project was supported by research grants from the Faculty of Information and Media Studies at UWO and by the American Association of Law Libraries. We are indebted to the members of the Canadian Library Association, who have been at the forefront of understanding the relationship between GATS and public libraries.

1

Introduction: What Has GATS Got to Do with Libraries?

This book explores the means by which the World Trade Organization's General Agreement on Trade in Services (GATS)[1] has the potential to impact government policies, programs, and funding arrangements for public library services. We seek to answer several interrelated questions about the GATS, such as what it is, what it does, why librarians and their associations should be concerned about it, and finally, what can be done to ameliorate some of the risks that international trade agreements like GATS pose to public library services.

Assessment of these risks will be situated in the broader context of growing tension between the principles underlying the provision and delivery of public services and those underlying trade liberalization through such institutions as the World Trade Organization (WTO) in the era of globalization. On the one hand, public library service is based on the values of providing universal access to information by promoting literacy, supporting authors and scholars in their research, preserving cultural heritage, and providing other needed information services to various communities. The mandate of the public library is grounded in broad societal goals that justify a model of service delivery that relies on public funding, that operates outside the constraints of private markets, and that is governed by models of democratic decision making.

On the other hand, the principles of progressive liberalization and the corresponding reliance on unregulated markets that inform the international trade system tend to view public services as unfair subsidies as well as unnecessary governmental interference with the market. From a trade perspective, such interventions amount to trade barriers that need to be removed. Recent controversies surrounding WTO meetings and summits have brought to the public's attention the concerns that the institutions of globalization could empower transnational corporations at the expense of the regulatory and subsidization powers of sovereign nations. While much attention has focused on the effects of globalization on labor, the environment, and human rights, there are also serious implications for information policy.

As the International Federation of Library Associations and Institutions (IFLA) puts it, there is "growing evidence that WTO decisions, directly or indirectly, may adversely affect the operations and future development of library services, especially in not-for-profit institutions in the near future."[2] The IFLA statement is significant because it reflects a growing consensus among library associations around the world that something is very wrong with an expansive international trading system that may override legitimate national policies. But despite growing recognition of the dangers posed by GATS and other agreements, those who have raised these issues have been marginalized and dismissed as spreading unwarranted "scare stories."[3]

Several difficulties in making confident predictions about the impacts of GATS should be noted. First, it is difficult to make accurate predictions about the impact of a services agreement that has no precedent and few analogues. The GATS agenda is ongoing and not always transparent. There is an underlying tension in reconciling the trade liberalization objectives of the GATS with the public policies required to ensure an ongoing and vital role for public sector libraries.[4] Second, while on its face GATS purports to protect public services by providing an exception for services offered under the auspices of a governmental authority, the governmental exemption is extremely limited and may not be effective in protecting public library services.[5] The GATS is still in an early stage of development, and there is a lack of authority that indicates how the exception will withstand scrutiny and challenge. Third, there exists a wide misunderstanding regarding the actual scope and effect of the GATS. The uncertainty is understandable considering the technical and often uncertain and untested meanings of significant GATS provisions. But even taking these difficulties into account, the problems that GATS creates for all public services, libraries being but an example, cannot be readily ignored.

The principal objective of this book is to initiate further discussion about the challenges posed by trade agreements within the context of public library policies, services, and funding arrangements. By explaining the structure of the GATS and how its various provisions operate, and by pointing to specific examples of library programs that could be at risk, we hope to make the discussion very concrete. Other objectives are to identify specific steps that individual libraries can take to avoid or ameliorate the potentially negative impacts and to suggest measures that library associations could take as part of their ongoing advocacy efforts.

THE PLAN OF THIS BOOK

So that it can meet these objectives, the book will proceed according to the following plan. This introduction will conclude by reviewing the background and structure of the general WTO framework. Tracing the historical development of the current international-trade scheme from the General Agreement on Tariffs and Trade (GATT) to the contemporary WTO framework evinces a marked expansion in the scope of international-trade agreements. The contemporary WTO framework now includes agreements on services and intellectual property in addition to its historical focus on goods.

In chapter 2, attention focuses on the scope of the GATS. As the agreement applies to governmental "measures by Members affecting trade in services"[6] the terms *measures* and *trade in services* will be defined. Chapter 2 also considers the general exemption for services provided under the auspices of governmental authority. At first glance, that exemption would seem to protect public library services from the reach of GATS. But since the exemption is available only to services offered neither on a commercial basis nor in competition with another service provider, it is very fragile, and libraries may not be able to rely on its protections. That discussion forms the basis for a more in-depth examination of particular library services and why they are potentially susceptible to the risk of challenges under GATS in chapter 4.

Chapter 3 outlines the general requirements of the GATS agreement and answers the basic question: What does it mean if a particular service is covered by GATS? In sorting through the complexities of the various GATS rules, known as *disciplines*, the discussion proceeds in nontechnical terms but with extensive references to primary sources as well as more technical works. The chapter also explains the classification scheme used by member states to differentiate the various service sectors and subsectors, and outlines the process by which member states "list" those sectors in individual schedules indicating the scope of their commitments in the area. The extent to which government programs, policies, and funding arrangements may be subject to GATS constraints depends on what the government has listed in its GATS schedules and whether the listing contains any express exceptions. The complexity of the listing process has generated considerable uncertainty about the extent of the commitments made by a country concerning any of the service sectors. Some GATS provisions apply across the board (horizontal, or "top-down," provisions such as Most Favoured Nation) unless a country claims a specific exemption. Other "bottom-up provisions" (such as the National Treatment and Market Access rules) apply only to services that have been specifically listed in a country's schedule. Since bottom-up obligations are the most onerous and present the greatest dangers to public libraries, the process by which countries list their commitments to particular services is significant. Chapter 3 also discusses the general issue of subsidies, how subsidies may be considered a violation of GATS disciplines, and what activities may be appropriately characterized as subsidies.

Building on the foundations provided in the earlier chapters, chapter 4 considers the various services offered by public libraries, particularly the newer, emerging services designed to meet the needs of the community in a changing environment, in terms of their susceptibility to GATS coverage. Since many of these services fall into the expanding area of overlap between the offerings of public libraries and the private sector, this analysis is central to an understanding of the potential problems posed by GATS. Examples of services that fall into this area of overlap, or zone of competition, include digital library services, Internet access services, fee-based services, homework-tutoring centers/services, virtual reference, and other areas of concern. As well, recent initiatives from the private sector to move into areas of service formally occupied primarily by public libraries are considered as examples within the problematic zone of competition.

Chapter 5 looks at the processes of commercialization and privatization of public library services utilizing the typology developed by Ruth Rikowski.[7] The chapter situates common library-related policies, such as outsourcing and contracting-out, within that typology and stresses the relationship between commercialization, privatization, and trade agreements such as GATS.

Chapter 6 asks what an individual library system or the profession in general can do to avoid or ameliorate the potential negative implications of GATS. We offer some practical considerations with regard to defining and publicizing services, along with an assessment of the downside of such practices as contracting-out, private-public partnerships, fee-for-service arrangements, and the characterization of library patrons as customers.

Chapter 7 considers how the library associations should respond to GATS in the context of their ongoing advocacy efforts. The chapter assesses how the issue of international trade agreements has fared as part of the advocacy agenda of the library associations and attempts to identify some of the barriers that stand in the way of developing more effective advocacy programs around the issue.

By way of conclusion, the final chapter considers the GATS as an instance of latent information policy. The discussion defines what is meant by the term *information policy*, distinguishes between "manifest" and "latent" policies, and argues that since the effects of GATS are not readily visible as information policy, the notion of latent policy is particularly applicable to the issue. The remainder of the chapter presents historical background that should help set the context for the specific treatment of the GATS that follows and closes with a short discussion of how the GATS relates to other international trade agreements.

THE BASIC FRAMEWORK OF INTERNATIONAL TRADE

The basic framework of international trade agreements is embodied in the General Agreement on Tariffs and Trade, which was established in 1947.[8] Successive rounds of trade negotiations had amended the framework prior to the conclusion of the Uruguay Round, starting in 1986 and ending with the 1994 WTO Agreement. While the original GATT framework applied only to trade in goods, the 1994 WTO Agreement expanded the scope of the trade regime to include annexes on trade in services (GATS) as well as on intellectual-property rights (TRIPS).[9]

The advent of the WTO agreements has elevated the importance of international trade agreements into areas that were previously matters of domestic policy. The WTO framework includes general provisions on dispute settlement and enforcement. GATT, GATS, and TRIPS (and other annexed agreements) are subject to the same general provisions.

While there have been numerous agreements between various nations on matters of trade for hundreds of years, the direct roots of the WTO system can be traced to the Great Depression in the 1930s. During that period, there was a reduction in international trade because of increased tariffs and other trade restrictions. In 1934, the U.S. Congress passed the Reciprocal Trade Agreements Act of 1934[10] in an effort to stem the tide of restrictive practices. Under the Act, the President was given the authority to negotiate a reduction in U.S. tariffs in exchange for similar reductions from trading partners. Over the next few years, the U.S. entered into bilateral agreements with more than twenty countries.[11] Even before the end of World War II, the U.S. and the U.K. had entered into numerous discussions looking toward a post-war trading system that would alleviate the practice of proliferating restrictive tariffs. At the United Nations Conference on Trade and Employment, held in Havana, Cuba, in 1947, the Havana Charter for the International Trade Organization (ITO) was adopted. The ITO was to serve as a formal organization under the auspices of the United Nations.[12] Meanwhile, a group of twenty-three countries negotiated a provisional agreement on tariff reductions that was known as the General Agreement on Tariffs and Trade (GATT). GATT was never intended to be a formal organization; that was to be left to the ITO. But for a variety of reasons, the agreement to establish the ITO as a permanent organization was never finalized. The GATT went into effect on January 1,

1948.[13] Jeffrey Thomas and Michael Meyer summarize the situation after the demise of the Havana Charter and the ITO:

> While a number of attempts were subsequently made to either revive the Charter or establish an organization similar to the proposed ITO, all would prove unsuccessful. Instead the global trading system was to develop in a much more *ad hoc*, piecemeal fashion over the next 40 years. With the failure of the ITO, the GATT remained, by default, the sole multilateral agreement then in place to deal with global trade issues, a role which it had never been designed to play.[14]

While the GATT was not a formal organization, it did emerge as the framework agreement for subsequent trade negotiations and lasted until it was replaced by the World Trade Organization in 1995. From the development of GATT through the end of the 1970s, there were seven separate rounds of negotiations.[15] The Uruguay Round is most significant because of its expanded negotiating agenda. Launched in 1986 at Punta del Este, Uruguay, the new round of negotiations was designed to expand the international trading system into the new areas of services and intellectual property.[16] Despite several impasses over the next few years, the agreement was concluded on December 15, 1993, and adopted by 124 governments at the Ministerial Conference held at Marrakesh in April 1994.[17] The WTO Agreement itself is merely an umbrella document, the particular agreements (on goods, services, intellectual property, the understanding on dispute settlements and others) are all attached as Annexes.

RELATIONSHIP BETWEEN WTO-GATS AND OTHER INTERNATIONAL TRADE AGREEMENTS

The utter complexity of the entire WTO system—which includes GATT, GATS, TRIPS, other substantive agreements, as well as a shared Dispute Settlement Understanding—is only a piece of the puzzle of the modern international-trade regime. In addition to the WTO, a variety of other international, regional, and bilateral agreements have some bearing on international trade. In North America, the most important of the other agreements is the North American Free Trade Agreement, which came into effect on January 1, 1994.[18] NAFTA is a multilateral agreement between the United States, Canada, and Mexico that includes a chapter on trade in goods, a chapter on intellectual property, and a chapter on investments and services. In many respects it duplicates the rules contained in GATT, GATS, and TRIPS, but in other respects it goes beyond what these WTO-related agreements contain. The most significant difference between the WTO and NAFTA is with respect to dispute-settlement provisions. Through what is known as state-to-state settlement, the WTO agreements limit standing in the dispute process to member nations. Individual claimants cannot bring cases to WTO bodies. A foreign national must persuade his or her country to bring the dispute forward. In addition to state-to-state disputes, NAFTA provides for investor-to-state disputes. The significance of that difference cannot be overemphasized, and without question, the most controversial aspect of NAFTA is its Chapter 11, on investor-state disputes. The Canadian government characterizes it as follows:

> Chapter 11 is the investment component of the North American Free Trade Agreement. It establishes a framework of rules and disciplines that provides investors from the NAFTA countries with a predictable rules-based investment climate, as well as dispute settlement procedures which are designed to provide timely recourse to an impartial tribunal.[19]

The organization Public Citizen provides a somewhat more critical description:

> The North American Free Trade Agreement (NAFTA) includes an array of new corporate investment rights and protections that are unprecedented in scope and power. NAFTA allows corporations to sue the national government of a NAFTA country in secret arbitration tribunals if they feel that a regulation or government decision affects their investment in conflict with these new NAFTA rights. If a corporation wins, the taxpayers of the "losing" NAFTA nation must foot the bill.[20]

It is important to recognize that these investor-state disputes cannot arise under the GATS or any of the other WTO agreements. However, the proposed Free Trade Area of the Americas (FTAA) agreement,[21] which would expand NAFTA throughout the rest of the Western Hemisphere (absent Cuba), would contain rules similar to NAFTA's Chapter 11.

NOTES

1. World Trade Organization, "General Agreement on Trade in Services: Uruguay Round Agreements, Annex 1B of the World Trade Agreement," *Legal Texts* (Geneva: WTO, 1994), www.wto.org/english/docs_e/legal_e/26-gats.pdf (accessed 9 July 2005). Cited hereafter as GATS.

2. International Federation of Library Associations and Institutions. *The IFLA Position on the World Trade Organization* (The Hague: IFLA, 2001), para. 4, www.ifla.org/III/clm/p1/wto-ifla.htm (accessed 8 July 2005).

3. See for example World Trade Organization, *GATS—Fact and Fiction* (Geneva: WTO, 2001). www.wto.org/english/tratop_e/serv_e/gatsfacts1004_e.pdf (accessed 8 July 2005).

4. See for example, Fiona Hunt, "Why the World Trade Organization Is a Threat to Libraries," *American Libraries* 32, no. 8 (September 2001): 32–33; and Ruth Rikowski, *Globalisation, Information and Libraries: The Implications of the World Trade Organisation's GATS and TRIPS Agreements* (Oxford: Chandos Publishing, 2005).

5. The exemption is contained in GATS Article I(3)(c) and is treated in depth in chapters 2 and 4. See also Wendy Newman [then president, Canadian Library Association] to Paul Robertson, Ottawa, Ontario, 23 October 2002, in *Correspondence*, Canadian Library Association (Ottawa: CLA, 2002), www.cla.ca/issues/robertson.htm (accessed 24 March 2005). This letter is reprinted in appendix D.

6. GATS, Article I(1).

7. Ruth Rikowski, "The Corporate Takeover of Libraries," *Information for Social Change* 14 (Winter 2001–2002), www.libr.org/ISC/articles/14-Ruth_Rokowski.html (accessed 9 July 2005).

8. World Trade Organization, "The General Agreement on Tariffs and Trade (GATT 1947)," *Legal Texts* (Geneva: WTO, 1986), www.wto.org/english/docs_e/legal_e/gatt47_01_e.htm (accessed 8 July 2005).

9. The texts of the various WTO agreements, including GATS, are available at World Trade Organization, *Legal Texts*, (Geneva: WTO, n.d.), www.wto.org/english/docs_e/legal_e/legal_e.htm (accessed 9 July 2005).

10. Reciprocal Trade Agreements Act of 1934, Public Law 73–316, *U.S. Code* 19, §§ 1001, 1201, 1351, 1354.

11. Jeffrey S. Thomas and Michael A. Meyer, *The New Rules of Global Trade: A Guide to the World Trade Organization* (Scarborough, Ont., Carswell, 1997), 3–4.

12. The Havana Charter was a comprehensive code that covered tariffs as well as such nontariff barriers as preferences, taxation, and regulation. It also touched on labor and employment issues.

13. The U.S. Congress failed to ratify the final ITO Charter, but the GATT, which was originally intended to be an agreement administered by the ITO, was finalized. The founding twenty-three members of the GATT were Australia, Belgium, Brazil, Burma, Canada, Ceylon, Chile, China, Cuba, Czechoslovakia, France, India, Lebanon, Luxembourg, Netherlands, New Zealand, Norway, Pakistan, Southern Rhodesia, Syria, South Africa, the United Kingdom, and the United States.

14. Thomas and Meyer, *The New Rules of Global Trade,* 5.

15. The early trade rounds (Geneva, 1946; Annecy, France, 1949; Torquay England, 1950–1951; Geneva, 1955–1956 and Dillon, 1960–1961) were limited mostly to the issue of tariff reductions. Starting in the Kennedy Round (1964–1967) and the Tokyo Round (1973–1979), the scope of the discussions expanded into nontariff barriers to trade.

16. The Punta del Este Declaration of 20 September 1986 is a significant document, as it set out the negotiating agenda for the Uruguay Round, including the "new issues" of services and intellectual property. See "General Agreement on Tariffs and Trade (GATT): Punta del Este Declaration, 20 September 1986," available at *SICE*

Foreign Trade Information System (Washington: Organization of American States, 2004), www.sice.oas.org/trade/Punta_e.asp (accessed 9 July 2005). Toward the ends of negotiating an agreement in these new areas, the declaration set up three formal bodies, one dealing with goods, one with services, and a trade negotiations committee to oversee the first two. The declaration also stated that the negotiations were to be completed within four years, an estimate that was overly optimistic since the final negotiations were not concluded until December 1993.

17. See World Trade Organization, "Agreement Establishing the World Trade Organization: Marrakesh, 15 April 1994, Uruguay Round Agreements," *Legal Texts* (Geneva: WTO, 1994), www.wto.org/english/docs_e/legal_e/04-wto.doc (accessed 9 July 2005).

18. North American Free Trade Agreement, 1992, *Legal Texts* (Ottawa, Mexico City, and Washington: NAFTA Secretariat, 1992), www.nafta-sec-alena.org/DefaultSite/index_e.aspx?DetailID=78 (accessed 9 July 2005).

19. See International Trade Canada, "Dispute Settlement, NAFTA, Chapter 11, Investment—Frequently Asked Questions, *Trade Negotiations and Agreements* (Ottawa: DFAIT, 2001), www.dfait-maeci.gc.ca/tna-nac/Mun-FAQs-en.asp (accessed 9 July 2005).

20. Public Citizen, "NAFTA Chapter 11: Corporate Cases," *Global Trade Watch* (Washington: Public Citizen, n.d.), www.citizen.org/trade/nafta/CH__11/ (accessed 9 July 2005).

21. See Free Trade of the Americas—FTAA [website], www.ftaa-alca.org/alca_e.asp 99 July 2005). The FTAA is a work in progress and has not been completed to date. See the latest released version of the agreement (November 2003), Free Trade of the Americas, "FTAA—Free Trade of the Americas Draft Agreement," FTAA.TNC/w/133/Rev.3, 21 November 2003, www.ftaa-alca.org/FTAADraft03/Index_e.asp (accessed 9 July 2005).

2

The Scope of GATS Coverage

The GATS[1] applies to all governmental measures affecting trade in services, including, among others, health care, education, public transit, automobile repair, and firefighting services. While the focus of the book is how the GATS applies to libraries, it is important to remain aware of how the GATS affects other public services. To that end, this chapter discusses important GATS definitions without specific reference to libraries. The purposes of this chapter are twofold: to demonstrate how the definitional scope of *measures* and *trade in services* is used to give the GATS a very broad mandate, and second, to demonstrate the method by which the GATS exemption for public services has been designed to reinforce the mandate rather than protect public services.

WHAT ARE "MEASURES AFFECTING TRADE IN SERVICES"?

The definitional starting point for discussing the scope of the GATS is Article I(1), which provides that "[t]his Agreement applies to measures by Members affecting trade in services." That definition, however, raises two crucial questions: What constitutes a "measure," and what does it mean to "affect trade in services"? These are important foundational questions for an understanding of the whole GATS agreement.

Defining *Measures*

Since all GATS provisions are based on "measures affecting trade in services," we begin by discussing how the GATS defines the term *measures*. Article I(3) states that "'measures by Members' means measures taken by: (i) central, regional or local governments and authorities; and (ii) non-governmental bodies in the exercise of powers delegated by central, regional or local governments or authorities." The circularity of the definition, where a measure means a measure, is evident. Measures are defined again in Article XXVIII(a) as "any measure by a Member, whether in the form of a law, regulation, rule, procedure, decision, administrative action, or any other form." Although that definition is also self-referential, it does provide examples of particular governmental actions that the WTO considers measures.

It is clear that the intention of the definition is to define the scope of GATS broadly and to include as much government activity at as many levels of government as possible. The activities of states, provinces, municipalities, townships, library boards, school districts, community-college districts, other special districts, and public universities are all "measures affecting trade in services." While actions taken by private service providers are not mentioned here, the activities of private associations are covered in the definition of measures if the entities are acting pursuant to any delegated authority from any level of government. For example, associations that license professional activities are often empowered to do so by statute, and the activities of such associations would be considered measures within the meaning of GATS to the extent of the statutory delegation.

Coverage within GATS is not limited to legislation in its formal sense but reaches virtually any official act undertaken by a governing body. The inclusion of the phrase "or any other form" in the third definition establishes that the scope of activities to be covered is open-ended. Even an activity that is not a "law, regulation, rule, procedure, decision or administrative action" may therefore be subject to inclusion as "any other form" in GATS. While it is not clear what these other forms may be, the meaning of the agreement is clear enough: If a government unit (or, importantly, a nongovernmental body under its jurisdiction) does something, it is considered a "measure," subject only to some very narrow exceptions (these exemptions, such as government procurement and authority, are discussed later in this chapter).

Defining *Affecting Trade in Services*: The Relationship Between GATS and GATT

At first, the distinction between the GATT and the GATS appears obvious: The former deals with trade in goods, while the latter addresses trade in services. In reality, however, the distinction is less clear. Previous WTO cases, specifically *European Communities (EC) Bananas*[2] and *Canada Autos*,[3] illustrate the close interrelationship between the GATS and GATT and highlight the broad scope of the term *affecting trade in services*. How can a measure affect both trade in goods and trade in services? In both *EC Bananas* and *Canada Autos*, WTO bodies found the GATS applicable to situations that appeared to pertain primarily to trade in goods.

EC-Bananas

The *EC-Bananas* case was launched in 1996 by the United States against the European Community, whose members were accused of preferentially importing bananas from former European colonies, mainly the Caribbean. This preference was a problem for the United States because American corporations, which control most Latin American banana crops, complained about not being granted this same "preferential" treatment by the EC. Though the case seems to have more to do with bananas than with the delivery of services, the Americans argued that both the GATT and GATS were applicable to the dispute. The focus of the case was the European Community's licensing regime for its banana imports.

But how can GATS rules apply to the trade of a good? It was the WTO that deemed the scope of GATS to be sufficiently broad to apply to this case: As the Appellate Body, which reviews the findings made by other decision-making bodies, especially with respect to appeals, explained in its findings, the GATS is intended to have a "broad reach" and there is "no legal basis for an a priori exclusion of measures from the scope of the GATS."[4] The EC argued that the GATS could not apply to its import-licensing procedures because those procedures were not measures "affecting trade in services" within the meaning of Article I(1). Both the Dispute Panel and Appellate Body agreed with the complaining parties, however, that the licensing regime was a measure affecting trade in services, notwithstanding the fact that GATT disciplines were also applicable. The Appellate Body put it this way:

> In our view, the use of the term "affecting" reflects the intent of the drafters to give a broad reach to the GATS. The ordinary meaning of the word "affecting" implies a measure that has "an effect on," which indicates a broad scope of application. This interpretation is further reinforced by the conclusions of previous panels that the term "affecting" in the context of Article III of the GATT is wider in scope than such terms as "regulating" or "governing."[5]

Therefore, while trade in bananas might have provoked the case, the focus turned quickly to services as it became clear that the GATS could be applied to any measures that affect the competition between domestic and foreign services (and service suppliers), even if those measures were also covered by the GATT.

As the measures were also covered by the GATT, it is useful to ask why the U.S. chose to base its challenge on GATS instead of the GATT in the first place.

Under the European Union Lomé Convention,[6] former European colonies are given the right to provide bananas directly and duty-free to the European market. The EU carefully negotiated exemptions for that Convention under the GATT to prevent exactly the kind of retaliatory action taken by the United States under the GATS. The U.S. team understood that the Lomé Convention was protected from GATT rules but that the broad definition of "measures affecting trade in services" under GATS could be the Convention's Achilles' heel. Ultimately, the United States won the case and was permitted to impose $191 million per year in trade sanctions against the EU in the form of import tariffs against products such as Roquefort cheese and cashmere.

Auto Pact

A broad scope was also applied to the term "affecting trade in services" in the *Canada-Autos* dispute. The Canada–U.S. Automotive Products Agreement of 1965, commonly known as the Auto Pact, permitted Canadian automobile manufacturers to import parts and vehicles from other countries so long as they met specific domestic requirements for assembly, content, and employment. Tariffs were applied to vehicles that did not meet those requirements (such as vehicles manufactured in Japan and Europe), in order to foster one of Canada's vital manufacturing industries. The Canada–U.S. Free Trade Agreement (CUSFTA) and NAFTA caused some of those tariffs to be phased out, though they still applied to non–North American imports. In 1999, Japan and the EU, on behalf of their automobile manufacturers, brought a case before the WTO courts to challenge the Auto Pact as a violation of the GATS. Canada argued that the GATS did not apply to the dispute because the measure's effect on trade in services was unsubstantiated:

> Canada submits that the measure at issue does not affect trade in services. In this case, Canada contends, the measure does not affect the supply of distribution services and does not affect wholesale distribution service suppliers in their capacity as service suppliers. It is true that the import-duty exemption "may affect" the cost of the goods. However, any effect this may have on the supply of distribution services is so "tenuous" that the measure clearly falls within the category of measures that should be scrutinized exclusively under the GATT 1994.[7]

The complaining parties asserted that the GATS was applicable because the Auto Pact *was* a "measure affecting trade in services" within the scope of the GATS definition and as such constituted an improper discriminatory measure. The Arbitration Panel, which works with the Dispute Settlement Body, the main WTO decision maker, to make its rulings, sided with the complainants. Canada appealed to the WTO Appellate Body, which in the end upheld most of the Arbitration Panel's rulings:

> Canada first appeals the Panel's finding that the measure is one "affecting trade in services" within the scope of Article I:1 of the GATS. It then appeals the finding that Canada does not accord immediately and unconditionally to services and service suppliers of any other Member treatment no less favourable than that it accords to like services and service suppliers of any other country contrary to its obligations.[8]

In its concluding report, the Appellate Body held that "at least two key legal issues must be examined to determine whether a measure is one 'affecting trade in services': first, whether there is 'trade in services' in the sense of Article I:2; and, second, whether the measure in issue 'affects' such trade in services within the meaning of Article I:1."[9] Concluding that trade in services was present, the Appellate body gave this summary:

> The complainants in this case allege that the "trade in services" here relevant is "wholesale trade services of motor vehicles," which is a category of services recognized in the Central Product Classification. Canada does not dispute that there are service suppliers of the United States, the European Communities and Japan which are established in Canada and which provide wholesale trade services of motor vehicles. Accordingly, we hold that the "trade in services" here in issue is wholesale trade services of motor vehicles supplied by service suppliers of certain Members through commercial presence in Canada.[10]

With regard to the second question, the Appellate Body concluded that the Arbitration Panel had failed to adequately support its decision that trade in services had been affected in the case.[11] That finding was further qualified by the Appellate Body:

> In coming to this conclusion, we do not suggest that the import duty exemption does not affect wholesale trade services of motor vehicles in Canada. Nor do we conclude that Canada accords no less favourable treatment to services and service suppliers of any Member than that which it accords to like services and service suppliers of another country consistently with Article II:1 of the GATS. We make no such conclusion. We mean only to say that the Panel, in this case, failed to substantiate its conclusion that the import duty exemption is inconsistent with Article II:1 of the GATS. As such, we have no choice but to reverse the findings and conclusions of the Panel relating to Article II:1 of the GATS.[12]

We define and discuss Article II(1) (Most Favoured Nation) in the next chapter; for now, the pertinent information to draw from the last quotation is that the Appellate Body came to its conclusion because it found the Arbitration Panel's reasoning flawed, not because it agreed with Canada's position. In the end, therefore, the WTO stood by its decision that the Auto Pact *was* an example of a "measure by [a member] affecting trade in services." The most alarming consequence of the ruling was the precedent it set with regard to requirements for Canadian content: The degree to which companies must invest, create employment, and purchase within Canada was significantly reduced. The overlap of regulation of trade in goods and trade in services is emphasized by Scott Sinclair and Jim Grieshaber-Otto:

> In practice, it is very difficult to draw a clear line between the production of goods and services. Services are embodied in tangible products, e.g. advertising in a magazine, which can be dropped on your foot. This is not a purely theological matter. It means that the WTO rules on trade in goods and services overlap and that government measures must conform to both.[13]

The tendency to construe the GATS broadly, even in the areas dealing primarily with trade in goods, is cause for concern because of its intrusion into domestic policy making. Marc Lee of the Canadian Centre for Policy Alternatives points to the Auto Pact case as an example "of a successful industrial development and trade policy that has been of huge benefit to Canada [that] was struck down by a WTO panel, even though autos are clearly 'goods.'"[14] Lee's concerns are echoed by others who point to the broad scope of GATS coverage as evidence that the Agreement is a threat to the integrity of legitimate policy tools enacted by sovereign states. As Sinclair and Grieshaber-Otto put it, "there is no trace of indecision or irony in the WTO panel decision that ruled that the Auto Pact, arguably Canada's most successful industrial policy ever, was GATS-inconsistent even though the panel acknowledged that the policy likely had no actual effect on trade in services."[15]

THE PUBLIC SERVICES EXEMPTION UNDER GATS

Considering the broad scope of its coverage, many countries would never have been signatories to the GATS without safeguards for public services. For these reasons, the GATS also contains an exemption for services supplied in the exercise of government authority, which include those public services that in no way compete or overlap with the private sector (traditionally services such as health care, education, and libraries). According to the definition given in Article I(3)(b), the services covered by the agreement are those "in any sector except services supplied in the exercise of governmental authority." That exception is qualified in the next subsection, I(3)(c), where the services exempted from the GATS are defined as "any service which is supplied neither on a commercial basis, nor in competition with one or more service suppliers."

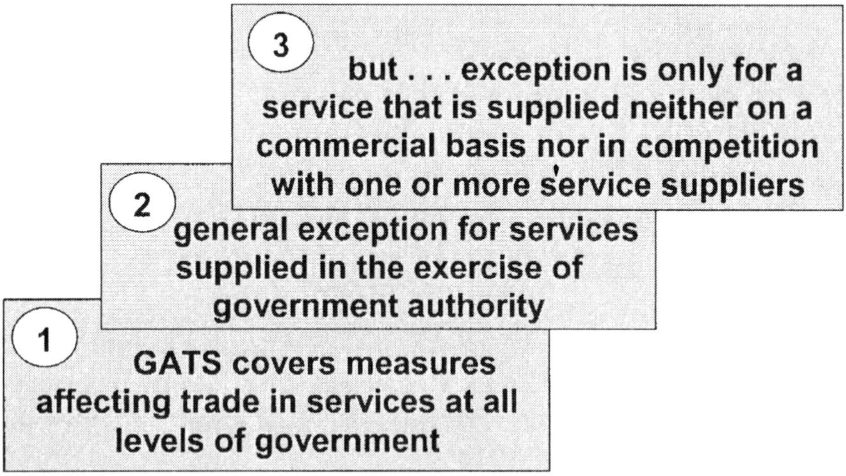

Figure 2.1. Rule of Coverage—Exception—Limitation on Exception

The meaning of these terms together (the exception and its corresponding limitation) is perhaps one of the most controversial aspects of GATS. A step-wise approach here, as illustrated in figure 2.1, may help clarify the problem. At the first level, the GATS applies to "governmental measures affecting trade in services."

At the level of the exception in subsection (b), the GATS does not apply to services supplied in the exercise of government authority. To some degree, it seems as if these two provisions cancel each other out. However, subsection

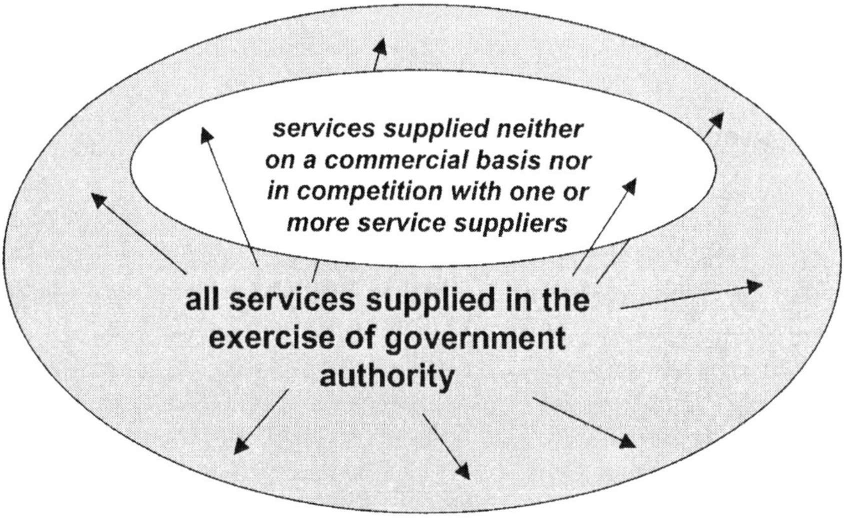

Figure 2.2. Services within the Exception Are Only a Subset of All Governmental Services

(c) limits the reach of the exception, and when taken together, subsections (b) and (c) are only about a subset of the total services supplied in the exercise of government authority as illustrated in figure 2.2. That is to say, the exception applies only to government services that are not supplied on a commercial basis or in competition with other service providers.

There is little consensus regarding the viability of the government-services exemption as a check on the broad GATS scope of coverage. On the one hand, critics charge that GATS threatens the ability of governments to provide public services without threat of challenge because of the very fragility of the exception. As Scott Sinclair writes, "Given that most public services are supplied through a mix of public and private funding and public, private, and not-for-profit delivery, the category of services provided purely by government without any commercial interest or competition is small, and in an age of widespread user fees and privatization, shrinking."[16] Furthermore, he suggests that "even attempts by government to influence the voluntary behavior of businesses, individuals, or other nongovernmental actors are measures subject to WTO oversight and challenge."[17]

On the other hand, GATS advocates claim that critics misunderstand the public-services exception. The WTO itself has gone to great lengths to attempt to rebut many of the claims made by critics. For example, a WTO report entitled *GATS—Fact and Fiction* characterizes many critics of the GATS as fearmongers:

> Recently . . . the negotiations and the GATS itself have become the subject of ill-informed and hostile criticism. Scare stories are invented and unquestioningly repeated, however implausible. It is claimed for example that the right to maintain public services and the power to enforce health and safety standards are under threat, though both are explicitly safeguarded under the GATS. How have serious people come to believe what is, on the face of it, out of the question? Why should any Government, let alone over 140 Governments, agree to allow themselves to be forced, or force each other, to surrender or compromise powers which are important to them, and to all of us?[18]

In other pronouncements, however, WTO officials seem to have acknowledged the general level of uncertainty surrounding the provision:

> A key issue is whether sales are made on a commercial basis. To begin with, it is not completely clear what the term "commercial basis" means. Nevertheless, if services were deemed to be supplied on a commercial basis, then, regardless of whether ownership was in public or private hands, the sector would be subject to the main GATS disciplines and to the negotiation of commitments under Articles XVI [Market Access] and XVII [National Treatment].[19]

A background report prepared by the government of British Columbia systematically demonstrated the fragility of the government-services exemption.[20] The report concludes with a recommendation that members should conduct an assessment of how their existing GATS commitments could affect the provision of public services.

> Members that fail to perform such assessments run a significant risk of covering services unintentionally in this and future rounds of negotiations. They may also introduce uncertainty into any new specific commitments they make—uncertainty that is likely to be clarified ultimately not by the member governments themselves but through dispute settlement. Moreover, in the absence of clear guidance to the contrary from member governments, it is very likely that dispute settlement panels will interpret the "governmental authority" exclusion narrowly. This could have the effect of diminishing governments' regulatory capability and undermining their existing public service systems.[21]

To date, no on-point GATS panel decisions have provided guidance on what the public-services exception really means. A similar public-services exception in the European Communities treaty, however, has been narrowly construed.[22]

CONCLUSION

At first glance, the government-services exception would seem to protect public library services from the reach of GATS. But inasmuch as the exception is available only to services that are offered neither on a commercial basis nor in competition with another service provider, the actual value of the exception to libraries is questionable. To introduce a framework for the discussion that chapter 4 takes up in further detail, figures 2.3, 2.4, and 2.5 illustrate the

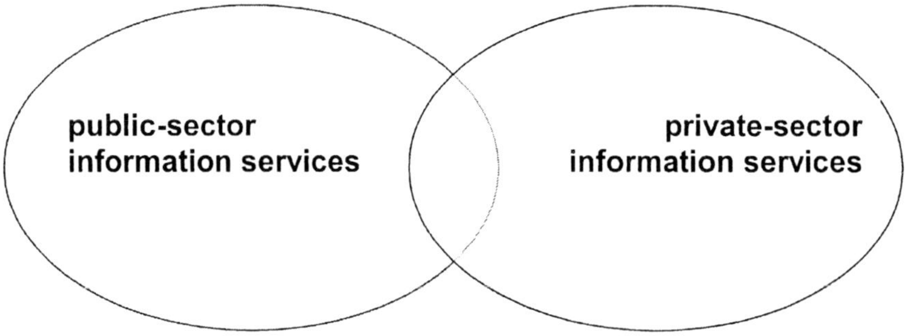

Figure 2.3. Traditional Relationship between Public and Private Information Services

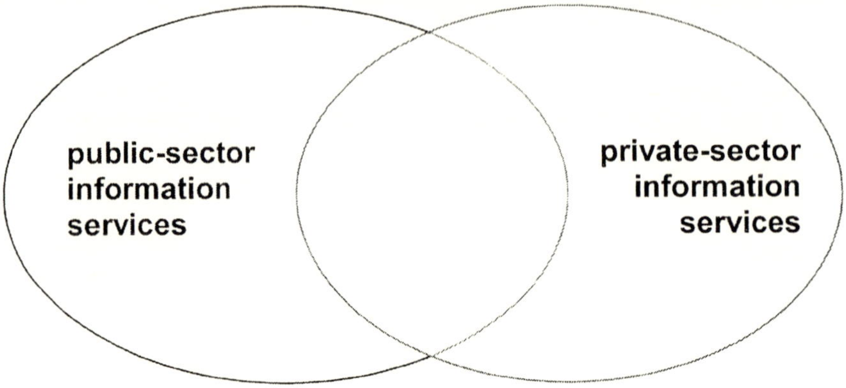

Figure 2.4. Developing Relationship between Public and Private Information Services

changing relationship between information services that are offered in the private and public sectors.

In figure 2.3, the traditional relationship shows only limited overlap, or competition, between the services provided by the public and private sectors. In figure 2.4, the area of overlap is growing as public libraries expand their range of services and as the private sector moves into areas previously occupied exclusively by public libraries. As the trend continues toward figure 2.5, the area of overlap becomes even larger. In all of these cases, the area of overlap represents that range of services where the public services exemption is the most fragile.

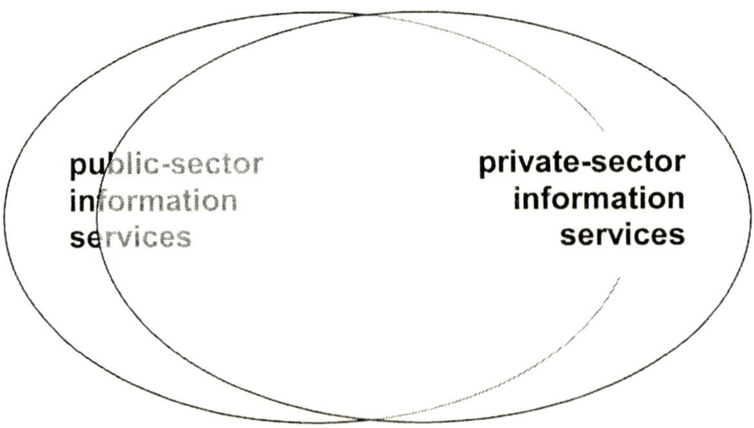

Figure 2.5. Ultimate relationship between public and private information services?

NOTES

1. World Trade Organization, "General Agreement on Trade in Services: Uruguay Round Agreements, Annex 1B of the World Trade Agreement," *Legal Texts* (Geneva: WTO, 1994), www.wto.org/english/docs_e/legal_e/26-gats.pdf (accessed 9 July 2005). Cited hereafter as GATS.

2. World Trade Organization, Appellate Body, *European Communities—Regime for the Importation, Sale and Distribution of Bananas: Report of the Appellate Body*, AB-1997-3, WT/DS27/AB/R, adopted 25 September 1997 (Geneva: WTO, 1997), www.worldtradelaw.net/reports/wtoab/ec-bananas(ab).pdf (accessed 6 July 2005).

3. World Trade Organization, Appellate Body, *Canada—Certain Measures Affecting the Automotive Industry: Report of the Appellate Body*, WT/DS139/AB/R, WT/DS142/AB/R, 31 May 2000 (Geneva: WTO, 2000), www.worldtradelaw.net/reports/wtoab/canada-autos(ab).pdf (accessed 8 July 2005).

4. World Trade Organization, Appellate Body, *European Communities—Regime for the Importation, Sale and Distribution of Bananas.*

5. World Trade Organization, Appellate Body, *European Communities—Regime for the Importation, Sale and Distribution of Bananas*, para. 220.

6. For a brief history of the Lomé Convention, see European Commission, *The Lomé Convention: Brief History*, Europa (Brussels: European Commission, 2004), http://europa.eu.int/comm/development/body/cotonou/lome_history_en.htm (accessed 8 July 2005).

7. See World Trade Organization, Appellate Body, *Canada—Certain Measures Affecting the Automotive Industry*, at para 20.

8. World Trade Organization, Appellate Body, *Canada—Certain Measures Affecting the Automotive Industry*, 48, para. 147.

9. World Trade Organization, Appellate Body, *Canada—Certain Measures Affecting the Automotive Industry*, 51, para. 155.

10. World Trade Organization, Appellate Body, *Canada—Certain Measures Affecting the Automotive Industry*, 51, para. 157.

11. World Trade Organization, Appellate Body, *Canada—Certain Measures Affecting the Automotive Industry*, 54, para. 165.

12. World Trade Organization, Appellate Body, *Canada—Certain Measures Affecting the Automotive Industry*, 60, para. 183.

13. Scott Sinclair and Jim Grieshaber-Otto, *Facing the Facts: A Guide to the GATS Debate*. (Ottawa: Canadian Centre for Policy Alternatives, 2002), 11, www.policyalternatives.ca/documents/National_Office_Pubs/facing_facts.pdf (accessed 8 July 2005).

14. Marc Lee, "Trade Agreements: What the New Alphabet Soup means for BC," *BC Commentary, A Quarterly Review of Provincial Social and Economic Trends* 4, no. 1 (Winter 2001), www.policyalternatives.ca/documents/BC_Office_Pubs/bc_commentary/bccwinter01.pdf (accessed 8 July 2005).

15. Sinclair and Grieshaber-Otto, *Facing the Facts*, 49–50.

16. Scott Sinclair, *GATS: How the WTO's New "Services" Negotiations Threaten Democracy* (Ottawa: Canadian Centre for Policy Alternatives, 2000), 57.

17. Sinclair, *GATS*, 106.

18. World Trade Organization (2001) *GATS—Fact and Fiction* (Geneva: WTO, 2001), 2, www.wto.org/english/tratop_e/serv_e/gatsfacts1004_e.pdf (accessed 8 July 2005).

19. World Trade Organization, Council for Trade in Services, Environmental Services, Background Note by the Secretariat, S/C/W/46/, 6 July 1998, 98-2690 (Geneva: WTO, 1998), www.wto.org/english/tratop_e/serv_e/w46.doc (accessed 8 July 2005); cited in Michelle Swenarchuk, *From Global to Local: GATS Impact on Canadian Municipalities* (Ottawa: Canadian Center for Policy Alternatives, Canadian Environmental Law Association, 2002), www.policyalternatives.ca/documents/National_Office_Pubs/gats_municipalities.pdf (accessed 8 July 2005).

20. See British Columbia, Ministry of Employment and Investment, *GATS and Public Service Systems: The GATS "Governmental Authority" Exclusion* (Victoria, B.C.: Government of British Columbia, 2001), http://members.iinet.net.au/~jenks/GATS_BC2001.html (accessed 8 July 2005).

21. British Columbia, Ministry of Employment and Investment, *GATS and Public Service Systems*, at text following note 64.

22. British Columbia, Ministry of Employment and Investment, *GATS and Public Service Systems,* at text accompanying notes 28–33, stating that the European Court of Justice has ruled that "the derogation provided for in Article 55 must be restricted to activities which in themselves are directly and specifically connected with the exercise of official authority."

3

The GATS Disciplines: Classification and Commitment of Services

The previous chapter discussed the ways in which definitions in the GATS text[1] are used to construe its broad scope and how public-service exemptions work in this context. This chapter explains the GATS requirements, also known as *disciplines*, for most favoured nation, national treatment, and market access. We also examine the method by which countries commit their services to and claim exemptions from GATS rules, and examine the implementation of the WTO's Services Sectoral Classification List. The dispute-resolution system under GATS is briefly described.

It is important to distinguish between the top-down and bottom-up provisions of GATS. GATS disciplines that apply across the board are termed *horizontal* or *top-down* provisions because the rules are applicable unless a country claims an exemption for an entire service or aspect of it. Disciplines are *bottom-up* if they apply to services that have been specifically listed in a country's schedule, or list, of commitments.

Schedules provide the source of two fundamental elements of GATS. The first is the list of commitments that each country has agreed to make to particular sectors and subsectors with respect to the bottom-up provisions, such as national treatment. The second is the limitations or exemptions it wishes to claim with respect to the top-down commitments, such as the most-favored-nation principle. If a schedule of commitments is silent on a particular sector, then the top-down provisions apply, and the bottom-up ones do not.

As discussed in chapter 2, the GATS agreement itself is only a framework document, laying out general parameters and requirements; the actual substance of the agreement is in a country's schedule. The bottom-up obligations, in particular the discipline of national treatment, are the most onerous and present the greatest danger to public libraries. Therefore, understanding the process by which countries subject their service sectors to the rules is crucial to understanding the general GATS threat to public libraries. The process by which a country develops its schedule of commitments is the heart of the ongoing process of GATS negotiations as shown in figure 3.1.

UNDERSTANDING "LIKE"

The kinds of services that are subjected to GATS are fundamental to an understanding of the issues impacting libraries. For a trade disagreement to arise under the GATS, two services have to be deemed similar enough to each other that a trade challenge is valid. Clearly, claiming that an automobile manufacturer is in unfair competition with a database company because of government support would be more difficult to substantiate than libraries being in competition with the same database providers. The designation of services being considered "like" is largely up to a WTO dispute-resolution panel. Therefore, the construction and use of this word is of critical importance.

What is a like service, and what is a like service supplier? In the context of trade disputes arising under the GATT, WTO panels and Appellate Bodies have discussed the general approach for interpreting "like or similar" products. As indicated in chapter 2, the same dispute-settlement system applies to GATT and GATS, which means cases that have construed the meaning of like products are relevant to the determination of like services. The WTO has in-

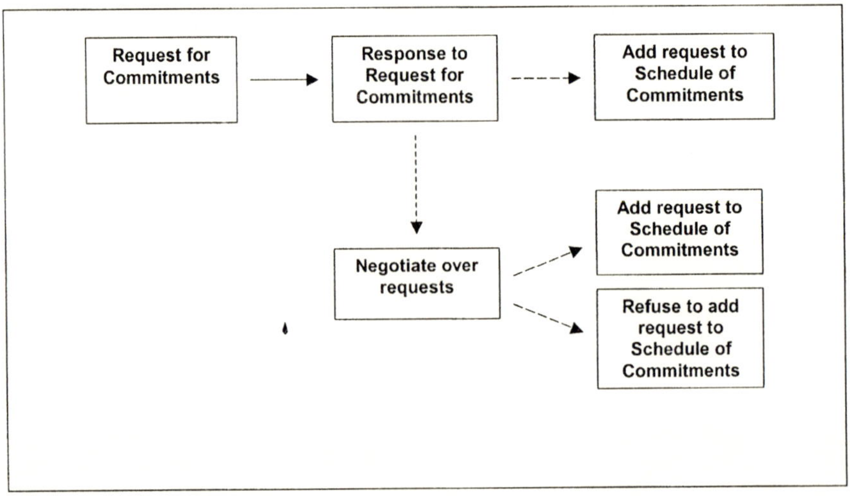

Figure 3.1.

dicated that the interpretation must be examined on a case-by-case basis and has suggested some criteria for likeness. These criteria include the product's end uses in a given market, consumers' tastes and habits, and the product's properties, nature, and quality.

The application of these standards is best illustrated by an example from a GATT challenge. In 1995, Japan's taxes on alcoholic beverages were challenged by the European Union, and to resolve the dispute, a domestic Japanese product, shochu, was compared with imported products such as gin, vodka, rum, brandy, and other distilled spirits. The panel concluded that shochu and vodka were like products because of similar physical characteristics, ingredients, and end uses, while other beverages, such as rum and brandy, with different ingredient lists and appearances, could not be considered like shochu (*shochu* in Japan is a fairly generic term for a distilled spirit made from any one of a number of different ingredients). Since Japanese taxes were higher on vodka than on shochu, the panel found an inconsistency with the GATT requirements and rejected Japan's arguments and insisted that shochu, vodka, and other distilled spirits receive the same tax treatment.[2]

Gaetan Verhoosel characterizes likeness as "one of the thorniest issues GATT/WTO panels have had to deal with in the past,"[3] and explains the two schools of thought on the likeness issue:

> On the one hand, there are those who posit that the likeness of two products should be determined solely on the basis of factors such as their physical similarity, tariff classification, consumer preferences, and end uses. On the other side of the spectrum are the proponents of the so-called aims-and-effects test, who take the view that a determination of likeness should take into account the regulatory objectives of the measure at hand.[4]

Those standards are probably far easier to apply to goods than to services. Indicia such as ingredients, appearance, and end use, for example, are not applicable where services are concerned. Nonetheless, in two leading WTO dispute decisions arising under the GATS (*EC-Bananas* and *Canada-Autos*), the onus of satisfying the likeness standard was set at a low and general level. In the *EC-Bananas* case, a panel held as follows:

> [T]he nature and the characteristics of wholesale transactions as such, as well as of each of the different subordinated services . . . are "like" when supplied in connection with wholesale services. . . . Indeed, it seems that each of the different service activities taken individually is virtually the same and can only be distinguished by referring to the origin of the bananas in respect of which the service activity is being performed. Similarly, in our view, to the extent that entities provide these like services, they are like service suppliers.[5]

In the *Canada-Autos* case described in chapter 2, a panel concluded that "[w]e agree that to the extent that the service suppliers concerned supply the same services, they should be considered 'like' for the purpose of this case."[6] In both of these instances, the panels declined to apply more exacting standards to satisfy the likeness requirement. Indeed, it would not be an exaggeration to claim that in the context of service disputes, the likeness requirement is so amorphous as to be of little value to a party facing a challenge. Looking back at Verhoosel's distinction between the physical similarity and aim and effects tests, it is hard to imagine how the distinction would be useful in a services setting.

INDIVIDUAL GATS DISCIPLINES

Top-Down: Most-Favoured Nation

The most-favoured-nation (MFN) principle is a foundational concept in international trade law. In the words of John H. Jackson, "MFN has been a central pillar of trade policy for centuries."[7] The obligation is not unique to the GATS; it is contained in the GATT as well, and in other traditional international trade agreements. *Most favoured nation* has traditionally meant that countries agree not to impose tariffs on another country higher than those levied on their best trading partner—for example, in the 1947 GATT agreement:

> With respect to customs duties and charges of any kind imposed on or in connection with importation or exportation or imposed on the international transfer of payments for imports or exports, and with respect to the method of levying such duties and charges, and with respect to all rules and formalities in connection with importation and exportation . . . any advantage, favour, privilege or immunity granted by any contracting party to any product originating in or destined for any other country shall be accorded immediately and unconditionally to the like product originating in or destined for the territories of all other contracting parties.[8]

The original 1947 GATT Agreement is incorporated and firmly entrenched in the 1994 version and is one of the key components of the WTO system. Since the same dispute-settlement system applies to both the GATT and the GATS, cases that have construed the terms in the GATT are also relevant in the context of the GATS. For example, decisions under the 1947 GATT using the term "like products" can be used by dispute panels to give meaning to "like services" under the GATS; hence the importance of the shochu case for understanding how the GATS works.

The term *most-favoured nation* is misleading because it implies favorable treatment of a particular trading partner. When implemented, however, MFN status actually works to disfavor the treatment of a trading partner. MFN is a rule of nondiscrimination and a guarantee of equal treatment. As GATS Article II(1) states: "With respect to any measure covered by this Agreement, each Member shall accord immediately and unconditionally to services and service suppliers of any other Member treatment no less favourable than that it accords to like services and service suppliers of any other country."

The purpose of the MFN provision is to avoid situations in which countries provide preferential treatment to some countries without affording that same treatment across the board, to all WTO member states. The goal is a "favour one, favour all"[9] approach:

> The MFN obligation . . . requires [WTO Members] to be even-handed in the application of measures to other countries. The MFN obligation has the effect of preventing trade measures from becoming a morass of special arrangements with individual trading partners. The MFN obligation also requires that the government carefully consider the impact of changing its trade policies because alterations must apply to all trading partners that are WTO members.[10]

The WTO's stated intention is to level the playing field among all trading partners and avoid side deals that enable specific countries to grant special treatment on an individual basis. That is, any provision regarding imports and exports given to one country must be extended to all other signatory countries. If country A provides preferential treatment to a service provider from country B, the service providers in countries C, D, E, and so on may all claim they are entitled to the same arrangement. The rule has been justified on the ground that it discourages discriminatory "national groupings," which may lead to national resentments at being left out.[11] In contrast, critiques of MFN provisions focus on the need to permit some forms of preference for legitimate circumstances, such as helping boost economies in developing regions.[12]

In the expanded scope of the modern international trade regime under the WTO, the MFN requirement has far-reaching implications beyond the simple setting of tariffs. As discussed in the previous chapter, the WTO regime is also concerned with nontariff barriers to trade such as internal subsidies. As such, the scope and implications of MFN are far-reaching.

The MFN obligation applies to *de facto* (i.e., in reality, as a matter of fact) as well as to *de jure* (i.e., as a matter of right or law) discrimination. Measures that are nondiscriminatory when taken on their face may still violate the MFN principle if in practice those measures restrict the free flow of one country's goods (in the case of the GATT) or services (in the case of the GATS). In the

GATS context, however, the MFN rules apply only in the case of like services and service suppliers (just as GATT rules apply only to like goods). According to the GATS, the only way a preferential measure granted to a foreign service provider of a particular country does not violate MFN is if such a service does not meet the like requirement.

On the assumption that two or more services *are* like, there are only two ways to bypass the MFN requirements, and they are laid out in parts 2 and 3 of the MFN treatment article. The first option is for a government to list a specific service as an exemption.[13] The second option allows countries to engage in regional trade agreements and afford preferential treatment by virtue of those agreements.[14]

Therefore, as a horizontal, or top-down, provision, the MFN requirement is applied across the board even to service sectors that have not been listed on a country's schedule of commitments, unless they have been specifically exempted. The complete coverage is in contrast to the bottom-up provisions, such as national treatment and market access, which we shall now discuss.

National Treatment

As is the case with MFN provisions, national-treatment requirements are found in the GATT and many other international trade agreements. One main difference between MFN and national treatment is that while MFN requires that all foreign service providers be treated equally, national treatment rules require that countries treat foreign service providers the way they treat domestic ones. GATS Article XVII(1) provides as follows:

> In the sectors inscribed in its Schedule, and subject to any conditions and qualifications set out therein, each Member shall accord to services and service suppliers of any other Member, in respect of all measures affecting the supply of services, treatment no less favourable than that it accords to its own like services and service suppliers.

Note that the provision applies only to services and suppliers deemed to meet the test of likeness. Another key difference between MFN and national treatment is their scope: Unlike the top-down nature of MFN, the national-treatment requirement is considered bottom-up—that is, it applies only to the sectors listed in a country's schedule of commitments. Stewart Young emphasizes this contingent aspect of GATS:

> GATS does not require all WTO members to cover all services because member countries are able to opt certain service industries in or out of GATS. Member countries can therefore choose which services they want to be subject to GATS,

> rather than having all of their service industries subject to GATS. Although GATS is supposed to regulate member countries so that they refrain from placing barriers to trade in services, it does not provide such protections to all services. According to the Schedule of Commitments, WTO member countries may determine which services in their country will be covered by GATS. Although a number of recognized services included by many WTO members are within their Schedule of Commitments, any country may omit services that it does not want covered by and subject to GATS. The effect is that GATS does not apply across the board to the same services for all WTO members.[15]

While Young's assessment is technically correct, his approach underemphasizes the complexity of the GATS and the danger that service areas could be subsumed by the requirements, even unintentionally. When compared to MFN, national-treatment provisions are generally considered more onerous and likely to become the subject of disputes. National treatment is also unlike MFN provisions in that it affects domestic rather than international policy:

> The national treatment obligation is often a source of complaint or dispute among nations. Because it refers to domestic regulatory and tax measures, it is intimately related to various governmental measures that are based on legitimate policy reasons not necessarily designed for purposes of restraining imports.[16]

As with MFN, a recurring problem of interpretation regarding the scope of the national-treatment obligation pertains to the difference between de facto and de jure discrimination. If a library provides free homework help to young patrons, there is no intent to discriminate against foreign service providers, and the measure is de jure nondiscriminatory. But if in reality a foreign-based private-tutoring firm loses business because it lacks the public library's advantage of governmental support, then an argument for de facto discrimination might be advanced. The fact that there was no intention to discriminate against foreign service providers becomes irrelevant. Therefore, even though a government measure is nondiscriminatory on its face and was enacted without any purposeful intent to discriminate, it can have the effect of somehow discriminating against a foreign product or service. The emphasis on effect is what is meant by de facto (or implicit) discrimination and broadens the potential scope of GATS challenges in the area of national treatment and MFN.

The requirement for national treatment is one of the more onerous of the GATS disciplines and is far more likely than the MFN requirement to collide with legitimate regulatory activities. Numerous examples of that problem in the context of library practice are considered in chapter 4.

Market Access

Market access refers to maximizing the domestic opportunities for foreign suppliers to deliver their services. The GATS market-access discipline in Article XV(1) explains that "[w]ith respect to market access through the modes of supply identified in Article I, each Member shall accord services and service suppliers of any other Member treatment no less favourable than that provided for under the terms, limitations and conditions agreed and specified in its Schedule."

That language defines market access as a GATS bottom-up discipline; consequently, market-access rules apply to sectors that are listed in a country's schedule of commitments. In addition, the modes of supply listed in Article I(2) are, in keeping with the GATS trend, construed very broadly.

The two major facets of market access in the GATS are both key to understanding its scope and purpose. The first addresses the modes of supply, or categories of ways in which services can be supplied, while the second lays out what private service providers can expect from governments. Article I(2) lists the four distinct modes by which services may be supplied:

> 2. For the purposes of this Agreement, trade in services is defined as the supply of a service:
>
> (a) from the territory of one Member into the territory of any other Member; in the territory of one Member to the service consumer of any other Member;
> (b) by a service supplier of one Member, through commercial presence in the territory of any other Member;
> (c) by a service supplier of one Member, through presence of natural *persons* of a Member in the territory of any other Member.

The first mode of trade in services corresponds to what is generally considered the normal form of trade in goods. According to the WTO, Mode 1 "is in many ways the most straightforward form of trade in services, because it resembles the familiar subject-matter of the GATT, not least in maintaining a clear geographical separation between seller and buyer: only the service itself crosses national frontiers."[17]

Mode 2, also known as consumption abroad, involves the supply of a service in the territory of one Member to a service consumer of another Member:

> [T]his will involve the consumer travelling to the supplying country, perhaps for tourism or to attend an educational establishment. Another example of consumption abroad would be the repair of a ship or aircraft outside its home country. Like cross-border supply, this is a straightforward form of trade which raises few problems, since it does not require the service supplier to be admitted to the consuming country.[18]

Mode 3 pertains to the supply of a service through the commercial presence of the foreign supplier in the territory of another WTO member:

> Examples would be the establishment of branch offices or agencies to deliver such services as banking, legal advice or communications. This is probably the most important mode of supply of services, at least in terms of future development, and also raises the most difficult issues for host governments and for GATS negotiations. A large proportion of service transactions require that the provider and the consumer be in the same place. But rules governing commercial presence are very different from the tariffs and other border measures that principally affect trade in goods. GATT has only gradually become involved in some sensitive domestic policy issues such as subsidies and technical standards. Right from the beginning, however, the GATS has been forced to grapple with internal policy issues such as rights of establishment that are inherent in the commercial presence of foreign interests. In doing so, and establishing multilateral rules that guarantee the opportunities for firms and individuals to establish themselves in a foreign market, the GATS has broken new ground.[19]

Mode 4 deals with the admission of foreign nationals into a country for the purpose of providing services there.[20]

Reviewing these four modes of supply makes evident that the scope of the agreement is very broad; the four categories encompass nearly every conceivable form of service provision. The market-access provisions create a series of rules for governments to follow when they list a service (or good, in the context of the GATT) on their schedule of commitments; specifically, governments cannot place limits on the number of service suppliers, the total value of service transactions or assets, the total number of service operations or output, or on the number of people employed. At the same time, governments may not require joint ventures, legal entity, or certain levels of domestic ownership. Article XV(2) sets forth the applicable limitations where such a commitment is made:

> In sectors where market-access commitments are undertaken, the measures which a Member shall not maintain or adopt either on the basis of a regional subdivision or on the basis of its entire territory, unless otherwise specified in its Schedule, are defined as:
>
> (a) limitations on the number of service suppliers whether in the form of numerical quotas, monopolies, exclusive service suppliers or the requirements of an economic needs test;
> (b) limitations on the total value of service transactions or assets in the form of numerical quotas or the requirement of an economic needs test;
> (c) limitations on the total number of service operations or on the total quantity of service output expressed in terms of designated numerical units in the form of quotas or the requirement of an economic needs test;

(d) limitations on the total number of natural persons that may be employed in a particular service sector or that a service supplier may employ and who are necessary for, and directly related to, the supply of a specific service in the form of numerical quotas or the requirement of an economic needs test;
(e) measures which restrict or require specific types of legal entity or joint venture through which a service supplier may supply a service; and
(f) limitations on the participation of foreign capital in terms of maximum percentage limit on foreign shareholding or the total value of individual or aggregate foreign investment.

The breadth of these provisions shows that making a market-access commitment in any particular sector will have serious implications for a country's ability to impose a variety of regulatory measures with respect to that service.

Subsidies

While subsidies do not comprise a separate GATS discipline, they play an important role in determining whether or not MFN, national-treatment, or market-access rules apply. It is important to establish that subsidies have a different meaning for a librarian and the WTO. For librarians, subsidies represent support given in the form of an appropriation, grant, or contribution. Libraries rely on such support for their sustenance and as the foundation for their operation. Without them, libraries would be limited in their ability to function as democratic institutions. Thus the inclusion of subsidies in the GATS is of particular concern to librarians and related information workers.

The WTO does not favor subsidies, for, as GATS Article XV(1) states, "subsidies may have distortive effects on trade in services."[21] According to a recent text on the WTO, "[b]roadly defined, a subsidy is a benefit that is not earned. In economic terms, a subsidy is a 'positive externality' that is, a benefit that comes from outside a business or firm. In lay terms, it is a 'windfall.'"[22] By windfall, the authors do not mean some sort of ill-gotten or even excessive gain; they mean subsidies are a net benefit for some that are not enjoyed by all competitors.

An important element of the subsidies article is its express requirement for ongoing negotiations. Article XV(1) gives further substance to that requirement:

> Members shall enter into negotiations with a view to developing the necessary multilateral disciplines to avoid such trade-distortive effects. . . . Such negotiations shall recognize the role of subsidies in relation to the development programmes of developing countries and take into account the needs of Members,

> particularly developing country Members, for flexibility in this area. For the purpose of such negotiations, Members shall exchange information concerning all subsidies related to trade in services that they provide to their domestic service suppliers.[23]

The foregoing clause is sometimes misinterpreted as express support for subsidies, particularly in developing countries; however, the opposite is the case, as the agreement actually calls for further disciplines to be developed for subsidies.[24] The purpose of additional disciplines would be to discourage subsidies that are seen as unfair policies that discriminate against like service suppliers in different modes of supply.

The flavor of the GATS view on subsidies is encapsulated in Article XV(2), which provides that "[a]ny member which considers that it is adversely affected by a subsidy of another Member may request consultations with that Member on such matters. Such requests shall be accorded sympathetic consideration."

The express requirement of "sympathetic consideration" potentially indicates an intent to give substance to the problem of subsidies as a separate discipline. Subsidies are potentially considered to be a form of a nontariff trade barrier. Consequently, subsidy issues can arise in cases involving the other GATS disciplines, such as national treatment, most favoured nation, and market access.

The wording of the subsidies article is noticeably more ambiguous than that of other GATS requirements, possibly because subsidies have never been treated as broadly as they are in this agreement. Another possibility is that WTO policy makers chose their words carefully in an attempt to assuage fear and dispel criticism. The subsidies article is not toothless, according to Jon Johnson:

> Domestic production subsidies are, in some respects, the least intrusive of the policy instruments addressed by the trade agreements. . . . However, subsidies become a trade problem when they enable domestic producers to compete unfairly in foreign markets, and export subsidies have caused serious distortions in the world trade in agricultural goods.[25]

While Johnson's analysis of subsidies is true to some extent, GATS sees subsidies as far more of a threat than do, say, the NAFTA or GATT agreements. The NAFTA specifically excludes subsidies from national-treatment and MFN rules, while the GATT allows countries to have production subsidies without fear of their being challenged under national-treatment provisions. Another important consideration for libraries is the extent to which they may be considered to be domestic producers competing unfairly in foreign markets by virtue of their receiving extensive subsidies. While such an outcome is as yet unknown since no cases have been launched against libraries, precedents like those set by the *EC-Bananas* and *Canada-Autos* cases suggest that such dangers cannot be dismissed out of hand. Exactly how problematic subsidies really are remains an issue of some dispute.

Virtually any governmental program may be characterized in some way as a subsidy, and the failure to make such benefits available to foreign service providers can be interpreted as a national-treatment problem. The GATS defines subsidies as measures, and by definition they must be treated in accordance with national treatment in sectors where specific commitments have been made. Any intention to restrict the availability of subsidies to national, as opposed to foreign, service suppliers must be specifically indicated in a country's schedule of commitments. Consequently, if a country lists a commitment in its schedule and does not reserve the right to subsidize nationals within that sector, the subsidy will be open to challenge. The issue of subsidies is further considered in the context of particular library services in chapter 4.

THE GATS CLASSIFICATION SYSTEM AND THE SCHEDULE OF COMMITMENTS

The complexity of the listing process has generated uncertainty regarding the extent of the commitments made by a country in particular sectors. In brief, the extent to which government prerogatives may be subject to GATS constraints depends on the listings a government enumerates in its GATS schedules and whether the listing contains express exceptions.

The WTO Services Sectoral Classification List

At the heart of this process is the classification system, which is used to distinguish and categorize the different service sectors. The WTO has a Services Sectoral Classification List,[26] which itemizes a series of service sectors that are divided into further subsectors. Because libraries are affected by many latent policies from sometimes seemingly unrelated sectors, the library community must be sensitive to the individual elements of the complete listing and not simply the portions that deal explicitly with library services. The twelve general sectors are as follows:

1. Business Services
2. Communication Services

3. Construction and Related Engineering Services
4. Distribution Services
5. Educational Services
6. Environmental Services
7. Financial Services
8. Health-Related and Social Services
9. Tourism and Travel-Related Services
10. Recreational, Cultural, and Sporting Services
11. Transport Services
12. Other Services Not Included Elsewhere

Of immediate interest to libraries is Sector 10, which is further subdivided:

A. Entertainment services (including theatre, live bands and circus services)
B. News agency services
C. Libraries, archives, museums and other cultural services
D. Sporting and other recreational services
E. Other

Unfortunately, as we just mentioned, the matter of determining the potential GATS coverage for services offered by libraries does not stop with subsector 10.C. A review of the entire classification system indicates that library services might be characterized in other sectors. For example, several of the subsectors of Business Services, such as Computer and Related Services (1.B), Research and Development Services (1.C), and Printing and Publishing Services 1.F.r), could potentially categorize certain library activities. In addition, subsectors covering Telecommunication Services (2.C), Audiovisual Services (2.D), and the entire Educational Services sector overlap considerably with many services now offered by libraries. The broad range of classification subsectors by which different aspects of library services may be subsumed gives ample reason for concern.

Even if a country does not make a commitment to library services specifically as classified under 10.C, listing services in any of these other sectors could potentially bring public libraries within the scope of GATS coverage. If a subsector is listed on the schedule of commitments, it does not matter that the same service may fall under another subsector that is *not* listed. Unless a specific exemption is claimed in the listing, the service is deemed to be covered by the GATS disciplines. Therefore, assurances from governments that library services will not be subjected to the GATS because no commitment is being made to 10.C are tenuous at best.

How the Classification System Is Used

Scott Sinclair underlines the importance of classification issues for the process of progressive trade liberalization. He argues that "[d]ecisions about how to classify services could affect the interpretation of existing commitments and definitely will shape how future commitments are made."[27] Sinclair points to various means by which classification issues may be used to maximize GATS coverage.

First, the description of excluded subsectors (in which governments have made the fewest commitments) may be narrowed. That can be interpreted as shifting definitions to suit different purposes: To the WTO, a government may be making a broader-than-expected commitment, while to the public unfamiliar with the definition shifts, governments may appear to have fully protected particular sectors.

Second, the description of included subsectors in which governments have made the most commitments may be broadened. This, again, is a case of shifting definitions in order to obtain different outcomes.

Third, particular service sectors may be disaggregated in a way that splits off subsectors targeted for liberalization by service corporations from other sectors. Such disaggregation, Sinclair argues, would make it easier to include such targeted services in the schedule of commitments while dodging public concerns that entire sectors are committed to the GATS.

Fourth, services may be clustered in order to make sure that subsequent commitments apply to the entire cluster of targeted services.

Finally, new and emerging services may be classified in such a manner as to be subsumed under previous commitments within an existing sector. Sinclair argues that in each of these cases, "nominally neutral classification issues can be manipulated to skew the results in favour of greater GATS coverage."[28] The issue of classification raises a number of particular problems in the field of library services, which will be discussed in detail in the next chapter.

PURPOSE OF GATS NEGOTIATIONS: PROGRESSIVE LIBERALIZATION

The disciplines discussed thus far form the overall framework for the GATS. But most of the details of how the GATS applies are to be filled in through ongoing negotiations. GATS Article XIX(1) outlines how that process is to take place, though, as we shall find, it raises as many questions as it answers:

> In pursuance of the objectives of this Agreement, Members shall enter into successive rounds of negotiations, beginning not later than five years from the date of

> entry into force of the WTO Agreement and periodically thereafter, with a view to achieving a progressively higher level of liberalization. Such negotiations shall be directed to the reduction or elimination of the adverse effects on trade in services of measures as a means of providing effective market access. This process shall take place with a view to promoting the interests of all participants on a mutually advantageous basis and to securing an overall balance of rights and obligations.

While details of the negotiations are delegated to the parties, the expectation is for the negotiations to proceed toward ever-higher levels of what is termed progressive liberalization. Nonetheless, subsection 2 seems to place limits on that imperative:

> The process of liberalization shall take place with due respect for national policy objectives and the level of development of individual Members, both overall and in individual sectors. There shall be appropriate flexibility for individual developing country Members for opening fewer sectors, liberalizing fewer types of transactions, progressively extending market access in line with their development situation and, when making access to their markets available to foreign service suppliers, attaching to such access conditions aimed at achieving the objectives referred to in Article IV.

In practice the course and outcome of the successive rounds of the negotiations reflect the relative power and bargaining strength of the individual members. As well, subsection 3 seems to qualify the generally open-ended nature of the process by requiring that "for each round, guidelines and procedures shall be established."[29] Subsection 4 once again emphasizes, in markedly mandatory terms, that the underlying goal of the negotiation process is the attainment of ever-higher levels of liberalization.[30]

To what degree, then, are members under an affirmative obligation to make concessions on their specific schedule of commitments? The text of Article XIX can be interpreted as fluctuating in its approach. Reading these four subsections resembles a ride on a roller coaster; but at the end of the ride there is a clear mandate for a strong version of progressive liberalization.

HOW COUNTRIES LIST SERVICES ON THEIR SCHEDULES OF COMMITMENTS

Countries may easily commit their services to GATS rules by listing them on schedules according to the rules in Article XX. But once they commit particular services or sectors to their Schedule, it is difficult for them to revise the commitments. Article XX(1) outlines the general contents of the actual schedule of commitments.

> [E]ach Schedule shall specify:
>
> (a) terms, limitations and conditions on market access;
> (b) conditions and qualifications on national treatment;
> (c) undertakings relating to additional commitments;
> (d) where appropriate the time-frame for implementation of such commitments; and
> (e) the date of entry into force of such commitments.

The assumptions that more commitments are better and that fewer commitments are a failure are persistent themes running through mainstream WTO discourse.

It is important to note that members do not have the unconditional right to modify their schedule of commitments. Article XXI sets forth the procedure for modification. A country (modifying member) may modify or withdraw any commitment in its Schedule after three years from the date on which that commitment entered into force.[31] However, the country must notify the Council for Trade in Services of its intentions at least three months before the proposed date of modification or withdrawal.[32] The right to modify or withdraw is not absolute: instead, it is subject to negotiation and compensation. For example, if other members fear that they will be adversely affected by a proposed change, the parties are required to try to reach an agreement on their own.[33] If an agreement cannot be reached, the matter is submitted to arbitration.[34] The arbitration may result in a compensation order, in which case the modifying member must comply with the payment order before modifying or withdrawing the commitment.[35] The procedures indicate that the ability of a country to modify its schedule will be directly related to its bargaining power vis-à-vis other members.

DISPUTE SETTLEMENT UNDERSTANDING

One of the most important features of the World Trade Organization is its unified system of dispute resolution. Regardless of whether a dispute arises under GATS, GATT, TRIPS, or any of the other WTO agreements, it is governed by the terms of the Understanding on Rules and Procedures Governing the Settlement of Disputes, Annex 2 of the WTO Agreement.[36] The purpose of the Dispute Settlement Understanding, or DSU, is described as "providing security and predictability to the multilateral trading system. The Members recognize that it serves to preserve the rights and obligations of Members under the covered agreements and to clarify the existing provisions of those agreements in accordance with customary rules of interpretation of public international law."[37] A Dispute Settlement Body, or DSB, is given broad powers. It has the authority to "establish panels, adopt panel and Appellate Body reports, maintain surveillance of implementation of rulings and recommendations, and authorize suspension of concessions and other obligations under the covered agreements."[38]

The dispute-settlement process has four general phases: consultation, referral to a panel, appeal to an Appellate Body, and finally, compliance and enforcement. The consultation process is outlined in Article 4 and can be invoked upon the written request of any member country to another member.[39] The resulting discussions are confidential,[40] and members are under an obligation to try to "attempt to obtain satisfactory adjustment of the matter"[41] before going on to the next stage in the procedure. If a settlement cannot be reached, the complaining party may request that Dispute Panel be established. The written request must "indicate whether consultations were held, identify the specific measures at issue and provide a brief summary of the legal basis of the complaint sufficient to present the problem clearly."[42] The composition of the panel is governed by Article 8:

> Panels shall be composed of well-qualified governmental and/or nongovernmental individuals, including persons who have served on or presented a case to a panel, served as a representative of a Member or of a contracting party to GATT 1947 or as a representative to the Council or Committee of any covered agreement or its predecessor agreement, or in the Secretariat, taught or published on international trade law or policy, or served as a senior trade policy official of a Member.[43]

Panels are composed of three members unless the parties to the dispute agree to a panel of five.[44] The function of the panel

> is to assist the DSB in discharging its responsibilities under this Understanding and the covered agreements. Accordingly, a panel should make an objective assessment of the matter before it, including an objective assessment of the facts of the case and the applicability of and conformity with the relevant covered agreements, and make such other findings as will assist the DSB in making the recommendations or in giving the rulings provided for in the covered agreements. Panels should consult regularly with the parties to the dispute and give them adequate opportunity to develop a mutually satisfactory solution.[45]

After hearing evidence and argument, the panel' submits its report to the DSB, and "within 60 days the report shall be adopted at a DSB meeting unless a party to the dispute formally notifies the DSB of its decision to appeal or the DSB decides by consensus not to adopt the report. If a party has notified its decision to appeal, the report by the panel shall not be considered for adoption by the DSB until after completion of the appeal."[46]

The third stage of the process involves taking the panel decision to an Appellate Body. These proceedings are confidential,[47] and the Appellate Body may "uphold, modify or reverse the legal findings and conclusions of the panel."[48] The report is sent to the DSB, which must adopt it unless they choose not to by consensus.[49]

After the final decision is adopted by the DSB, the compliance and enforcement process begins. These procedures are set out in Articles 21 and 22. Article 21(1) states the general expectation that "[p]rompt compliance with recommendations or rulings of the DSB is essential in order to ensure effective resolution of disputes to the benefit of all Members." Within 30 days of the DSB's decision, "the Member concerned shall inform the DSB of its intentions in respect of implementation of the recommendations and rulings of the DSB. If it is impracticable to comply immediately with the recommendations and rulings, the Member concerned shall have a reasonable period of time in which to do so."[50] After a decision is adopted, the DSB retains jurisdiction over the issue to make sure it is being complied with. Article 21(6) provides as follows:

> The DSB shall keep under surveillance the implementation of adopted recommendations or rulings. The issue of implementation of the recommendations or rulings may be raised at the DSB by any Member at any time following their adoption.

If the recommendation of the DSB is not implemented, the DSB may consider sanctions, including compensation or the suspension of concessions. If possible, concessions should be suspended in the same sectors that were at issue in the dispute. If, however, the same-sector approach is not practical or effective, the sanctions can be applied to a different sector in the same agreement. If "same agreement" sanctions are not practicable or effective, the suspension of concessions may be made under a different agreement.[51]

CONCLUSION

It is crucial to recognize the entities that govern the scope of the GATS as defined by the coverage of its disciplines and process of scheduling commitments. There is a trend toward broadening the scope of the agreement in order to promote trade liberalization in the following GATS-related areas:

- defining the disciplines;
- determining which services may be considered "like";

- listing modes of service supply;
- establishing what subsidies constitute "measures";
- creating very malleable rules for its classification scheme; and
- making it very easy for commitments to be made but very difficult to withdraw them.

It is important to understand how the power of creating or manipulating definitions ultimately lies within the scope of dispute-settlement procedures. It is fair to say that this fundamental power has not been retained by the individual governments, much less by their citizens.

NOTES

1. World Trade Organization, "General Agreement on Trade in Services: Uruguay Round Agreements, Annex 1B of the World Trade Agreement," *Legal Texts* (Geneva: WTO, 1994), www.wto.org/english/docs_e/legal_e/26-gats.pdf (accessed 9 July 2005). Cited hereafter as GATS.

2. World Trade Organization, *Japan—Taxes on Alcoholic Beverages, Report of the Panel*, WT/DS8/R, WT/DS10/R, WT/DS11/R, 11 July 1996 (Geneva: WTO, 1996), para. 6.22, www.worldtradelaw.net/reports/wtopanelsfull/japan-alcohol(panel)(full).pdf (8 Jul 2005).

3. Gaetan Verhoosel, *National Treatment and WTO Dispute Settlement: Adjudicating the Boundaries of Regulatory Autonomy* (Oxford: Hart Publishing, 2002), 23.

4. Verhoosel, *National Treatment and WTO Dispute Settlement.* See also Robert Hudec, "GATT/WTO Constraints on Domestic Regulation: Requiem for an 'Aims and Effects' Test," *International Lawyer* 32 (1998): 623. For a thorough analysis of the problem of "like products," see Won-Mog Choi, *"Like Products" in International Trade Law: Towards a Consistent GATT/WTO Jurisprudence* (Oxford: Oxford University Press, 2003).

5. World Trade Organization, *European Community—Regime for the Importation, Distribution and Sale of Bananas, Complaint by Mexico: Report of the Panel*, WT/DS27/R/MEX (Geneva: WTO, 1997), para. 7.322, www.worldtradelaw.net/reports/wtopanels/ec-bananas(panel)(mex).pdf (accessed 8 July 2005).

6. World Trade Organization, *Canada—Certain Measures Affecting the Automotive Industry: Report of the Panel*, WT/DS139/R, WT/DS142/R, 11 February 2000 (Geneva: WTO), 2000, para. 10.248, www.worldtradelaw.net/reports/wtopanels/canada-autos(panel).pdf (accessed 8 July 2005).

7. John H. Jackson, *The World Trading System: Law and Policy of International Economic Relations,* 2nd ed. (Cambridge, Mass.: MIT Press, 1997), 157.

8. World Trade Organization, "The General Agreement on Tariffs and Trade (GATT 1947)," *Legal Texts* (Geneva: WTO, 1986), www.wto.org/english/docs_e/legal_e/gatt47_01_e.htm (accessed 8 July 2005). Article I(1) provides as follows: "The 1947 GATT Agreement is incorporated into the 1994 GATT Agreement, which forms part of

the WTO system." As indicated in chapter 2, the same dispute-settlement system applies to GATT and GATS, which means cases that have construed the meaning of like product are relevant to the determination of like services. As discussed below, the likeness requirement is also contained in the national treatment rule. Some of the problems of interpreting likeness as a threshold issue will be discussed after the national treatment is introduced.

9. World Trade Organization, *Trading into the Future*, 2nd ed. (Geneva: WTO, 2001), 21, www.wto.org/english/res_e/doload_e/tif.pdf (accessed 8 July 2005).

10. Jon R. Johnson, *International Trade Law* (Toronto: Irwin Law, 1998), 53.

11. Jackson, *The World Trading System*, 159.

12. Jackson, *The World Trading System*, 159–160.

13. GATS, Article II(2), provides as follows: "A Member may maintain a measure inconsistent with paragraph 1 provided that such a measure is listed in, and meets the conditions of, the Annex on Article II Exemptions."

14. GATS, Article II(3), provides as follows: "The provisions of this Agreement shall not be so construed as to prevent any Member from conferring or according advantages to adjacent countries in order to facilitate exchanges limited to contiguous frontier zones of services that are both locally produced and consumed." The inclusion of this exception for regional-trade-agreement overrides seems counterintuitive given the stated purpose of MFN as avoiding exactly this sort of favoritism. Encouraging such side agreements by allowing this exemption does seem to fly in the face of the otherwise salutary purposes of a nondiscrimination rule.

15. Stewart Young, "Whistleblowing in a Foreign Key: The Consistency of Ethics Regulation under Sarbanes-Oxley with the WTO GATS Provisions," *Denver Journal of International Law and Policy*, 32, no. 1 (Winter 2003): 55.

16. Jackson, *The World Trading System*, 213.

17. World Trade Organization, Secretariat, Trade in Services Division, *An Introduction to the GATS* (Geneva: WTO, 1999), 2, www.wto.org/english/tratop_e/serv_e/gsintr_e.doc (accessed 8 July 2005).

18. World Trade Organization, Secretariat, Trade in Services Division, *An Introduction to the GATS,* 2–3.

19. World Trade Organization, Secretariat, Trade in Services Division, *An Introduction to the GATS,* 3.

20. World Trade Organization, Secretariat, Trade in Services Division, *An Introduction to the GATS,* 3.

21. GATS, Article XV(1).

22. Mitsuo Matsushita, Thomas J. Schoenbaum, and Petros C. Mavroidis, *The World Trade Organization: Law, Practice and Policy* (Oxford: Oxford University Press, 2003), 260. www.lexis.com/research/retrieve?_m=08375a567600534aaf685798fa77c078&docnum=8&_fmtstr=FULL&_startdoc=1&wchp=dGLbVzb-zSkAz&_md5=edc2ca919c89abcff96ddc2ceb972fc1&focBudTerms=title%28GATS%29&focBudSel=all—n11.

23. GATS, Article XV(1).

24. Scott Sinclair, *GATS: How the WTO's New "Services" Negotiations Threaten Democracy* (Ottawa, Ont.: Canadian Centre for Policy Alternatives, 2000), 85.

25. Johnson, *International Trade Law*, 9.

26. See World Trade Organization, *Services Sectoral Classification List,* MTN.GNS/W/120, 10 July 1991 (Geneva: WTO, 1991), www.wto.org/english/tratop_e/serv_e/mtn_gns_w_120_e.doc (accessed 8 July 2005).

27. Sinclair, *How the WTO's New "Services" Negotiations Threaten Democracy*, 68.

28. Sinclair, *How the WTO's New "Services" Negotiations Threaten Democracy*, 9.

29. GATS, Article XIX(3), continues: "For the purposes of establishing such guidelines, the Council for Trade in Services shall carry out an assessment of trade in services in overall terms and on a sectoral basis with reference to the objectives of this Agreement, including those set out in paragraph 1 of Article IV. Negotiating guidelines shall establish modalities for the treatment of liberalization undertaken autonomously by Members since previous negotiations, as well as for the special treatment for least-developed country Members under the provisions of paragraph 3 of Article IV."

30. GATS, Article XIX(4), provides as follows: "The process of progressive liberalization shall be advanced in each such round through bilateral, plurilateral or multilateral negotiations directed towards increasing the general level of specific commitments undertaken by Members under this Agreement."

31. GATS, Article XXI(1)(a).

32. GATS, Article XXI(1)(b).

33. GATS, Article XXI(2)(a).

34. GATS, Article XXI(3)(a).

35. GATS, Article XXI(4)(a). And under subsection (4)(b), if the modifying member fails to comply with arbitration findings, the other member that participated in the arbitration then has the right to withdraw substantially equivalent benefits that are in conformity with the findings.

36. World Trade Organization, "Understanding on Rules and Procedures Governing the Settlement of Disputes, Annex 2 to the World Trade Organization Agreement," *Legal Texts* (Geneva: WTO, 1994), www.wto.org/english/docs_e/legal_e/28-dsu.pdf (accessed 8 July 2005). Cited hereafter as DSU.

37. DSU, Article 3(2).

38. DSU, Article 2(1).

39. DSU, Article 4(4) provides as follows, "Any request for consultations shall be submitted in writing and shall give the reasons for the request, including identification of the measures at issue and an indication of the legal basis for the complaint."

40. DSU, Article 4(6).

41. DSU, Article 4(5).

42. DSU, Article 6(2).

43. DSU, Article 8(1).

44. DSU, Article 8(5).

45. DSU, Article 11.

46. DSU Article 16(4).

47. DSU Article 17(10).

48. DSU Article 17(13).

49. DSU Article 17(14).

50. DSU Article 21(3).

51. DSU Article 22(3).

4

Do Public Libraries Operate on a Commercial Basis and Compete with Other Service Suppliers?

INTRODUCTION

In 2001, the International Federation of Library Associations and Institutions (IFLA), representing the opinion of the international library community, published a position statement regarding the potential impact of the General Agreement on Trade in Services (GATS). The statement claimed that the agreement "has the potential to open up all aspects of a national economy to foreign competition including public sector services such as libraries." The IFLA is concerned that "[w]ith the advent of for profit on-line content providers targeting individual users of education services and public libraries, the potential for GATS challenges to traditional library service is increasing." IFLA warned that the tax-supported status of public-sector libraries at the national, regional, and local levels would be undermined by such challenges.[1] Those fears are justified on the grounds that the GATS is the broadest-ranging international trade agreement that specifically covers services; it is backed by the WTO's powerful dispute-resolution process, and it is being shaped outside the sphere of public scrutiny. The IFLA is keenly aware that library services fall directly into the GATS definition of what a service is. As discussed earlier in this book, the GATS general exemption for services provided under the auspices of government authority *does not apply* when services are offered either on a commercial basis or in competition with the private sector. Therefore, it is very important to seek out the instances of overlap between private suppliers and public libraries. Librarians and in fact all citizens need to be cognizant of how cost-cutting privatization and commercialization measures put all public libraries at risk for trade challenges.

The purpose of this chapter is to examine ways in which certain practices threaten the GATS exemption for services "provided in the exercise of governmental authority." We also consider how the encroachment of the private sector onto service areas traditionally in the domain of public libraries is creating a zone of competition in which GATS challenges could apply. While we begin with a fairly theoretical analysis, the rest of the chapter is basically a description of library activities that inadvertently put libraries at risk to threats from international trade.

The discussion begins by reviewing what we mean by *traditional* (or *core* or *basic*) services, in contrast with those that are often identified in much of our literature as *nontraditional* or *new*. We examine how each of these services is or is not challenging the GATS exemption, either by the complicity of libraries in adopting the market model or by private-sector provision of like services. It is our hope that this information will provoke thought and discussion about how we manage and operate our resources and services.

PUBLIC LIBRARY SERVICES

For more than a century, public libraries have provided collections and a public space where users can read, work, and (yes) sometimes snooze. Libraries have typically offered services beyond the simple circulation of library collections to local users; they have also provided information and reference services to help patrons find the materials they need via local holdings and interlibrary loans. According to Michael H. Harris, because of a perceived lack of use of public libraries after the Second World War, librarians took "a more aggressive stance in the area of service and . . . initiated numerous 'outreach' programs to increase the availability and use of library facilities."[2] They offered a variety of activities for children and adults that were often reading-related, such as adult basic literacy training, book clubs or discussion groups, and ESL classes. They also showed films, held workshops and courses on nonreading subjects (current events, flower arranging, nutrition, etc.), and provided a space where community groups could meet. Some libraries allowed patrons to rent or borrow film projectors, typewriters, and toys. The purpose of the nonreading-related services was partly to entice nonusers into the library so that they could become comfortable with the environment and eventually become regular patrons. Realistically speaking, however, some of these programs were meant to increase library-use figures in order to impress funding agencies. Nevertheless, public libraries succeeded in creating truly public spaces funded by public taxes and were open to all in the communities they served.

Traditional versus Nontraditional Services

The kinds of services mentioned above are often described as basic, core, or traditional. Defining the terms became very important with the advent of outsourcing, which is defined by the *Online Dictionary for Library and Information Science* as "the contracting of library services formerly performed in-house to an outside service provider, usually a for-profit enterprise."[3] Outsourcing is often seen as an effective and efficient way to control costs and cut staff, particularly in budget-strapped libraries where there is increasing financial pressure to outsource services deemed noncore and hence not covered by public library legislation. This trend has generated much literature attempting to identify and define core services. The Public Library Association notes that the "designation of 'core' mission functions assumes that a library has both core and noncore functions or services that might be provided by either internal or external resources."[4]

Defining Core Library Services

Defining "core" services can have serious consequences in terms of GATS challenges; therefore, it is important to examine what a variety of definitions do or do not contain and why organizations have chosen to include particular terms. The American Library Association Task Force on Outsourcing, for example, defined core services as:

> those professional activities that define the profession of librarianship. These include collection development and organization; gathering and providing information; making the collection accessible to all library users; providing assistance in use of the collection; and providing oversight and management of these activities.[5]

Meanwhile, the California Library Association argues that each local library should define its own basic public library services but adds that in general, "library services include access to and circulation of any type of resource, reference and information services, and admission and access to facilities and programs."[6] In its guidelines for services to people with disabilities, the Canadian Library Association speaks of "standard library services available to all readers" and notes that they include reader-advisory services, reference, user education and orientation, community-information services, and interlibrary loans.[7] Each of these definitions uses different terminology, and none is actually trenchant.

In many countries, core library services are defined in national or provincial/state legislation. Consider the case of Denmark:

> Core services are defined as access to borrowing and using the library's materials—including Internet access, but this principle is combined with the principle of the

> municipal libraries being allowed to request payment for special services. This means that—at a fee—the libraries may offer a variety of services ranging from express delivery of library materials to consultancy and training services to companies, public institutions and citizens.[8]

If *core* does not necessarily mean *free*, it is not surprising that there is some confusion about what constitutes a core service. The ALA Outsourcing Task Force had difficulty with the concept—as noted in a follow-up proposal to ALA Council in which Liz Bishoff and Sally G. Reed conceded that there are "widely varying beliefs about what services are core to libraries" and that the Task Force could not reach consensus on what services were appropriate for outsourcing.[9]

These organizations are trying to come up with definitions simply because there are consequences, some severe, for services that are considered noncore. As one New Zealand librarian writes, "If we accept the core functions of a public library to be information, education, enculturation, recreation, [then] technical services are not core operations, but only contribute to the core functions, so these areas are prime targets for outsourcing."[10] Clearly, how an organization chooses to define a core service can reflect its opinion on outsourcing.

Traditional and Nontraditional Services

Rather than choosing one of the many definitions of *core*, we shall fall back on the terms *traditional* and *nontraditional*. At the outset, we must be clear that those dichotomous terms are merely a useful way to arrange a chapter; the separation is not an implicit policy recommendation. While some library services are clearly nontraditional in nature—computer-based document delivery service, for example—others, like cataloging, are clearly traditional. There is a very large and gray continuum of service between the two extremes; we hesitate to draw lines, particularly since nontraditional services tend to evolve into traditional ones as they become widely adopted and accepted. Some librarians may disagree with how we've chosen to separate our two main categories of service, but we use the terms descriptively, not prescriptively.

Many librarians argue that traditional services (a) are offered by most public libraries; (b) have "always" been provided; and (c) are provided free of charge. Our discussion then makes a distinction between traditional services commonly provided free of charge in most public libraries and newer nontraditional services, many of which began to be provided in public libraries in the years following the advent of computers and the Internet. Karen Hyman argues that this penchant can be identified as the Rule of 1965, which holds that anything a library did prior to 1965 is basic and that everything else is extra.[11]

Today, most librarians see nontraditional services as simply different ways of providing what they've always offered—but with new technology. These services, however, are still often described as new or nontraditional; therefore some libraries apply fees to their delivery.

GATS Risks and the Traditional/Nontraditional Service Dichotomy

Defining some services as nontraditional gives the impression that public libraries are extending their reach by adding new services and, in doing so, are deviating from their mandate. There is, in fact, overlap with the private sector, as businesses also offer many of the new services. Just as book and video stores occasionally complain about library lending, newer library services—such as those that provide access to computers, information-literacy training, digitized materials, and the Internet—can be considered in competition with the private sector's growing information industry.

While libraries can argue that their collections only peripherally compete with bookstores on the basis that library holdings are necessarily retrospective, their computer-based services can make no such claim. Almost all of the materials, including training and other services, that are available on a library's computers are available from private-sector firms. Many of the firms are transnational corporations that provide cross-border services and could therefore direct trade challenges at libraries.

An increasing overlap between public library services and commercially available ones is evident. In fact, as more commercial providers take on functions that libraries perform, and as libraries add computer-based services, a zone of competition develops (see figures 2.3 to 2.5, in chapter 2 for an illustration of the zone of competition). That zone is where publicly funded libraries can become increasingly subject to GATS challenges. As we have already seen, public libraries are subsidized, and because the WTO frowns on subsidies, multinational private service providers could issue GATS challenges to public providers of library services.

Even traditional services such as book and video lending could be threatened. If public libraries are commercializing their services at the same time that overlap with the private sector is growing, they are placing themselves under the jurisdiction of GATS rules. By providing any services on a commercial basis, libraries may no longer have the protection offered to services in the exercise of government authority (an exemption described in chapter 2). While newer, nontraditional services are most at risk to GATS challenges, some traditional services are changing in ways that make them vulnerable, too. Indeed, whole public library systems can be privatized, and the potential GATS implications of such possibilities are worrisome, to say the least.

In the following pages, we discuss some of the specific traditional and nontraditional services that are offered increasingly on a commercial basis or that can be seen to compete with private-sector enterprises. We begin by looking at traditional services such as collections, including collection development, acquisitions and cataloging, lending and renting, and government information; reference and research services, including interlibrary loan and document delivery, photocopying, printing and faxing; and user services and programs, including room rentals and services for children, adults, and businesses. The chapter concludes with analyses of newer, nontraditional technology-based services such as digital collections, Internet-access services, information-literacy training, and virtual reference.

COLLECTIONS SERVICES

Historically, libraries have served their users by acquiring, storing, preserving, and organizing materials, and by providing assistance to individuals in locating the information they needed.[12] These are easily identified as traditional services: those that create and support library collections and serve library patrons. Unfortunately, while we mentioned the threat of outsourcing to nontraditional services earlier, recent trends toward outsourcing even the most basic library services make GATS challenges possible.

Collections Development, Acquisitions, and Cataloging

The acquiring and organizing of books, along with their cataloging and classification, are long-standing traditional services that are implicit in the idea of a library. Until the 1970s most of that work was done in-house by professionally trained staff. By as early as 1901, the Library of Congress began distributing cataloging cards to libraries, and since the early 1970s, bibliographic utilities such as the Online Computer Library Center (OCLC) have enabled libraries to access common cataloging data. Meanwhile, many libraries have contracted acquisitions work to book jobbers and serials vendors, which provide both cataloging records and shelf-ready materials, thereby reducing the number of staff needed in technical services departments. The financial benefits are obvious, but there could be serious consequences if GATS rules become an issue. As we discuss later in this chapter and again in greater detail in chapter 5, several organizations have distinguished between contracting out certain internal tasks to an outside supplier and contracting out decision-making and managerial responsibilities.[13]

Outsourcing Collection Development

Approval plans have been used as an outsourcing mechanism for collection development since the initiation of the Greenaway Plan in 1928. The Greenaway Plan began at the Philadelphia Free Library as a program whereby publishers would send copies of books to librarians who could determine whether those books met their collection needs. In that way, the professional process of book selection was enhanced, though partially commercialized.[14] With the explosive growth in the number of new academic and public libraries in the 1960s and early 1970s, vendors expanded to help libraries establish "opening-day collections" by providing full acquisitions, cataloging, and book-preparation services. Material selection was based on profiles developed by the library staff and vendors, as well as on standard lists, such as the Association of College & Research Libraries' *Opening Day Collection*.[15] In public libraries, opening-day collection builders could use *Public Library Catalog*.[16] Even today, Brodart, a company that offers a range of library-oriented services and supplies, actively markets its opening-day partnerships with public libraries.[17]

In recent years, under the influence of budget cuts and ideologically driven government outsourcing policies, even long-established public libraries have begun to outsource their entire collection-development process. Since the early 1990s, collection-development functions, including selection, have been increasingly contracted out to private-sector national and international jobbers and vendors that provide either complete collections or materials for specific subject areas. Though collection policies and the broad limits of library profiles are usually still developed in-house, vendors make many of the decisions regarding individual titles, along with cataloging and book-preparation activities. Next to cataloging, collection development is perhaps the most commonly outsourced service in public libraries. While, as we discussed earlier, outsourcing is an obvious, efficient, and effective way to cut spending on staff in budget-restricted libraries, there is no consensus as to whether outsourcing is always appropriate.

There have been some notable failures. The most controversial of these are described in a 2000 study for the ALA done by Robert S. Martin and others at Texas Woman's University. In 1996, as a result of budget cuts, the Hawaii Public Library System outsourced its entire collection-development process to Baker and Taylor, a North Carolina book vendor. The contract "covered selection, acquisitions, cataloging, processing, and distributing books, spoken word, audio, video and multi-media titles."[18] The unfortunate result was that the library collection suffered a multitude of mishaps, including, for example, receiving sixty-one copies of Newt Gingrich's novel, along with geographically inappropriate books such as *A Practical Guide to*

Lambs and Lamb Caring. The contract was terminated due to a barrage of public and staff complaints and the corporation's poor performance in meeting the terms of its contract with the library system.

What's Wrong with Outsourcing and Contracting Out Collections Services?

According to the Public Library Association, the need to obtain goods and services from commercial vendors is seldom questioned. Furthermore, "the relationship between publishers, public librarians, book jobbers, subscription services, and a host of library suppliers is critical for the institutional viability of libraries of all types."[19] The Public Library Association, however, also acknowledges the critics of outsourcing who "maintain that outsourcing of core functions threatens public library institutional viablility, diverts local control, and diminishes the contributed value of professional librarians."[20] As regards the last point, it is clear that outsourcing cataloging and collection development take some of the most professional of responsibilities out of the hands of public librarians. The ALA Task Force on Outsourcing recognized that, too, with its statement that "[q]ualified professional library staff members are critical to developing and maintaining collections responsive to user needs of serviced communities and providing access to information."[21]

Outsourcing turns a publicly subsidized service into a market for private firms. While many government services are already outsourced, the GATS introduces a new level of potential threats to which libraries may not be immune. Libraries that outsource their services put themselves in a competitive zone that could enable large companies that provide services to libraries to demand that all library work be outsourced, on the premise that no publicly subsidized library should be providing like services in competition with the private sector. Contracting out and outsourcing as forms of privatization are discussed in detail in chapter 5.

LENDING AND RENTING

The third traditional service offered by any public library, after building collections and organizing them for access, is lending materials to library patrons—usually members of the community who fund the library by paying taxes. Public libraries have always *lent* books and other materials, often with some restrictions for varying formats, but some libraries allow patrons to *rent* certain items. Thus we consider various aspects of lending and renting, and the extent to which that service, when offered on a commercial basis or in competition with private-sector providers, may become a problem.

Library Cards

In recent years, some public libraries have begun to charge community members for library cards. A wave of fee impositions occurred in Alberta following provincial budget cuts to libraries, and it is not surprising that Alberta libraries discovered that charging fees for borrowing privileges meant that fewer people used libraries.[22]

While most public libraries have managed to provide free access for local users, many do charge a fee to individuals who are not members of the community when they want a library card to borrow books. Do fees for library cards imply commercialization? Yes: As discussed in chapter 2, charging fees for any service means that a library is operating on a commercial basis and therefore opening itself to a potential GATS challenge on that basis.

Lending Books and Other Print Materials

When they were first being established, public libraries were disliked by booksellers, which often saw them as unfair competition because libraries lent books instead of selling them. Over the years it became apparent that libraries encouraged book reading, which in turn encouraged book buying. One review of research on public library use noted that "[r]esearch going back to the 1940s consistently shows that those people who regularly buy books are more likely to belong to a library. Library members own more books than nonmembers."[23] Librarians argue that library collections do not compete with but rather complement bookstores by providing access to older, out-of-print books and items that do not sell well. Given the history of public library book lending, a GATS challenge from that direction would seem unlikely. The increasing consolidation and strength of bookstore chains such as Barnes & Noble and online book vendors such as amazon.com, however, suggest that the GATS does open the door to challenges to the publicly subsidized lending of books.

Lending Audio—Records, Cassettes, and Compact Discs

In addition to its vast array of books, almost any library also has a collection of sound recordings, including but not limited to audiobooks, language materials, and music. Public libraries began providing sound recordings when vinyl discs became available, and many libraries had "extensive collections of 78 rpm records by the end of the 1950s."[24] Since then, vinyl recordings and tapes have been augmented or replaced with CDs. In public libraries, the collections are commonly weighted toward audiobooks and educational or instructional materials, rather than music, and thus do not appear to be in great competition with music stores. Franchised music stores, however, are an ever-expanding international business; both new and used audiobooks are sold by Internet marketers based around the world. As those stores become ubiquitous and dominate more of the market, they may want to increase that market share by trying to eliminate music recordings from library collections. Here, too, the GATS grants a potential means by which these companies could challenge public libraries that lend such recordings.

Lending Films, Videos/DVDs

By the 1940s North American public libraries began to include 8mm and 16mm films in their collections,[25] and in the 1980s libraries collected videotape recordings as well. When those collections were first introduced, private video-rental operators raised objections to what they claimed was unfair competition. The counterargument, however, was and is that public libraries "include the types of quality documentary and educational materials and the hard-to-find international cinema works that patrons are unlikely to encounter in the local video store."[26] That kind of concentration on collecting for cultural and educational value has been changing, however, as Wendy Newman told the director of the Services Trade Policy Division, Department of Foreign Affairs and International Trade, when she was president of the Canadian Library Association:

> [I]t does appear that libraries were careful to diffuse . . . criticism by not competing with the video rental outlet's core business—recent Hollywood feature films. In the early years it was common for library video collections not to contain any feature films. Since the early days of these collections, the prohibition on current Hollywood features has relaxed considerably in most libraries. While libraries do apply critical standards to the acquisition of video, there has been an increasing overlap between library holdings and the collections offered by commercial rental outlets.[27]

The problem is that while video stores began mostly as neighborhood mom-and-pop operations, most of them have been replaced by large multinational franchises, such as Blockbuster. In her 2002 letter to Canada's Department of Foreign Affairs and International Trade, Newman wrote that video collections are now part of "overall library services" that "extend beyond the strict definition of library and archive services provided by the World Trade Organization." She further asserted that

> provincial legislation in most jurisdictions prohibits libraries from charging for the lending of items whether they be books or such items as video tapes. Given

the legislated free provision of tax funded video and DVD collections in direct competition with commercial entities, this service appears to CLA to be a candidate for a GATS challenge.[28]

Renting Library Materials

Renting library materials to patrons or charging for the use of certain types of materials, such as those easily damaged or in high demand, is not unknown in public libraries. Some also charge for use of audiocassettes and videos, as they earlier charged for the use of long-playing vinyl discs and 16mm films. In addition, many libraries use rental services that enable them to supplement collections with high-use reading materials. Multiple copies of popular books, for example, may be rented from commercial providers such as Brodart, through its McNaughton Plan.[29] To pay for that service, libraries usually charge the patron a nominal fee to help cover the costs of the rental service. The practice is fairly common in many of North America's smaller public libraries.

Edward Evans explains that the fees for borrowing videos from libraries were low "when compared with stores" and, further, that "in some cases videos became a source of revenue in times of budget cuts."[30] While that observation may reflect the pragmatic truth, Evans was clearly unaware of potential GATS implications; his statements illustrate how public libraries that are renting out materials are doing so directly—even if completely unintentionally—in competition with other service suppliers and are therefore by definition subjecting themselves to GATS scrutiny.

GOVERNMENT INFORMATION

In both the United States and Canada, many public libraries receive government publications free of charge as part of depository programs. They also receive electronic versions of government information, which were first issued on CD-ROM and are now usually available via password-protected Internet access. The programs are obvious forms of government subsidization, which has always been justified on the ground that the public needs free access to government information in a democratic society. Depository programs ensure that current government information is widely available across the country. Public libraries that do not have depository status (often small libraries or branches) tend to have poor government-information collections.

Where deficiency is the case, particularly in the United States, private-sector vendors are quick to offer government publications for sale; depository libraries that want extra copies of particular publications may obtain them from these companies. One such vendor, Bernan Associates, distributes more than 45,000 publications and describes itself as a "one-stop source for publications by hundreds of U.S. government agencies and intergovernmental organizations."[31] Vendors like Bernan have had a long and fruitful relationship with libraries in many countries. But under the GATS, the argument could be made that that publicly subsidized depository libraries are competing unfairly with such vendors and that, in fact, those libraries are benefiting unfairly from depository programs. For that matter, the depository program itself may be vulnerable to a challenge.

In addition to depositories and related vendors, American citizens have yet another way to obtain government information. While Canada protects its government documents with Crown Copyright and republication is possible only with permission from the government that is rarely given, in the United States, government information is often republished and made accessible to libraries from commercial firms. When the U.S. government itself seeks to make information readily available, it is sometimes challenged by the private sector. The Software & Information Industry Association, for one, argued as follows:

> Government initiatives to disseminate public information electronically should not result in expanding the role of government in providing commercial information services. Rather, government efforts to disseminate information should take full advantage of public–private partnerships or independent private services and products to efficiently and effectively provide the desired added value for the public.[32]

Governments, they are arguing, should not be making certain information available for free. In fact, proposals by the U.S. National Technical Information Service to provide free access to its information brought this response to NITS's associate director of business development from Ken Wasch, president of SIIA:

> NTIS' proposal to increase the level of information and services provided to the public for free, while maintaining a fee structure for vendors to re-disseminate the NTIS database, represents a direct subsidization of services provided free around the world by private sector resellers. . . . Clearly, any move to provide free, comprehensive access to even a subset of the NTIS database would establish NTIS as a competitor to its private sector vendors.[33]

Private-sector players are quick to argue that publicly subsidized agencies should not compete with private-sector ventures. Another telling example is the discontinuance of PubSCIENCE, a freely accessible database from the U.S. Department of Energy that provided access to abstracts of scientific articles published in peer-reviewed journals. The ALA's Washington Office Newsline (ALAWON) described how this database, which was available from 1999 to November 2002, was shut down because of private sector concerns, specifically from Cambridge Scientific Abstracts and Elsevier Science Inc. Those companies argued that PubSCIENCE was an unfair competitor. ALAWON went on to show how the decision to discontinue PubSCIENCE was made:

> While there were only 7 comments in favor of ending PubSCIENCE, there were nearly 240 public comments, many from librarians and other PubSCIENCE users, pressing for continuance of the indexing service. Negative comments generally originated from members of the information industry and some publishers. This group has, since 2000, targeted PubSCIENCE because they perceive it to be in competition with two private sector indexes—Scirus (owned by Reed Elsevier) and Infotrieve. Scirus and Infotrieve currently provide no cost indexing services to the public. However, this could change to a fee-based subscription service at any time.[34]

The Association of Research Libraries (ARL) argued that PubSCIENCE did not "directly compete with Scirus, Infotrieve or other fee-based commercial services" because it targeted the scientific and research community in energy-related fields, while "the other resources are being marketed primarily to corporations and other large entities rather than the public."[35] One commentator sums up the issue:

> DOE [Department of Energy] touts PubSCIENCE as a significant taxpayer benefit. The private sector never saw it that way. Since its inception, PubSCIENCE has been a target. Database producers and some scholarly publishers felt threatened by the free availability of peer-reviewed scientific information. The Software & Information Industry Association (SIIA) is on record as opposing what it sees as unfair competition from the government.[36]

The story of PubSCIENCE's demise shows how susceptible governments are to lobbying from the private sector and how easily those governments can eliminate public access to information if pressured. That said, it might be naïve and overly optimistic to anticipate a more positive response from governments that are subject to pressure from the World Trade Organization.

REFERENCE AND RESEARCH SERVICES

Public libraries began to provide reference services in the 1880s. These services were and continue to be routinely offered by professional staff and trained paraprofessionals to walk-in patrons. Telephone reference service became available in the early 20th century, supplemented later by fax and e-mail.[37] More recently, libraries started to use digital collections and began to provide structured virtual reference services using e-mail and chat technologies. The next sections will examine a range of research and reference services that are provided either for a fee or in inadvertent competition with private suppliers. Digital collection and virtual reference are discussed under the heading "Newer Technology-Based Services."

Research Services

In addition to reference help, larger public libraries with research-level collections may offer research services to individual patrons, advanced students, and, sometimes, businesses (specific services for businesses will be discussed in more detail later in the chapter). While research help may also be offered by a library's reference desk, the implication is that more time and effort are spent on requests coming to a research service than to a reference desk. That is why the enhanced help is often offered on a fee-for-service basis to both in-house and distance users. For example, the New York Public Library's NYPL Express offers personalized services from its information specialists at rates ranging from $75 an hour for standard service to $125 an hour for expedited service, with "database fees, photocopies, tolls calls, etc.," being extra.[38] Similarly, the Minneapolis Public Library offers INFORM, which, on MPL's website, is described as a "nonprofit, cost recovery, research service. Our specialists have a professional, creative approach to serving your personal or business information needs. INFORM has served thousands of clients worldwide. No project is too big or too small."[39]

Clearly these public libraries are providing the service on a commercial basis. While they are not for-profit, the services *are* generating revenue. They are not necessarily in competition with the private sector, as few private-sector research services offer the kind of general research assistance available from large public libraries. However, as we discuss in the Services for Business section, many private-sector research services have been established specifically to serve the business community. A private-sector firm serving business clients might not distinguish between general and business research services in the public library, which means that any research service has the potential to be perceived as unfairly competitive.

Interlibrary Loan and Document Delivery

Interlibrary-loan and document-delivery services enhance collections by providing materials that are not locally available. Interlibrary loan (ILL), another of the long-standing traditional library services, achieves that goal by lending tangible materials from one library to another. The service has been provided in libraries since the early 1900s and the first ILL codes were developed in 1917.[40]

Photocopying and faxing expanded the types of items (e.g., articles, chapters) available and increased the speed with which they could be sent. Originally the service was provided free of charge to users; today, however, many libraries levy fees when they lend materials or fax items to other libraries. The charge is either absorbed by the borrowing library or passed on to individual requestors.

The Cleveland Public Library charges no fee to send materials to other Ohio libraries but charges out-of-state and foreign libraries $10 and $20 per item, respectively.[41] While there is little competition with private service providers or intent to go beyond cost recovery, libraries are still operating on a commercial basis and are therefore vulnerable to GATS rules.

Document-Delivery Services

Some public libraries offer document-delivery services (DDS) to supplement interlibrary loans. There is no doubt that document-delivery services are convenient: They retrieve or locate the needed publication and often send it to an offsite requester electronically. In fact, many public libraries advertise that service to local small businesses. The *Online Dictionary for Library and Information Science* explains that DDS is generally a fee-for-service transaction:

> The provision of published or unpublished documents in hard copy, microform, or digital format, usually for a fixed fee upon request. In most libraries, document delivery service is provided by the interlibrary loan office on a cost-recovery basis. . . . Also refers to the physical or electronic delivery of documents from a library collection to the residence or place of business of a library user, upon request.[42]

Libraries generally pass fees they incur on to the requesting patron, and some have an additional service charge. Thus by charging for ILL and document delivery, the library is providing a traditional service on a commercial basis. Again, while there is no profit motive, the activity could contribute to a library's being subject to a trade challenge.

Public Libraries as Commercial Document Delivery Suppliers

In addition to locating needed materials through ILL or DDS, some large public libraries established themselves as document-delivery suppliers in a more directly commercial manner. For example, NYPL Express is open to everyone who can pay the fee, which ranges from standard service for $15 (for three- or four-day service) to express service for $50 (documents within three hours).[43]

When public libraries establish document supply services in a commercial manner, they are obviously competing with private-sector firms such as, for example, Instant Information Systems. That company charges for paper or electronic copies on a sliding scale, depending on the speed of service requested. Typical costs include a base fee ranging from $7.75 to $19.75, depending on turnaround time, plus a charge of $0.25 per page for mailed paper copies, $1 per page for fax delivery, or $0.50 per page to receive an electronically delivered PDF document.[44] There is clearly room for profit to be made by library entrepreneurs.

Providing document-delivery services in libraries is justified on the grounds that they are a natural extension of traditional ILL and that libraries have no intent to make a profit. As explained in the Canadian Library Association letter regarding the GATS, the fees charged for such services are typically "based on the recovery of direct costs, but not recovery of the full indirect costs, which would include a proportion of the costs of acquiring, processing and maintaining collections, general administrative costs, and the physical building infrastructure." The letter goes on to state that, in fact, "[p]roportionally the indirect costs far exceed the direct costs, and therefore these services are heavily subsidized . . . [and] compete with commercial ventures and are therefore potentially exposed to a challenge under the provisions of GATS."[45]

Photocopying, Printing, and Faxing

Photocopying is perhaps one of the oldest technology-based services in libraries. Public libraries began to provide photocopiers soon after the first commercial Xerox machines appeared on the market in the 1960s, but the machines were fairly rare in libraries until the 1970s. At that time, while libraries charged for photocopy services, they generally charged less per page than did the rapidly proliferating private copy shops. Libraries were able to subsidize copying because providing access to the machines was seen as an extension of traditional library services. Accordingly, overhead costs were not included in the price per copy. The cost of photocopying, however, rose inexorably over time, not so much because of private sector pressure as because librarians saw the machines as a way to generate much-needed revenue and cover some of the staff costs of servicing the copiers.

Most libraries developed policies regarding fees for photocopying and faxing. The Seattle Public Library, for example, charges "for faxes, photocopying and printing at public-access computers to defray financial costs, conserve resources and ensure equity-of-access standards."[46] Whatever the rate or justification, charging fees implies operation on a commercial basis. At the same time, competition with private-sector providers is increasing as international franchises such as Mail Boxes Etc. spring up to provide copy, printing, and computer services.[47]

Some libraries are contracting out photocopying services in their entirety to commercial firms such as Xerox Corp. In early 2004, a press release issued by Xerox described how libraries in Memphis, Nashville, New Orleans, and San Francisco are "achieving the goal of many public entities—simultaneously offering improved patron services and saving money—through contracts signed with Xerox Corporation's Global Services Division." The release continues:

> At the Memphis/Shelby County Public Library and Nashville Public Library, printing services were streamlined to reduce equipment, maintenance and supply costs, allowing staff to focus on their primary mission of helping patrons locate information. The solution also helped the Memphis/Shelby County Library to offer new color printing services. In addition, the *on-site Xerox employee* [italics added] at the Memphis/Shelby County Public Library maintains and administers the system and collects card fees.[48]

That precedent demonstrates that any public library providing similar photocopying services directly to patrons, regardless of the rate level, is competing with a private-sector supplier.

USER SERVICES AND PROGRAMS

Librarians have provided "more than lending" services for decades, and programs directed at particular user groups have a long history in libraries. Originally primarily book based, more recently these programs have become extremely varied. In the discussion that follows, we name some services that are directed at specific categories of users and identify the extent to which providing them services is placing libraries in a vulnerable position vis-à-vis trade challenges.

Services for Children and Young Adults

Children's services have been offered by libraries since the end of the nineteenth century; their purpose has been to promote literacy, reading, and creativity. The services are seen as essential, especially in light of the fact that most users of public libraries are children and young adults.[49] The programs are important: National Center for Education Statistics indicates that about 49 million American children attended library programs nationwide in 2000.[50] Young people use libraries for the range of services they offer, including, most often, lending, activity programming, and homework help.

Book-Based Services

Children are encouraged to come to libraries to be introduced to books and reading and to take books home—sometimes to homes where no other books can be found. In communities that do not have school libraries, children are usually taken to local public libraries with their classes for what is often their first exposure to public library services and materials.

With those ends in mind, librarians try to develop collections for various reading levels and provide fresh and new materials on a regular basis. Children are encouraged to borrow many books and at the same time learn to care for them and return them to the library by their due date. Librarians also provide a number of ancillary book-based services, such as story-times, which help develop children's reading skills. Book clubs for older children, book discussion groups for teens, competitions for book prizes, and summer reading programs are also very common.

Activity Programming

Other activities that bring children into libraries but that are not primarily book based include arts-and-crafts programs, computer training, and so on. While these activities are attractive to children and do bring them into the library, they might cross over into the zone of competition with for-profit children's enterprises.

The number of private-sector providers of these services is increasing. Many are franchises that encourage franchisees to rent space in malls or other storefront settings. One of these, Gymboree Play and Music (with franchises in twenty-six countries), explains on its website that it "is looking to locate in commercial locations, such as strip malls, shopping centers and regional malls. Commercial sites best represent the brand and have greater potential to deliver on all aspects of the business."[51] Some of the franchises are parent-child play centers, while others provide child-care services and still others offer courses or regularly scheduled programs. They supply a wide range of activities that public libraries might also offer, such as art classes, preschool computer education, and after-school drama programs.[52]

These franchises are growing quickly in popularity, size, and importance, as Entrepreneur.com notes: "Franchises that blend education with fun are still hot, as are a variety of cutting-edge child-related businesses, ranging from baseball camps to Victorian tea parties. Children themselves are proving to be no minor market—they make or influence almost $150 billion in purchases each year."[53] While the services were undoubtedly created to meet a perceived need and fill a market niche, publicly subsidized library services that are "like" could be seen as competing unfairly with private-sector ventures.

Homework Assistance and Tutoring

Another area of competition is created when franchised educational services offer homework assistance and tutoring. Many libraries already provide homework-assistance links that can be accessed from home computers; one example is the New York Public Library's Teen Link site.[54] Many libraries are embarking on new programs to provide in-library assistance to schoolchildren doing their homework. In 2002, Cindy Mediavilla predicted that while only one in seven public libraries was currently offering formal after-school homework help, the need for homework-related library services would increase dramatically in the coming years.[55] The County of Los Angeles Public Library is trying to meet that growing need with an innovative program that provides enhanced resources, computer technology, and homework helpers to support the educational needs of students in targeted communities. The program is supported by a combination of grants and other community-based resources, and as of November 2004, thirty-one centers had been established in the Los Angeles area.[56]

The Cleveland Public Library also offers special assistance to students. In addition to targeted training, such as its special services for those students preparing for statewide proficiency tests, the library system offers online homework help, using chat technology to link to the State Library of Ohio's "Homework Now" website.[57] Its service links students to assistance from "live, online professional tutors from 2:00 p.m. to 10:00 p.m." However, the Cleveland Public Library site fails to inform its patrons that the tutors are not local library staff members. In fact, the service is run by librarians from across the state during business hours and in off-hours by Tutor.com, a private firm. On its website, Tutor.com's "Live Homework Help" is described as its "flagship service" that "works side by side with virtual reference services." Libraries such as Cleveland's subscribe to Tutor.com, though rates for libraries are not given on the corporation's website, in order to provide students with free access to tutors who are "certified teachers, college professors, professional tutors, graduate school students and undergraduates from top universities." The company's website markets the service to libraries with the following information:

> Tutor.com works with every client to ensure a successful program. This includes assigning a Program Manager who will work with you throughout your program and is available via email [*sic*] or phone to answer questions and consult on your program. Your library will also receive 4-color promotional materials including customizable posters and bookmarks and access to a client website with templates for newsletters, press releases, presentations and more![58]

The Tutor.com example illustrates a possible avenue of private-sector involvement in the provision of public library service; public/private partnerships of that kind give libraries opportunities to offer services that would be too expensive or complicated for the library to run on its own. However, such partnerships also raise questions about competition: Does a public library that provides its own homework service free of charge compete with private companies like Tutor.com? Probably. We will leave this for now and return in chapter 5 to discuss the GATS implications of public–private partnerships in detail.

Even as libraries are expanding their services to provide homework assistance and tutoring, some of the same private services are going directly to potential customers. Students who do not have access to Tutor.com through their public library, for example, can obtain private tutoring and personal live homework help subscriptions directly from the company. Private tutoring costs $20 an hour, and live homework help subscriptions cost $99 per month ("first week free!").[59] Again, that service has potential to become a very lucrative industry. Tutor.com lists the public libraries in each state that have contracted to offer free homework help service, though only the names of the libraries are provided; there are no easy links to the free services. In that way Tutor.com is surely making a tidy profit from competing with the public service from which it also benefits financially.

Other private companies are part of the quickly expanding supplemental-education sector. They differ from companies like Tutor.com in that they do not also contract with public libraries to provide services. One example is Kumon, a worldwide franchise that started in Japan in 1958 and that as of 2004 had 1,180 outlets in the United States, 340 in Canada, and 23,050 more in other parts of the world.[60] Kumon's service, which costs $80 to $110 a month per student, is described in the following excerpt from the company's website:

> Located in nearly every corner of the world and with an enrolment [*sic*] of more than 3 million children, Kumon pre-school to high school, the Kumon Method empowers students to reach their full potential by helping them to master, step by step, the skills and knowledge they need for success in higher level math and reading comprehension.[61]

Other education businesses, such as Sylvan Learning Centers[62] (now part of Educate Inc., which provides live online tutoring on "eSylvan"), and Oxford Learning Centres[63] (originally a Canadian franchise), are expanding their commercial presence aggressively and soliciting potential franchisees throughout the world. As these companies expand internationally, the GATS offers them an opportunity to challenge the existence of publicly subsidized homework centers in libraries.

Services for Adults

Public libraries offer a variety of book-based services to adults too, including large-print books, book clubs and discussions, author evenings, and so on. Basic adult-literacy classes are also common, both in libraries and in other publicly subsidized organizations. Generally, with the exception of private tutoring, there is little private-sector involvement in such training. Libraries also provide courses and workshops that are not specifically book based. These can range from job skills workshops to cooking classes and specific arts and crafts sessions, some of which are conducted by library staff and some by outsiders. Public libraries often plan special events, and some even have an employee designated as a special events coordinator.

An examination of almost any large public library's website reveals a wide variety of programs. At the Cleveland Public Library, one can learn how to preserve family heirlooms, at the Indianapolis Public Library how to play chess, and at the Boston Public Library about tenants' rights and responsibilities. Like children's activities, adult programs are designed not only to teach classes that are of interest to the public but also to bring people to the library and perhaps make patrons out of visitors. If fees are charged for any of these activities, however, not only are patrons less likely to attend, but libraries are also clearly operating on a commercial basis. Even if no fees are charged, such services fall within the growing zone of competition.

Some specific programs designed for adults are also offered by private firms, and therefore might fall in the zone of competition with respect to the GATS. For example, English as a Second Language (ESL) training has a rich history in public libraries. More recently, income tax assistance programs have been introduced. These services are offered with the best of intentions, and we believe that libraries should continue to offer them. Libraries must be aware, however, that there could be challenges for providing them in a publicly subsidized environment, especially since there are so many private suppliers.

ESL Training

Public libraries tend to provide both ESL collections and classes. In the United States, library-based ESL classes were available for immigrants by the early twentieth century. Since the 1980s, increasing waves of immigrants and refugees have resulted in public libraries establishing themselves "as centers for literacy education. Some provide space and promotion for small group or one-on-one ESL instruction, often in cooperation with local literacy providers and volunteer organizations."[64]

Many public libraries offer ESL classes for no charge. The Dallas Public Library's website lists courses at almost all of its branches. The Toronto Public Library offers a range of ESL programs for adults, summer programs for children, and opportunities for ESL classes to visit libraries. In all of these, the adult courses charge only for the cost of materials.

While public libraries are offering expanded ESL programs, however, a growing number of independent language schools offer similar classes. Hundreds of such schools throughout the world are listed on numerous Internet directories, and they are joining forces to develop what they call a language industry. In Canada, for example, accreditation agencies such as the Canada Language Council (CLC) monitor, set standards, and promote such schools.[65] Another agency, the Canadian Association of Private Language Schools (CAPLS) "represents the interests of Canadian private language schools both at the international and national level." CAPLS, in turn, is a member of the Global Alliance of English Language Associations.[66] Another organization, the Language Industry Association (AILIA) was launched in Canada in 2003 "to make Canada a world leader in the language industry" and to be "the voice of the Canadian language industry."[67] In the United Kingdom, Quality English is "a sales and marketing company which is committed to promoting high quality English language schools and their courses to international students." While the company is currently U.K.–based, it is planning to expand internationally.[68] An international program based in France, The Eurolingua Institute, offers classes throughout the world, as well as one-on-one tutoring in many languages.[69]

These developments illustrate an increasing "industry" approach to ESL education. As these various associations become more powerful and international, they may object to competition from publicly subsidized organizations such as libraries. Public libraries generally do not charge for ESL classes and so cannot be considered to be operating in a commercial manner. They are, however, clearly in the zone of competition with private ESL schools, at least insofar as they offer classes to clientele who would otherwise have to pay for private tutoring.

Income Tax Assistance

Several governments help citizens fill out income tax forms. The U.S. government runs the Volunteer Income Tax Assistance (VITA) program, which offers free income tax return preparation assistance to seniors, people with disabilities, low-income persons, and others at thousands of locations throughout the country. Many of these programs are housed at public libraries during tax season. For example, the Las Vegas–Clark County Library District provides space for VITA as well as AARP Tax Counseling for the Elderly program.[70] The overlap with commercial services such as H&R Block is evident.

Services for Business

We have seen that public libraries provide research and document delivery services that can be used by businesses and other patrons. Small businesses especially can often find many items of interest in public library collections. Libraries may also target particular services at this group. The Arlington County Public Library in Virginia does so by offering free business programs on such topics as starting a small business, business-plan writing, tax preparation, and financial planning.[71]

Many public libraries also provide fee-based information-retrieval services specifically designed to serve business communities. Large public libraries, such as the New York Public Library with its NYPL Express service, serve an enormous and potentially nationwide business community. These kinds of services are well established in some cases: The Tulsa City-County Library has offered a fee-based service called Research Wizard for twenty-five years. Its website offers "you and your company information that is customized to meet your business needs and maximize your time and profits." Beyond the normal business information provided in libraries, the service offers business intelligence, customer prospecting, market research, industry analysis, and so on. The fee is "$60 per hour plus associated project costs, which may include online database, document retrieval, special delivery and long distance charges." Businesses can also subscribe to a membership plan for reduced rates on these services.[72]

In providing these fee-based services, public libraries are competing with a variety of commercial ventures. A typical private information provider is Factiva, a large company owned by Dow Jones & Reuters. In addition to providing extensive news and business information to the business community, Factiva provides individualized advice and expertise.[73] Independent information brokers (many of whom are freelance librarians) work in most cities providing those kinds of personalized services to businesses. Numerous business-information providers also offer some free information on their Internet sites, with invitations to pay for more advanced information services.[74]

While many libraries offer business-research help on a cost-recovery basis, the fact that they are charging at all means that they are operating commercially and are also in competition with private-sector information services. Unaware of possible GATS implications, Martha Gregory, Director of Tulsa's Research Wizard project, noted that "libraries in general must work to stay competitive in this environment. We have lost customers to the Internet and to the new information provider companies that have sprung up via the Internet."[75] In actual fact, what libraries need to do is evaluate very carefully what it means to "stay competitive"—especially where they provide services that are "like" those supplied by the private sector.

Public Libraries as Public Space: Room Rentals

From their earliest days, libraries have provided a free public space for readers to sit quietly (and warmly) without being harassed or urged to "move on." Public library reading, newspaper, and periodical rooms were commonly full to bursting with readers who wanted to scan a large number of publications or who could not afford to buy local newspapers, let alone books and magazines. Instead of the comfortable chairs we know so well today, libraries were usually and traditionally equipped with large tables with six or eight wooden chairs around them. Now, however, as libraries try to compete with the attractions of big-box bookstores, public reading areas are becoming more comfortable and inviting, and seats in public libraries tend to be filled with readers. The public reading spaces are one of the many contributions that libraries make to social advancement and self-education.

Other rooms in the library are often made available for community activities, workshops, and library programs. Use of these spaces is usually free to nonprofit groups, though many public libraries in recent years have begun to charge rent for their use. Typical library policies, such as that of the Lafayette Public Library in Colorado, restrict rentals to "individuals and organizations engaged in educational, cultural, intellectual, or charitable activities," and charge varying rates to nonprofit groups—from $10 per hour to $15 and $45 for three hours of use, with some free use for communitywide events.[76]

In some instances, libraries rent space to private firms. The Los Angeles Public Library does so quite extensively, though as far as booking privileges are concerned, the library lists such firms as third in priority, after the library itself and the Library Foundation of Los Angeles. Rates range up to $5,000 for a minimum four-hour rental at the central library.[77] By charging rent for these rooms, libraries may be operating on a commercial basis, and to the extent that the rooms are publicly subsidized, libraries may also be seen to be competing unfairly with private rental facilities such as hotels and conference centers.

NEWER TECHNOLOGY-BASED SERVICES

As the above discussion illustrates, advances in technology enabled libraries to provide a number of traditional services in new ways. These services are often described as new or nontraditional, the implication being that they are not core or basic to the library's mission. However, over time, some nontraditional services have become core. Microforms, for example, were once a new technology that helped libraries develop collections of materials that would not otherwise have been available. Though assisting users with reader-printers was often the low point of many a librarian's day, there was general agreement about the need to acquire microforms and their related technology. So now, microform-related services are no longer described as nontraditional. Photocopying was another nontraditional service that is now taken for granted. Many of the nontraditional services that we talk about today relate to using computers to provide access to information. Arguably, these services are simply extensions of traditional services using new technology and, as we discussed earlier in this chapter, these are the kinds of services that fall somewhere on the constantly shifting traditional/nontraditional continuum.

We have already described how technological advances were incorporated into some traditional services. Now we consider four services that some might categorize as nontraditional: digital collections and libraries, Internet access services, Internet training, and virtual reference. We believe that each of these is simply an extension of traditional collections, reference, and user services. However, the public—and some librarians—may not necessarily consider them to be core functions of, or funding priorities for, public libraries. In addition to that challenge, libraries must contend with the fact that they are moving steadily into a zone of competition with the private sector, which is constantly seeking to sell these new technology-based services directly to consumers.

Digital Collections and Digital Libraries

As the technology became available, many libraries moved aggressively toward providing digital collections and related services. The movement includes access to commercial and noncommercial digital materials as well as participation in both digitization projects and creating "born-digital" products. This activity is a natural expansion of the library's traditional collection, as was, say, the incorporation of microforms in the 1960s. The fact that we use computers to access digital collections does not make the provision of such collections nontraditional any more than did providing microform readers.

The presence of electronic information in libraries leads quite naturally to the concept of a digital library, which is defined by the *Online Dictionary for Library and Information Science* as a library "in which a significant portion of the resources are available in machine-readable format (as opposed to print or microform) accessible by means of computers. The digital content may be locally held or accessible remotely via computer networks."[78] As the definition suggests, many people think of digital libraries as physical libraries that have expanded their collections to include digital content. However, an alternative to this model is the kind of large, publicly funded digital library that is not specifically connected to a physical library and is established utilizing digitized collections and links to outside sources. One of many examples is the Perseus Digital Library, which describes itself as an "evolving digital library" and describes its goal as being "to bring a wide range of source materials to as large an audience as possible." That digital library is a university-based project funded by the National Endowment for the Humanities (and other public and private agencies and foundations) to provide free access to resources via the Internet.[79] Other organizations, such as the Association for Computing Machinery,[80] host digital libraries containing their own publications, though access to them is often limited to organization members.

While many digital libraries are repositories of scholarly work, others are designed for use by the general public. A key example is the Internet Public Library, a nonprofit "online library" located at the University of Michigan that provides library services to anyone with access to the Internet. IPL can serve the same population as public libraries, but because it has a presence only online, it is less tied to local users. It aims to "enhance the value of the Internet to its ever-expanding and varied community of users."[81] As a nonprofit organization, IPL is very unlikely to consider public libraries as competition for its services; in fact, it refers its users to their local libraries whenever possible.

Commercial Digital Libraries

As more and more materials are digitized, a variety of commercial digital libraries, such as netLibrary, HighBeam Research (formerly eLibrary), and Questia, are proliferating. Most recently, Google has entered the market. Each of these particular companies operates on a different digital library model, and while each has its own set of implications for public libraries with respect to the GATS, the general threat each has in terms of offering a like service is similar.

In the first model, a commercial digital library mimics the traditional idea of a book vendor's serving libraries. An example is NetLibrary, now a division of OCLC, which markets itself to all types of libraries and acts as a vendor by providing access to "full text digital books, journals, newspapers and other published works." A library can purchase a collection of electronic titles "just as they would print titles and netLibrary handles all of the technology and hosts the eBooks from [its] servers." The library pays the publishers' list prices for the ebooks, with discounts for volume plus a service fee to netLibrary; the fee is not published on netLibrary's website.[82] That kind of digital library is unlikely to present a GATS challenge because publicly funded libraries are its main market.

HighBeam Research and Questia, however, are examples of commercial digital libraries that market services directly to individuals and bypass any connection to physical libraries. According to its own website, HighBeam Research, the new name for a company that bought out earlier digital libraries, including eLibrary and encyclopedia.com, "delivers sophisticated research tools for serious business, education and personal research with convenient, customizable access to the free Web, selected online services and HighBeam™ Research's proprietary eLibrary database." The company provides its members with access to their "extensive archive of more than 35 million documents from over 3,000 sources—a vast collection of articles from leading publications, updated daily and going back as far as 20 years. Save your searches, save articles and set up alerts to save time and increase your efficiency." It provides a web-searching interface and offers a reference and research service, along with free access to the *Columbia Encyclopedia*. Members can also search "over 20 different encyclopedias, almanacs, dictionaries, and thesauri. Over 299,000 fact filled reference documents to help you find your answer faster." HighBeam is a subscription service, offering a free "basic" and a priced "full" membership. Basic members can search the eLibrary database, though they face restrictions, such as not being able to see, save, or download full-text articles. The monthly subscription rate for a full membership was US$19.95, or $99.95 annually in 2005.[83]

While HighBeam markets itself and its "productivity enhancing research tools" primarily to executives, entrepreneurs, and graduate students, Questia, as an example of a third model, targets high school and undergraduate students. It describes itself as an online library with (as of February 2005) "over 50,000 books and 400,000 journal, magazine, and newspaper articles." It provides access to materials on a wide range of research topics and claims to make "paper writing easy" as it "creates footnotes and bibliographies automatically" and "organizes your work with highlighter and project folders." Questia's website offers "24 × 7 access, every title is always available—the library is never closed." Automatically renewable subscriptions range from US$19.95 a month to $99.95 a year. Subscriber quotes "raving" about Questia are included on the site; among them: "WOW! (speechless momentarily) that was the BEST 'trip' I've ever taken to the library" and "I thought Questia was very easy to use and I loved the fact that it put together the bibliography for you in the end. I didn't have to leave my house to do a research paper. I got an A– in my senior class."[84] Quotes such as these, which are displayed by the company to try to prove that its services are more helpful than those offered by a library, should give any librarian pause.

The number of items available from commercial libraries is usually limited when compared with many urban public libraries. However, improved access for students and people in smaller communities, remote locations, or countries with limited public library service is an obvious selling point. That said, a surprising number of subscriber testimonials are from people in large urban centers with prominent public libraries.

Digital libraries such as HighBeam and Questia are providing the same materials and services that public libraries offer; therefore, they could make the claim that publicly subsidized institutions have an unfair competitive advantage in the market. Gregory Crane of the Perseus Project observes that electronic libraries are being created with collections that include tens of thousands of books, "[a]nd they are growing fast: although modest by the standards of print collections, these commercial digital libraries already dwarf even the largest non-profit [digital] collections."[85] A stunning example of the potential growth of digital libraries is the Google Print program, which digitizes new books and makes them available online along with targeted advertisements and "Buy-This-Book" links. Google claims that the "Buy-This-Book" links assist publishers and authors by generating sales. In December 2004, Google announced an expansion of Google Print: It had agreed to digitize collections from Harvard, Stanford, and Oxford universities, the University of Michigan, and the New York Public Library.[86] One journalist who praises the company for its expensive investment claims that the move will make Google the most comprehensive digital library in the world; however, he notes that access will be limited since users of Google Print will not be able to download, copy, paste, or save the books they see on Google. Furthermore, due to copyright restrictions, people may be limited to viewing a few pages, or sometimes only a few sentences of particular works. Even so, the expanded digitzation project will include thousands of books that are in the public domain, and hence no longer protected by copyright.[87]

The Google example illustrates the growth potential of commercial digital libraries and the potential overlap with the public library domain: As the company itself says, "Google's mission is to organize the world's information and make it universally accessible and useful."[88] (Last we checked, that was what librarians are also trying to do!) The GATS simply raises a new level of concern. As Paul Whitney, Director of the Vancouver Public Library warns, commercial e-content providers whose ventures have failed may pose a problem because their "inability to charge for what libraries offer for free may lead to questions regarding public subsidies when other companies try similar formats."[89] Google sees an overlap, too, though it is careful to declare that its actions are "not intended to replace or discourage funding for the efforts of others working to digitize library collections."[90] The degree to which that is true remains to be seen.

Internet Access Services

Public libraries provide Internet access as part of their commitment to intellectual freedom and access equity. According to the American Library Association, "Libraries in America are cornerstones of the communities they serve. Free access to the books, ideas, resources, and information in America's libraries is imperative for education, employment, enjoyment, and self-government."[91] Furthermore, the association explains, "As a profession, librarians share a commitment to equity of access. They have a long tradition of providing books and information to people who are geographically, physically or culturally isolated—in the earliest days, by foot and horseback. Today, librarians use the Internet and other new technologies to make their services accessible to all."[92]

The same principles are echoed in the Canadian Library Association's *Statement on Intellectual Freedom*, which says that libraries are expected "to acquire and make available the widest variety of materials in order to guarantee and facilitate access to all expressions of knowledge and intellectual activity."[93] Coupled with the CLA's *Statement on Internet Access,* which gives a broad justification for providing Internet related services in public libraries as part of the library's mission,[94] the CLA's *Information and Telecommunication Access Principles* places the convergence of computers and high-speed telecommunication networks within the context of universal access, literacy, and communication rights.[95]

Public libraries around the world have moved quickly to provide Internet access. In Australia, for example, there were 3,011 public access terminals in libraries, representing 63 percent of the nation's library service points, by the year 2000. The number of terminals, however, was insufficient to meet local demands; most libraries imposed time limits and booking systems for Internet use.[96]

In North America, about 10 percent of the population uses the Internet in public libraries. In Canada, 3,153 public libraries provided Internet service in 2000, accounting for 100 percent of all libraries that wanted to be connected (seventy-six libraries refused connections).[97] Meanwhile, Statistics Canada data for 2003 showed that 8.7 percent of all Canadian households had at least one person who used the public library to access the Internet, and the percentage of users was greatest (9.8 percent) for the highest income quartile.[98]

In the United States in 2000, a U.S. National Commission on Libraries and Information Science (NCLIS) study prepared by John Carlo Bertot and Charles

R. McClure reported that 94.5 percent of American public libraries provided Internet access, with an average of 8.3 workstations per outlet. The services are funded by municipal operating grants, various state sponsors, and private foundations.[99] By 2004, according to the Bill and Melinda Gates Foundation's *Toward Equality of Access* report, there was a slight increase in the percentage of libraries offering the service (95 percent) but a decrease in the number of workstations (7.5 per location). Also, according to this report, about 10 percent of Americans access the Internet through public library computers.[100]

Funding Internet Access

In many countries, Internet services in public libraries are funded, at least partly and usually mostly, by governments—commonly through a combination of municipal and state/provincial support. Therefore, as a publicly subsidized service, computer and Internet access is free of charge in most public libraries. In fact, American Library Association policies "oppose the charging of user fees for the provision of information services by all libraries and information services that receive their major support from public funds."[101]

The Canadian Library Association claims to support the UNESCO *Public Library Manifesto*, which bluntly states that "[t]he public library shall in principle be free of charge."[102] However, the CLA is unclear about its own position on user fees for Internet access, merely writing in its *Statement on Internet Access* that it encourages libraries to "offer Internet access with the fewest possible restrictions."[103] In reality, most Canadian public libraries offer free Internet access, certainly at least where they were initially funded by the federal government's Community Access Program (CAP). That program provided money for equipment, connections, staff, training, and technical support beginning in the mid-1990s. It did so by distributing funds to nonprofit organizations that in turn allocated money to provide Internet access to communities. In 2003 CAP supported "up to 10,000 public Internet access sites in rural, remote and urban communities";[104] In 2004, the program was reconfigured, and funding was largely reallocated. Some libraries do charge nominal fees for Internet access. In Australia, for example, "access to the Internet is free, generally speaking, in all states except Queensland and Tasmania." Some public libraries do not impose fees on members but do charge fees to nonmembers. Some charge all users equally; the Sydney Public Library, for example, charges all library patrons A$2 per hour.[105]

In some countries, charging fees for Internet use violates specific legislation and regulations regarding free access. For example, in the United States, libraries are prohibited from charging for access to the electronic collection of government publications that are provided free of charge by the Federal

Depository Library Program.[106] Understanding how Internet access fits into the legislation under which public libraries are established is more problematic, however. While the legislation usually has specific requirements regarding free access, what defines "free" can vary by jurisdiction. Under the Library Act in British Columbia (*RSBC* 1996, c. 264), for example, "public library collections must be accessible on site without charge and every library board must allow residents and electors of the area served by the library board to borrow library materials free of charge."[107] Interpreted narrowly, the legislation could limit free public access to library collections and not extend it to the Internet. Another example is from Australia, where most public libraries are legally required to provide core services for no charge. Depending on the relative affluence or philosophical bent of each library, some make extremely generous provisions for users, while others charge (usually modest amounts) for noncore services. Other librarians rely on the discretion of their staff to determine how much and for what services to charge.[108] In addition to the variations in service levels that these differences imply, the Australian legislation raises the question of defining *core*, which, as noted earlier in this chapter, has significant implications for the provision of funding and services. Clearly today, with so much information being provided electronically, Internet access should be defined as a core service, and weak policy statements, such as the CLA's, must be strengthened and made more inclusive.

Competing with the Private Sector in Providing Internet Access

It should be obvious that most public libraries are not providing Internet access on a commercial basis. Are they, however, competing with private service providers? As the seemingly exponential growth in the number of Internet cafés throughout the world demonstrates, there is no shortage of private-sector participation. While some Internet service providers, or ISPs, are independent operations, many are actually controlled by franchises, of which many are large international conglomerates. Greg Keizer, writing for *PC World*, reported that in a survey of that magazine's subscribers, "fewer than 25 percent subscribe to a local service. More than half connect via a national provider, and 16 percent use a regional ISP." That trend suggests that the ISP sector is growing in strength and clout. He continues:

> The ISP business is huge. According to *Boardwatch*, a publication that covers the ISP market, more than 7,400 Internet service providers now compete for consumer and small-business customers. But the big daddy remains America Online. With membership estimated at 21.4 million by Internet analyst firm Jupiter Communications, AOL dwarfs every other ISP.[109]

In addition to the ISP-specific companies, large telephone and telecommunications corporations usually provide Internet services, as do cable companies. Most ISPs charge subscribers on a monthly use basis, but as Keizer points out, some have formed affinity groups (partnerships between ISPs and unrelated businesses or organizations) to offer free or cheap Internet access. Those companies, of which NetZero is one example, do so by soliciting other businesses that have highly visible advertisements on the company's Internet sites.

The GATS implications of this growing national and international commercial ISP sector were noted by Wendy Newman of the Canadian Library Association in her letter to the DFAIT:

> There is no direct government measure that legislates free public access to the Internet. Direct and indirect government involvement in developing the infrastructure to facilitate broad access [has taken place], but exploitation of the infrastructure is available to public sector and private sector organizations alike. As public use and interest increases, [*sic*] so will commercial Internet service providers see opportunities for the expansion of fee-based services. In this environment, the access provided free of charge to the public by libraries, may well be seen as subsidized competition.[110]

As we have discussed, where like services are perceived as subsidized, a GATS challenge could arise. Clearly, librarians must become and remain aware of potential trade threats to free and universal access to vital online resources.

Information-Literacy Training

While it is widely recognized that providing Internet access in public libraries is key to guaranteeing access to information, it is also true that library patrons need skills and knowledge to use information technology. The Gates Foundation report cited earlier recognizes that much of today's technology training is done through one-on-one instruction, as "almost all libraries provide basic computer and Internet training on a daily basis through individual assistance from librarians," and that "informal one-on-one assistance from librarians has the additional benefit of teaching computer skills in the context of the patron's own search for information."[111]

While individualized assistance is probably the most effective way to provide information-literacy training, it is very staff-intensive and hence costly. In order to teach patrons more efficiently, many public libraries offer group workshops on the use of computers and the Internet. The 2000 NCLIS report found that 62.3 percent of American library outlets in the U.S. offered Internet-access training services.[112] However, an evaluation of the Gates Foundation's U.S. Library Program reported that only 40 percent of libraries receiving foundation assistance offered formal computer classes. Moreover, the report explains, "the urban/suburban and mixed libraries are more likely to report patron training classes (about 60%) compared with rural and small town libraries (35%). Central libraries are most likely to say they offer patron training (50%) compared with branch libraries (34 percent). Independent libraries fall between these extremes (42%)." Low figures for formal training were explained by claims of lack of space and that libraries "don't have enough computers to offer 'classes' to more than 2 or 3 people at a time and, even then, only if they deny other patrons access while the classes are being held."[113]

Many public libraries offer courses directed at particular age groups, such as children or seniors. Libraries also focus on training for new immigrants, minority groups, job seekers, low-income groups, or seniors in an attempt to overcome the digital divide. Short courses and workshops are offered for development and enhancement of personal skills and knowledge. Courses for seniors are particularly common and successful. An example is at the Cleveland Public Library, which "offers classes that are geared toward enabling seniors to become full participants in the digital age. The classes are well attended, and seniors report feeling more confident with the technology."[114] While technology training programs are invaluable in libraries, they are also offered by the private sector, as the next section will discuss.

Competing with the Private Sector in Information-Literacy Training

When public libraries offer formal training programs, they are usually heavily subscribed to and, in the United States and Canada, are often offered free of charge to library members. The programs include both short sessions and longer courses. The Cleveland Public Library offers sixty-nine courses, including one-hour classes, one entitled "Creating Tables in Word," and a two-hour course titled "Internet Skills Training for Seniors." The East Brunswick Public Library in New Jersey offers some twenty different two-hour courses. Some libraries offer both in-house and online courses. The Buffalo and Erie County Public Library, for example, offers workshops with follow-up online tutorials.

Some Canadian libraries are charging nominal fees for Internet training; that move appears to be mainly a result of municipal-budget cutbacks. The fees tend to range from $5 to $15 per class. However, charging at all for training means that the libraries are providing services on a commercial basis. Whether courses are given for free or for a nominal cost, publicly subsidized libraries are clearly competing with private-sector firms, of which there are many, offering computer training. For-profit vocational schools teach classes, while local computer stores, Internet cafés, and independent entrepreneurs offer one-on-one and small-group training. Online training courses are also marketed widely.

A growing number of franchises also offer classes that address various aspects of Internet literacy. Some of the franchises are directed at the same audience as are public library courses. For example, Computer U Learning Centers offer computer training to adults fifty years and older.[115] Another franchise, Computertots/Computer Explorers, which teaches computer technology to children, was acquired in 2003 by the International Center for Entrepreneurial Development (ICED), a holding company that also owns a number of other franchises such as Kwik Kopy, Women's Health Boutique, and Parcel Plus. The ICED describes itself as "a global organization with eight franchise brands and more than 800 locations" and claims that it is "a global leader in childrens [*sic*] computer classes."[116]

While at this point it appears that none of the private-sector firms offering computer and Internet training are sufficiently large to seek a GATS challenge, the last example illustrates the industry's capacity for growth. The kind of consolidation demonstrated by the ICED may empower the franchise industry enough to challenge public libraries as subsidized competitors.

Virtual Reference Services

Virtual reference is one of many terms being used to describe a service that enables users to reach a librarian electronically. Other common terms include *electronic*, *digital*, or *online* reference. We prefer the designation *virtual reference* because it appears to be the most commonly used term. The service is defined by the ALA's Reference and User Services Association as follows:

> Virtual reference is reference service initiated electronically, often in real-time [*sic*], where patrons employ computers or other Internet technology to communicate with reference staff, without being physically present. Communication channels used frequently in virtual reference include chat, videoconferencing, Voice over IP, co-browsing, e-mail, and instant messaging. While online sources are often utilized in provision of virtual reference, use of electronic sources in seeking answers is not of itself virtual reference. Virtual reference queries are sometimes followed-up [*sic*] with telephone, fax, in-person and regular mail interactions, even though these modes of communication are not considered virtual.[117]

Virtual reference services are growing quickly, and many public libraries are establishing such services, as well as frequently participating in regional or even worldwide consortia that allow electronic reference questions to be answered around the clock. Individual public libraries have moved quickly to provide either e-mail or chat reference help. Several state and provincial systems, such as QandANJ in New Jersey and the Saskatchewan Libraries' Ask Us service, and national consortia, such as Virtual Reference Canada, link libraries together to provide the service. Some are sponsored by particular government agencies. One example is the Virtual Reference Desk AskA+ Locator; it is a U.S. Department of Education–sponsored database that provides links to both general and specific virtual reference sites operated by libraries and other publicly funded organizations.[118]

The Library of Congress was at the forefront of establishing worldwide services in cooperation with major libraries around the world. It developed QuestionPoint, which is now a collaborative project between the Library of Congress's Global Reference Network and OCLC. Libraries can use QuestionPoint to access worldwide cataloging data and subject specialists in libraries and other organizations around the world.[119] Smaller libraries are participating in global networks as well. One good example is Global Librarian, a service provided by four libraries: one in Southampton, England; two in Canada, in Vaughan, Ontario, and in Surrey, British Columbia; and one in Adelaide, Australia, which work together to provide a 24/7 virtual reference desk.[120] Other publicly funded services are not tied to a single group of libraries. The Ask a Question program, for example, is offered by the Internet Public Library, which invites the public to submit questions that are then answered by volunteer librarians and library school students from around North America.

Most librarians see virtual reference as yet another extension of traditional reference service using new technologies, just as face-to-face service was extended by the use of telephones and fax machines. As users become more computer literate and as more library resources become available online, the importance of these services will grow. However, there is also an increasing private-sector presence, as fee-based question-answering services are emerging quickly. For example, the Google search engine provides Google Answers for fees ranging from $2.50 to $200. Questions are answered by "researchers," some of whom are freelance librarians who receive 75 percent of the user fee.[121] Tutor.com, cited earlier, offers its Librarians by Request service to answer questions in both English and Spanish. That particular service markets itself to libraries with its guarantee that it will provide "high quality reference support around the clock and during your most demanding service hours. This subscription service provides your customers with online access to Tutor.com's experienced reference librarians."[122] Steven Coffman and Linda Arrett argue that libraries should contract out their virtual reference services to commercial firms wherever possible because these services are so expensive and staff intensive.[123] Since both Coffman (an executive with LSSI, a firm that provides outsourcing services to libraries) and Arrett (an independent digital reference service consultant) represent private-sector interests, one wonders if their arguments are completely ingenuous. Many public services are expensive and staff intensive and yet are fully justified by the public-good nature of the service.

Because of public subsidization, public libraries could be construed as being in unfair competition with private virtual reference providers. In her 2002 letter to Paul Robertson, Wendy Newman wrote that "the development of the Web and ubiquitous use of the Internet have led to commercial ventures and the perception that there are significant opportunities in the sphere of information mediation and distribution and research services. As a result, a challenge to publicly funded institutions that offer virtual reference services is possible under the GATS discipline."[124] Librarians, seeing virtual reference as an extension of traditional reference service and recognizing that those projects have been validated by specific federal, state, and provincial government grants, may want to remain abreast of library and trade issues in this area.

PUBLIC LIBRARY SERVICES: COMMERCIAL AND COMPETING?

The wide variety of public library services available illustrates the extent to which libraries are either operating in a commercial manner or competing with private-sector suppliers. On either account, libraries cannot rely on the GATS exemption for services provided under the auspices of government authority. The main problem is that while libraries are developing new services and programs, the private sector is busily doing the same. The more entrepreneurial both sides become, the greater the area of overlap and competition, hence greater potential for losing the governmental exemption for public services. Areas that are purely in the domain of public service are most often those susceptible to market failure. Wherever market failure occurs, the private sector cannot or will not provide required services. One of the things libraries and governments do is aim to fill the holes left by market forces; we discuss that more in chapter 6. In the meantime, suffice it to say that librarians have to be aware of an overwhelmingly great number of directions from which potential trade challenges can come. What we have tried to do with this chapter is reduce the number of blind spots. Our next chapter addresses how trends toward privatization and commercialization impose further challenges in terms of international trade; we wait until chapter 6 to focus on some alternatives and avenues of advocacy within the library profession.

NOTES

1. International Federation of Library Associations and Institutions. *The IFLA Position on the World Trade Organization* (The Hague: IFLA, 2001), para. 4, www.ifla.org/III/clm/p1/wto-ifla.htm (accessed 8 July 2005).

2. Michael H. Harris, *History of Libraries in the Western World*, 4th ed. (Metuchen, N.J.: Scarecrow Press, 1995), 248.

3. *Online Dictionary for Library and Information Science (ODLIS)*, comp. Joan M. Reitz (Westport, Conn.: Libraries Unlimited, 2004), http://lu.com/odlis/odlis_o.cfm (accessed 24 March 2005).

4. Public Library Association, *Outsourcing: A Public Library Checklist* (Chicago: ALA, 2000), 5, www.ala.org/ala/pla/plaorg/reportstopla/outsourc.pdf (accessed 24 March 2005).

5. American Library Association Outsourcing Task Force, *Outsourcing & Privatization in American Libraries* (Chicago: ALA, 1999), 3, www.ala.org/ala/oif/iftoolkits/outsourcing/outsourcingamericanlibs.htm (accessed 24 March 2005).

6. California Library Association, *Fees for Public Library Services* (Sacramento, Calif.: CLA, 1997), www.cla-net.org/aboutcla/policies.php (accessed 24 March 2005).

7. Canadian Library Association, *Canadian Guidelines on Library and Information Services for People with Disabilities* (Ottawa: CLA, 1997), www.cla.ca/about/disabils.htm (accessed 24 March 2005).

8. Jens Thorhauge, "Nordic Public Libraries: Denmark," in *Danish Library Policy: A Selection of Recent Articles and Papers*, ed. Vibeke Cranfield (Copenhagen: Danish National Library Authority, 2002), 4–11, www.ifla.org/VII/s8/annual/cr02-dk.pdf (accessed 24 March 2005).

9. Liz Bishoff and Sally G. Reed, *ALA Proposal on Outsourcing and Privatization* (Chicago: ALA, 2001), www.ala.org/Template.cfm?Section=outsourcing&Template=/ContentManagement/ContentDisplay.cfm&ContentID=19799 (accessed 24 March 2005).

10. Andrew Kerkham, "Outsourcing" (paper presented at Library Information Association of New Zealand Aotearoa Conference, Napier, October 2003), www.lianza.org.nz/conference/conference03/papers/kerkham.pdf (accessed 24 March 2005).

11. Karen Hyman, "Customer Service and the Rule of 1965," *American Libraries* 30, no. 9 (October, 1999): 55–58.

12. G. Edward Evans, *Introduction to Library Public Services,* 6th ed. (Englewood, Colo.: Libraries Unlimited, 1999), 2.

13. See for example Public Library Association, *Outsourcing: A Public Library Checklist.*

14. American Library Association, Outsourcing Task Force, *Outsourcing & Privatization in American Libraries*, 5.

15. Association of College and Research Libraries, *Opening Day Collection: A List of 1,776 Books the Editors of CHOICE Feel Should Be on the Shelves of Every Academic Library When It Opens Its Doors* (Chicago: ACRL, 1967).

16. *Public Library Catalog* (New York: Wilson, 1968–).

17. Brodart Books, *Opening Day Services* (Williamsport, Pa.: Brodart, 2004), www.books.brodart.com/plibraries/opendayserv.htm (accessed 10 July 2005).

18. Robert S. Martin, et al., *The Impact of Outsourcing and Privatization on Library Services and Management* (Denton, Tex.: School of Library and Information Studies, Texas Woman's University, 2000), 29–31.

19. Public Library Association, *Outsourcing: A Public Library Checklist.*

20. Public Library Association, *Outsourcing: A Public Library Checklist.*

21. American Library Association, Outsourcing Task Force, *Outsourcing & Privatization in American Libraries*, 8.

22. Shelley Mardiros, "Spreading the Word: Banff's Very Public Library," *Alberta Views* 4, no. 1 (January/February 2001): 37–39, www.albertaviews.ab.ca/issues/2001/janfeb01/janfeb01social2.pdf (accessed 24 March 2005).

23. Ian Smith, "Some Myths about Public Library Use," *Impact, the Journal of the Career Development Group* 2, no. 1 (January 1999): 11, www.tees.ac.uk/depts/lis/lisresearch/research/chapter6.pdf (accessed 24 March 2005).

24. Evans, *Introduction to Library Public Services*, 299.

25. *Encyclopedia of Library and Information Science*, ed. Allan Kent, Harold Lancour, and Jay E. Daily (New York: Marcel Dekker, 1977), s.v. "Non-Print Material: Sound Recordings, Motion Pictures, and Pictures" (by Andrew M. Modelski).

26. Pat Lora, "Public Library Video Collections: Evolving Issues in Media Management," in *Video Collection Development in Multi-Type Libraries: A Handbook*, ed. Gary P. Handman (Westport, Conn.: Greenwood, 1994), 18.

27. Wendy Newman to Paul Robertson, Ottawa, Ontario, 23 October 2002, in *Correspondence*, Canadian Library Association (Ottawa: CLA, 2002), www.cla.ca/issues/robertson.htm (accessed 24 March 2005).

28. Newman to Robertson.

29. Using the McNaughton Plan, a library can lease appropriate quantities of popular titles when they are most popular. The books are then returned to Brodart when no longer heavily used. Brodart Books, *McNaughton: Popular Reading* (Williamsport, Pa.: Brodart, 2004), www.books.brodart.com/products/mcnaughton.htm (accessed 17 March 2006).

30. Evans, *Introduction to Library Public Services*, 358.

31. Bernan Associates (Lanham, Md.: Bernan, 2005), www.bernan.com (accessed 24 March 2005).

32. Software & Information Industry Association, *Ensuring a Diversity of Information Sources in the Digital Era* (Washington: SIIA, 2001), www.siia.net/govt/docs/pub/gip_brief_gip_01.pdf (accessed 24 March 2005).

33. Ken Wasch to Walter Finch, 13 September 2001, www.siia.net/sharedcontent/govt/issues/ip/09-13-01.html (accessed 7 May 2004; site now discontinued).

34. American Library Association, "PubSCIENCE is Discontinued," *ALAWON: American Library Association Washington Office Newsline* 11, no. 89 (12 November 2002), www.ala.org/ala/washoff/washnews/20026/89nov12.htm (accessed 24 March 2005).

35. Association of Research Libraries, *PubSCIENCE: A Unique and Needed Scientific Resource* (Washington: ARL, 2002), www.arl.org/info/frn/nsletter/pubscience02.html (accessed 24 March 2005).

36. Marydee Ojala, "PubScience Joins the Endangered Species List," *Information Today* 19, no. 9 (2002): 22–23, www.infotoday.com/newsbreaks/nb020819-2.htm (accessed 24 March 2005).

37. Charles A. Bunge and Richard E. Bopp, "History and Varieties of Reference Services," in *Reference and Information Services: An Introduction*, ed. Linda C. Smith and Richard E. Bopp (Englewood, Colo.: Libraries Unlimited, 2001), 4–5.

38. New York Public Library, *NYPL Express: The Express Link to a World of Information* (New York: NYPL, n.d.), www.nypl.org/express/index.html (accessed 24 March 2005).

39. Minneapolis Public Library, "INFORM" (Minneapolis, Minn.: MPL, 2005), www.mplib.org/inform.asp (accessed 24 March 2005).

40. Evans, *Introduction to Library Public Services*, 174.

41. Cleveland Public Library, "Interlibrary Loan" (Cleveland, Ohio: CPL, 2002), www.cpl.org/Locations.asp?FormMode=IL (accessed 24 March 2005).

42. *Online Dictionary for Library and Information Science.*

43. New York Public Library, *NYPL Express*.

44. Instant Information Systems, *DocDel.net* (Germantown, Md.: Instant Information Systems, n.d.), www.docdel.net (accessed 24 March 2005).

45. Newman to Robertson.

46. Seattle Public Library, *Fees for Printing, Photocopying, and Faxing* (Seattle: SPL, 2005), www.spl.org/default.asp?pageID=about_policies_printingfees (accessed 24 March 2005).

47. *Mail Boxes Etc*. (San Diego, Calif.: MBE, 2005), www.mbe.com (accessed 24 March 2005).

48. Xerox Corporation, "Public Libraries Check Out Xerox Solution to Increase Patron Service, Decrease Costs," press release, *Business Wire* (San Francisco: Business Wire, 25 February 2004), www.businesswire.com/webbox/bw.022504/240565039.htm (accessed 24 March 2005).

49. Mary K. Chelton, "Three in Five Public Library Users Are Youth; Implications of Survey Results from the National Center for Education Statistics," *Public Libraries* 36, no. 2 (March/April 1997): 104–8, www.ifla.org/VII/s10/irayls/users.htm (accessed 24 March 2005).

50. Adrienne Chute, et al., "Public Libraries in the United States Fiscal Year 2000," *Education Statistics Quarterly* 4, no. 3 (2003), http://nces.ed.gov/programs/quarterly/vol_4/4_3/5_1.asp (accessed 24 March 2005).

51. Gymboree Play and Music, "Franchise Information" (San Francisco: Gymboree, n.d.), www.playandmusic.com/b2c/customer/franchisee.jsp (accessed 24 March 2005).

52. See examples at Franchise Zone, "Educational Services," Entrepreneur.Com, comp. *Entrepreneur Magazine*, 2005, www.entrepreneur.com/franzone/cats/0,6587,12-12-1-EDUC,00.html (accessed 24 March 2005); and Franchise Solutions, "Children's Franchises," Franchise Solutions Corp., 2004, www.franchisesolutions.com/childrens-franchises (accessed 24 March 2005).

53. Janean Chun, "Franchise Frenzy," *Entrepreneur Magazine* 25, no. 1 (January 1997): 160, 162–163, www.entrepreneur.com/mag/article/0,1539,226846,00.html (accessed 24 March 2005).

54. New York Public Library, *Teen Link* (New York: NYPL, 2004), http://teenlink.nypl.org/HomeworkHelp.cfm (accessed 24 March 2005).

55. Cindy Mediavilla, *Creating the Full-Service Homework Center in Your Library* (Chicago: ALA, 2001), 2.

56. County of Los Angeles Public Library, *Homework Centers* (Downey, Calif.: COLA, 2001), www.colapublib.org/children/parents/hmwork.html (accessed 24 March 2005).

57. Ohio State Library, *Homework Now* (Columbus: State Library of Ohio, n.d.), www.homeworknow.net (accessed 24 March 2005).

58. Tutor.com, *Live Homework Help* (New York: Tutor.com, 2004), www.tutor.com/products/lhwh.aspx (accessed 24 March 2005).

59. Tutor.com, website (New York: Tutor.com, 2004), www.tutor.com (accessed 24 March 2005).

60. Entrepreneur.com, website, "Kumon Math and Reading Centers" (Irvine, Calif.: Entrepreneur Media, Inc., 2004), www.entrepreneur.com/franzone/details/0,5885,12-12-282507-,00.html (accessed 24 March 2005).

61. Kumon Math and Reading Centers, website (Teaneck, N.J.: Kumon North America, Inc., 2004), www.kumon.com (accessed 24 March 2005).

62. Sylvan Learning Centers, website (Baltimore, Md.: Educate, Inc., 2004), www.educate.com/homepage.html (accessed 24 March 2005).

63. Oxford Learning, website, (London, Ont: Oxford Learning Centres Inc. and Learning Centres of America, 2004), www.oxfordlearning.com (accessed 24 March 2005).

64. Shelley Quezada, "The Role of Libraries in Providing Services to Adults Learning English," *ERIC Digest*, ED334868 (Washington: National Clearinghouse on Literacy Education, 1991), www.ericdigests.org/pre-9220/libraries.htm (accessed 24 March 2005).

65. Canada Language Council, website (Ottawa: CLC, 2005), www.c-l-c.ca (accessed 15 December 2004).

66. Canadian Association of Private Language Schools, website (Surrey, B.C.: CAPLS, n.d.), www.capls.com (accessed 24 March 2005).

67. Language Industry Association/Association de l'industrie de la langue, website, *Mission and Objectives* (Montreal, Que.: AILIA, 2004), www.ailia.ca/tiki-index.php?page=About_en&bl (accessed 24 March 2005).

68. Quality English Ltd., website (Abingdon, U.K.: Quality English Ltd., 2005), www.quality-english.com (accessed 24 March 2005).

69. Eurolingua Institute, website (Douglas, U.K.: Eurolingua Institute, 2004), www.eurolingua.com (accessed 24 March 2005).

70. Las Vegas–Clark County Library District, "Tax Assistance," *Research: Info Guides* (Las Vegas, Nev.: Las Vegas–Clark County Library District, 2005), www.lvccld.org/library/info_guides/guide.cfm?guideID=36 (accessed 24 March 2005).

71. Arlington, Virginia, Dept. of Libraries, *Arlington Public Library: Putting the World within Reach* (Arlington, Va.: City of Arlington, n.d.), www.co.arlington.va.us/lib/biz (accessed 24 March 2005).

72. Tulsa City-County Library, *Research Wizard* (Tulsa, Okla.: Tulsa City-County Library, 2001), www.researchwizard.org (accessed 9 July 2005).

73. Factiva, website (New York: Dow Jones & Reuters, 2005), www.factiva.com (accessed 24 March 2005).

74. See, for example, Entrepreneur.com, which provides how-to guides and other useful information for free, while "sponsored partners" advertise fee-based services and products, www.entrepreneur.com (accessed 24 March 2005).

75. Martha Gregory, "Entrepreneurial Focus: Fee-Based Service, Tulsa City-County Library, Research Wizard," handout for an Infopeople.org workshop, "Secrets of a Successful Entrepreneurial Library," California State Library, 2002 (Tulsa, Okla.: Tulsa City-County Library, 2002), www.infopeople.org/training/past/2002/entrepreneur/handout2_tulsa.pdf (accessed 24 March 2005).

76. Lafayette Public Library, *Rental Charges* (Lafayette, Colo.: LPL, 2004), www.cityoflafayette.com/page.asp?navid=266 (accessed 24 March 2005).

77. Los Angeles Public Library, "Los Angeles Public Library Rental Facilities" (Los Angeles: LAPL, 2004), www.lapl.org/facilities (accessed 9 July 2005).

78. *Online Dictionary for Library and Information Science.*

79. Perseus Digital Library, website (Medford, Mass.: Dept. of the Classics, Tufts University, n.d.), www.perseus.tufts.edu (accessed 24 March 2005).

80. Association for Computing Machinery, *The ACM Digital Library* (New York: ACM, 2005), http://portal.acm.org/dl.cfm (accessed 9 July 2005).

81. Internet Public Library, website (Ann Arbor: School of Information, University of Michigan, n.d.), www.ipl.org (accessed 9 July 2005).

82. Online Computer Library Center, "Collection Management," *NetLibrary* (Dublin, Ohio: OCLC, 2004), www.oclc.org/services/collection/default.htm (accessed 24 March 2005); Online Computer Library Center, NetLibrary, "Public Library FAQs" (Dublin, Ohio: OCLC, 2005), http://legacy.netlibrary.com/about_us/public/faq.asp (accessed 24 March 2005).

83. HighBeam Research, website (Chicago: HighBeam Research, Inc., 2005), www.highbeam.com (accessed 9 July 2005).

84. Questia, website (Houston, Tex.: Questia Media America, Inc., 2005), www.questia.com (accessed 9 July 2005).

85. Gregory Crane, "Commercial Digital Libraries and the Academic Community," *D-Lib Magazine* 7, no. 1 (2001), www.dlib.org/dlib/january01/crane/01crane.html (accessed 24 March 2005).

86. Google Press Center, "Google Checks Out Library Books," press release, 14 December 2004), www.google.com/press/pressrel/print_library.html (accessed 9 July 2005).

87. Steve Johnson, "How Google Will Scan the World, 1 Book at a Time," *Chicago Tribune*, 25 February 2005, www.chicagotribune.com/technology/chi-0502250033feb25,1,3962945.column?ctrack=1&cset=true (5 March 2005). This article is available online only to people who register with chicagotribune.com. It is worth noting that the privacy policy, which can be found at www.chicagotribune.com/services/site/chi-privacy.story, indicates that any personally identifiable information collected may be used to promote "products and services offered by Chicagotribune.com and other Tribune Company affiliates and partners, administration of sweepstakes and contests, processing e-commerce transactions and other topics we think you might find of interest," and that Chicagotribune.com reserves "the right to share this information with other Tribune Company business units and affiliates." Furthermore, user information may be among transferred assets when the company sells, buys, merges, or partners

with other companies or businesses; and the information may also be given to law-enforcement authorities without prior notice.

88. Google, "Company Overview," *Corporate Information* (Mountain View, Calif.: Google, 2005), www.google.com/corporate/index.html (25 Mar. 2005).

89. Paul Whitney, "Libraries Up for Grabs," *Now Magazine Online Edition* 22, no. 42 (19–25 January 2003), www.nowtoronto.com/issues/2003-06-19/news_story2_p.html (accessed 24 March 2005).

90. Google Print, *Library Project* (Mountain View, Calif.: Google, 2005), http://print.google.com/googleprint/library.html (accessed 9 July 2005).

91. American Library Association, *Libraries: An American Value* (Chicago: ALA, 1999), www.ala.org/ala/oif/statementspols/americanvalue/librariesamerican.htm (accessed 24 March 2005).

92. American Library Association, *Equity of Access* (Chicago: ALA, 2004), www.ala.org/ala/ourassociation/governingdocs/keyactionareas/equityaction/equity-brochure.htm (accessed 24 March 2005).

93. Canadian Library Association, *Statement on Intellectual Freedom* (Ottawa: CLA, 1974, amended 1985), www.cla.ca/about/intfreed.htm (accessed 24 March 2005).

94. Canadian Library Association, *Statement on Internet Access* (Ottawa: CLA, 1997, revised 2000), www.cla.ca/about/internet.htm (accessed 24 March 2005).

95. Canadian Library Association, *Information and Telecommunication Access Principles* (Ottawa: CLA, 1994), www.cla.ca/about/access.htm (accessed 24 March 2005).

96. Australia, Parliament, Senate, Environment, Communications, Information Technology and the Arts Committee, "Libraries in the Online World," *Libraries in the Online Environment* (Canberra: Senate, 2003), 15–16, www.aph.gov.au/senate/committee/ecita_ctte/completed_inquiries/2002-04/online_libraries/report/index.htm (accessed 24 March 2005).

97. Industry Canada, LibraryNet, *Internet Connectivity in Public Libraries* (Ottawa: Industry Canada, 2003), http://ln-rb.ic.gc.ca/e/connect/table4.asp (15 July 2004). The LibraryNet program was discontinued in March 2004, and this document has been removed from the Industry Canada website.

98. Statistics Canada, "Internet Use Rates by Location of Access and Household Income," *Household Internet Use Survey* (Ottawa: Statistics Canada, 2003), www.statcan.ca/english/Pgdb/arts56e.htm (accessed 24 March 2005).

99. John Carlo Bertot and Charles R. McClure, "Summary Findings and Data Tables," *Public Libraries and the Internet 2000* (Washington: NCLIS, 2000), www.nclis.gov/statsurv/2000plo.pdf (accessed 24 March 2005).

100. Bill & Melinda Gates Foundation, *Toward Equality of Access: The Role of Public Libraries in Addressing the Digital Divide* (Seattle, Wash.: Bill & Melinda Gates Foundation, 2004), 15, www.gatesfoundation.org/nr/Downloads/libraries/uslibraries/reports/TowardEqualityofAccess.pdf (accessed 10 July 2005).

101. American Library Association, *Access to Electronic Information Services and Networks* (Chicago: ALA, 2004), www.ala.org/alaorg/oif/electacc.html (accessed 24 March 2005).

102. UNESCO and IFLA, *Public Library Manifesto* (Paris: UNESCO, 1994), www.ifla.org/VII/s8/unesco/eng.htm (accessed 24 March 2005).

103. Canadian Library Association, *Statement on Internet Access*.

104. Industry Canada, "Community Access Program" (Ottawa: Industry Canada, 7 August 2003), http://cap.ic.gc.ca/english/5200.shtml (accessed 24 March 2005).

105. Australia, Parliament, Senate, *Libraries in the Online Environment*, 70.

106. Federal Depository Library Program, "FDLP Internet Use Policy Guidelines," *Administrative Notes* 20, no. 2 (January 15, 1999), www.access.gpo.gov/su_docs/fdlp/mgt/iupolicy.html (accessed 24 March 2005).

107. British Columbia, Ministry of Aboriginal, Community and Women's Services, *Public Library Services. Public Libraries in British Columbia: Policy and Legislation* (Victoria: Government of British Columbia, 2004), www.mcaws.gov.bc.ca/lgd/public_libraries/index.htm#policy (accessed 24 March 2005).

108. Australia, Parliament, Senate, *Libraries in the Online Environment*, 70.

109. Greg Keizer, "The Best and Worst ISPs," *PC World*, November 2000, www.pcworld.com/reviews/article/0,aid,18624,00.asp (accessed 24 March 2005).

110. Newman to Robertson.

111. Bill & Melinda Gates Foundation, *Toward Equality of Access*, 21.

112. Bertot and McClure, "Summary Findings and Data Tables," 5.

113. Margaret T. Gordon, Elizabeth J. Moore, and Andrew C. Gordon, *Sustainability in First Ten States to Receive Gates Awards: Most Libraries Maintaining Public Access Computing Programs, but 25 Percent Are Still Fragile: A Report to the Bill & Melinda Gates U.S. Library Program* (Seattle: Public Access Computing Project, Evans School of Public Affairs, University of Washington, 2004), 19, www.gatesfoundation.org/NR/Downloads/libraries/eval_docs/word/sustaina-final-2-13.3.doc (accessed 24 March 2005).

114. Bill & Melinda Gates Foundation, *Toward Equality of Access*, 8, 19–20.

115. Devlin Smith, "Back to School: Computer U Franchise Teaches Seniors How to Travel on the World Wide Web," *Entrepreneur Magazine* 28, no. 6 (June 2000): 188G. www.entrepreneur.com/mag/article/0,1539,275124,00.htm (accessed 24 March 2005).

116. International Center for Entrepreneurial Development, website (Cypress, Tex.: ICED, n.d.), www.iced.net (accessed 10 July 2005).

117. Reference and User Services Association, "Guidelines for Implementing and Maintaining Virtual Reference Services," *RUSA Guidelines* (Chicago: ALA, 2005), www.ala.org/ala/rusa/rusaprotools/referenceguide/virtrefguidelines.htm (accessed 10 July 2005).

118. Virtual Reference Desk, website, "Ask-A-Locator" (Syracuse, N.Y.: Information Institute of Syracuse, n.d.), www.vrd.org/locator (accessed 10 July 2005).

119. Online Computer Library Center, *QuestionPoint: Cooperative Virtual Reference* (Dublin, Ohio: OCLC, 2004), www.oclc.org/questionpoint/default.htm (accessed 10 July 2005).

120. *Global Librarian*, website (Vaughan, Ont.: Global Librarian, 2004), www.globallibrarian.info (accessed 10 July 2005).

121. Jessamyn West, "Information for Sale: My Experience with Google Answers," *Searcher* 10, no. 9 (2002), www.infotoday.com/searcher/oct02/west.htm (accessed 24 March 2005).

122. Tutor.com, *Librarians by Request* (New York: Tutor.com Inc., 2004), www.tutor.com/products/lbr.aspx (accessed 24 March 2005).

123. Steve Coffman and Linda Arrett, "To Chat or Not to Chat—Taking Another Look at Virtual Reference, Part 1," *Searcher* 12, no. 7 (July/August 2004), www.infotoday.com/searcher/jul04/arret_coffman.shtml (accessed 24 March 2005); "To Chat or Not to Chat—Taking Another Look at Virtual Reference, Part 2," *Searcher* 12, no. 8 (September 2004), www.infotoday.com/searcher/sep04/arret_coffman.shtml (accessed 24 March 2005).

124. Newman to Robertson.

5

The Perils of Privatization: Commercialization and Privatization of Public Libraries and Library Services

The GATS exemption for services provided under the auspices of government authority is not available when the services are offered on a commercial basis, nor are exemptions offered when they compete with other service suppliers. In chapter 4 we examined specific public library services and how their delivery might result in libraries' losing that exemption. Our discussion now expands to analyze the trend toward commercialization and privatization in (and of) public libraries, and librarians' increasing acceptance of market models. The analysis is based on a typology of commercialization and privatization put forward by Ruth Rikowski.[1] Rikowski's typology is particularly useful for two reasons: first because it specifically focuses on public libraries, and second because it offers a framework for identifying and analyzing both commercialization and privatization in public library systems.

We discuss the construction of the word *privatization* and how the related terms *outsourcing* and *contracting out* can be used to disguise the privatization of library policy making and management. We also examine various forms of privatization (again, using Rikowski's typology) and public–private partnerships in libraries, and conclude by showing how trends toward commercialization and privatization relate directly to the GATS.

COMMERCIALIZATION IN PUBLIC LIBRARIES

As with any discussion in library and information science, it is important first to define the terms employed. *Commercialization* is generally known as the act or process of commercializing something or making it a tradable good. The *Random House Dictionary of the English Language* provides the following definition of *commercialize*: "(1) to make commercial in character, methods, or spirit; (2) to emphasize the profitable aspects of; (3) to offer for sale; make available as a commodity"; and *commercial* is defined as "pertaining to or characteristic of *commerce*." *Commerce*, in turn, is defined as "the interchange of goods or commodities; trade, business."[2] For the purposes of our discussion, all three definitions of commercialize are valid and applicable to public libraries.

Since the 1970s, governments have argued that commercialization measures are means of generating revenue from and/or recover costs for the work they do. A wide range of government information, resources, services, and goods have been subject to commercialization, and different public sectors have been required or encouraged to charge for services that were formerly offered at either low or no cost to the end user. Government-service commercialization generally means that control over those services remains within the public sector without any involvement from the private sphere. By retaining such control, however, a government can put itself in competition with private-sector suppliers (where they exist) of the same service. Therefore any fees a government agency charges need to be high enough that the agency will not be seen by the private sector as a competitor with the unfair advantage of public support (and therefore subject to things like the GATS), but still low enough that people are not discouraged from using the service.

The need to establish this balance emerges from the cyclical nature of the commercialization process. The cycle begins with a government's touting the benefits of private over public funding. Once people are convinced that this is true, government can begin to divert money away from a variety of public services, leaving those service providers feeling as though they have no option but to commercialize their goods or services to meet their new budget constraints. In that way, many public service providers, including libraries, find innovative ways to make do with less funding. Unfortunately, governments often see that as justification and permission to make further cuts. The commercialization impulse has infiltrated public libraries partly because of budget cuts and partly because of the neoconservative ideology permeating the entire sphere of public administration. We shall discuss the origins and implications of that trend more fully in chapter 6.

Types of Commercialization

Rikowski describes four kinds of commercialization in public libraries: (1) the creation of markets or quasi markets; (2) libraries being viewed as a place for selling products and services; (3) libraries becoming venues for private enterprises to promote their products; and (4) libraries being used as sites for extracting money (specifically in the form of small payments for particular services). Examining each kind is important to understanding the scope of commercialization in libraries.

The Creation of Markets or Quasi Markets

This type of commercialization occurs when "library users are transformed into 'consumers' and market research is undertaken in order to gather information on library and information consumers' wants, needs and their potential future wants and needs." Rikowski argues that while data gathered in such market research might give librarians information about patron needs, "once in place, its purpose can easily be shifted into a competitive market scenario, particularly if, in the future, the library supplier is a private company and not the local authority."[3] Librarians have watched the acceptance of a market model develop in public libraries for some time. When, for instance, did the chief librarian become the CEO? Why did some librarians start calling patrons "customers"? We will discuss both that topic and the hazards of the market approach to language in chapter 6.

Library as a Site for Selling Products and Services

This kind of commercialization is a process that Rikowski notes is "well underway [*sic*], with notions of income streams and income generation already well established."[4] Chapter 4 dealt with a number of examples wherein public libraries levy fees to patrons who use a service.

Product sales are another facet of commercialization that could subject subsidized libraries to a potential GATS challenge. Many libraries now have book and gift shops that sell marginally library-related items. Increasingly, libraries also offer food and drinks from in-house coffee shops and other food venues. Sometimes the shops are operated by "Friends of the Library" volunteers, in which case libraries are competing with private-sector retail shops. Alternatively, some libraries rent floor space to private vendors, and where that space is rented for less than its market value, private companies could raise issues about unfair competition.

The presence of shops in libraries is a relatively new phenomenon that is quickly becoming normalized. Newer urban central libraries, such as the one in Seattle, are placing retail outlets in the main floor areas. The New York Public Library, which established a library shop in the mid-1980s, sells books for readers, writers, and collectors, along with other paraphernalia, both in its three shops and on its website.[5] Clearly, such offerings are outside the library's real mandate, but library administrators often see these shops as ways to draw in both library patrons and supplementary revenue.

As the retail effort becomes more visible, it is also worth looking at other nonprofit organizations that try to expand their incomes with specialty shops. Museums, for example, have done so for decades. The Museum Store Association, representing "museum retail professionals" working in nonprofit institutions, claimed in its 2004 conference announcement that museum stores are "the number one source of earned revenue for museums" and that conference attendees could learn more about "money-saving and profit-enhancing ideas."[6] Such nonprofit retailers compete with for-profit enterprises, including online museum stores. Libraries need to consider very carefully, especially where the GATS is concerned, whether or not they want to go down that road.

Product Promotion in Libraries

Rikowski explains that "[l]ibraries are viewed by private enterprises as sites for the promotion of their products: advertising, public relations exercises and product promotions are the primary mechanisms here." By way of example, she cites the Bill & Melinda Gates Foundation programs that provide public libraries in low-income areas with access to computers, the Internet, and digital information. Rikowski argues that the programs tie recipient libraries to Microsoft software and that the benefits for the corporation are twofold: first, the partnership helps "place Bill Gates in a very favourable light," and second, "Microsoft is being promoted in our public libraries."[7]

Another corporation with a growing presence in public libraries is Starbucks. In addition to renting library space for its coffee shops, it provides grants of between $5,000 and $20,000 to nonprofit organizations in the United States, Canada, and the United Kingdom. For example, through the Starbucks Foundation's Power of Literacy program and other grants, it supports a Reading Is Fundamental program in numerous U.K. public libraries.[8]

In 2003, the Multnomah Public Library in Portland, Oregon, announced a new Starbucks grant that would fund puppet shows, craft programs, and educational opportunities. In total, the corporation agreed to support about 140 programs in sixteen library locations. The library's website quotes Starbucks' regional marketing manager, who says that "Starbucks is happy to be sponsoring these fun and enriching programs." She goes on to say that the company "is committed to improving young lives through the support of literacy programs throughout our community. The library has been an ongoing partner and is great for this effort!" The library's website explains that this is not the corporation's only contribution to the library system: "Starbucks has supported numerous Multnomah County Library projects in the last six years, including donating to the annual library gala (which benefits Summer Reading), hosting Everybody Reads book groups this winter and promoting children's library card sign-ups."[9] There is a Starbucks espresso bar in the Multnomah County Library.[10]

Starbucks' involvement is an example of libraries being, as Rikowski says, "viewed by private enterprises as sites for the promotion of their products." As another example, the Seattle Public Library's website says that the Starbucks Foundation was created in 1997 "to benefit local literacy programs in communities where Starbucks has coffeehouses."[11] A slight twist to the story is given by GrantsAlert.com, which claims that the foundation's Power of Literacy grants are given to nonprofit charities that "provide opportunities for Starbucks partners and stores to be integrated in a meaningful way."[12]

Another way to establish a commercial presence in a library, according to Rikowski, is for a business to provide a free service in the library and in that way promote itself. She explains that in the United Kingdom,

> [information technology] centres are being set up by private companies and some are running training courses in IT—they can be allocated a small room within a large central library, for example. There will be no big posters on the door advertising the company, but there will be a small sign outlining who is sponsoring the centre. In this way, the company is being advertised.[13]

Named space is another variation on commercialization. In that case, donations are solicited from corporations or private individuals and foundations in return for rights to name a particular building or space within that building. The Seattle Public Library's website lists all of the library's named spaces and respective donors, who had to give $250, 000 or more to the building of the main branch in order to name a space, including the Starbucks Teen Center on the third level of the new building.[14]

Fundraising websites sometimes list "naming opportunities" in particular libraries. For example, on its own site, the Providence Public Library lists more than forty such opportunities (and the amount of the suggested gifts) for its Knight Memorial Library branch: The circulation desk, board room, study rooms, window reading nooks, reading benches, picture book collection—and much more—are all available for branding.[15]

While there is a long history of naming buildings based on foundation money—consider, for example, the Carnegie libraries—the increasing reliance on corporate money and the use of that money to sponsor *parts* of libraries is new. When library spaces are named after corporations, those spaces play an important role in the promotion and favorable public relations of the donor corporation, which, in addition to reasonably priced, long-term advertising, receives a tax deduction for its generosity.

Libraries as Sites for Extracting Money

According to Rikowski, this form of library commercialization occurs when libraries are "used as sites for extracting money (and this money can then be distributed to various private companies), which in turn helps to provide investment and thus to ensure the continued success of global capitalism." Micropayments are an example of that kind of commercialization: A library might charge patrons pennies to access the Internet, and any transactions (such as copying and pasting, downloading, printing) could also be charged to the user. By levying micropayments for access to digital content, libraries would also be engaging in the second kind of commercialization noted above, where libraries are viewed as sites for selling products and services.

The argument in favor of a library's using microfees is the expected one: Public libraries could raise money by charging micropayments for access to digital library materials.

> Long a center of photocopying, libraries may soon be "Web entrepreneurs" and deliver content online via micropayment systems. Instead of visiting your local library and hunting through microfiches of archived newspapers or magazines, the library of the future may deliver that content online for an e-cash payment of 10 cents, 50 cents or perhaps a dollar or two, which may cover both the fee of copyright permissions and library services.[16]

That proposal overlooks two important questions: (1) To what extent are public library patrons willing to pay even very small amounts for digital content? and (2) If micropayment schemes become universal, will libraries have to pay someone else for their own access to the Internet?

Micropayment schemes have been adopted for a number of online commercial providers but they have been far more successful in selling music, for example, directly to customers, than in selling content in libraries. One commercial electronic content provider, *ebrary*, originally sought to generate income using micropayments. Its idea was to provide academic libraries with electronic content, such as ebooks, at no charge to individual libraries; the revenue stream would come from students and other library users who viewed all the titles in the *ebrary* collection but would pay a small fee to the company to view the actual texts. The library, for its part, would receive a small portion of the charges as micropayments from *ebrary*. In the end, that pricing model was abandoned as being "too problematic."[17]

Libraries are frequently cited as institutions that could benefit from charging micropayments. However, those schemes clearly violate access goals since people have to pay for information that would otherwise be free. Moreover, the future of micropayments is questionable: Though they were much lauded in the late 1990s, they were not so successful as their cheerleaders had hoped.[18] Micropayments are far more likely to work successfully for online shopping through companies such as BitPass, which enables people to make small purchases of music, articles, video clips, and other digital content using prepaid accounts.[19]

THE PRIVATIZATION OF PUBLIC LIBRARIES

Since the late 1970s and early 1980s, privatization has become one of the most popular means by which governments try to achieve the goal of economic growth. Paul Starr, professor of sociology at Princeton University, made note of its ideological basis in conservative governments in Great Britain, France, and the United States. He explained that privatization has come to mean primarily "(1) any shift of activities or functions from the state to the private sector; and, more specifically, (2) any shift of the production of goods and services from public to private."[20]

The key distinction between privatization and commercialization is the shift of control from public to private that occurs in privatization but not under commercialization. Since the separation between the two ideas is not so clear in libraries, an example from a different sector might help introduce the distinction. If a state builds and operates a highway for which tolls are charged or billboards are installed, the highway is commercialized. If in building that highway the state contracts to a private-sector road builder, then the construction is privatized but paid for with public funds. Ownership remains with the state, and its management reverts back to the state when the highway is completed. If, however, the state sells the completed highway to a private-sector firm (i.e., a company charges tolls), then it is completely privatized. In the context of libraries, the difference between privatization and commercialization is far muddier since the definition of privatization itself is hotly debated. We will discuss this issue later; suffice it to say for now that both commercialization and privatization are closely tied to trade liberalization. Allan G. Tupper and Bruce Doern explain that trade liberalization is included within the concept of privatization:

> In its narrowest sense privatization encompasses the whole or partial sale of state owned companies but more broadly and importantly it also embraces actions to reduce the role of government and enhance market forces to produce a more competitive economy. In this larger sense, privatization includes deregulation, trade liberalization, and the increased contracting out of government services.[21]

Are Contracting Out and Outsourcing in Libraries Really Privatization?

Public libraries have been contracting for goods, such as photocopiers, and services, such as maintenance, for decades. As our discussion of the terms *contracting out* and *outsourcing* explains, contracting for equipment or services is not a problem where trade agreements are concerned; neither is contracting for materials acquisition from vendors and subscription agents. However, as we said in chapter 4, many public libraries are outsourcing other aspects of collection development and in the process are moving decision-making power from the public to the private sector. That activity is no longer contracting or outsourcing: It is blatant privatization.

What Do We Mean by Outsourcing *and* Contracting Out*?*

The terms *contracting out* and *outsourcing* are used interchangeably, though outsourcing is a neologism that has been widely accepted only since 1979. Their interchangeability implies that the two terms are synonymous, though some, such as Peter Bendor-Samuel, the "world's top outsourcing authority" (according to OutsourcingCenter, from whose website the following statement is taken), argue that they are not:

> [T]hese two terms are often confused, but they are not the same at all. Contracting is when a company (buyer) purchases goods or services from another company (supplier or vendor). In this situation, the buyer "owns" and controls the process. In outsourcing, the buyer turns over the control ("ownership") of the process to the supplier. The buyer tells the supplier what results it wants the supplier to achieve, but the supplier decides how to accomplish those results.[22]

A library, then, would be considered a buyer, and according to Bendor-Samuel's distinction, if a library process or service is outsourced, control moves to the supplier. It is common in the library context, however, to treat the terms synonymously. The *Online Dictionary of Library and Information Science*, for one, defines outsourcing as "the contracting of library services formerly performed in-house to an outside service provider, usually a for-profit enterprise,"[23] while the ALA Task Force on Outsourcing defines outsourcing as "the contracting to external companies or organizations, functions that would otherwise be performed by library employees."[24] Neither definition addresses the issues of control and ownership Bendor-Samuel raises.

In 2000, the Public Library Association (PLA) concluded that a distinction indeed can be made between contracting out and outsourcing. Where contracting out is concerned, the library may transfer certain internal tasks or specific limited functions to an outside supplier. Outsourcing, however, involves transferring "recurring internal activities that are not core to the mission of the library" to "a third party,[25] outside vendor, or contractor, or independent workers, or providers" through contractual agreements.[26] While the PLA suggests that the transfer of decision rights and management is privatization, it avoids stating whether outsourcing core services is included in this scope, noting only that when outsourcing involves activities that are core to the mission of the library, "the gravity of the decision increases particularly with privatization."[27]

As Patricia Glass Schuman argued passionately, the all-encompassing use of the term *outsourcing* "masks the encroachment of privatization" and while "some say that outsourcing in libraries simply reflects private industry trends," the claim "disguises the reality that the management of public assets is being turned over to private interests. There are public policy sea changes going on that will have long-term—perhaps irreversible—effects on how, at what price, and for whom the knowledge base of this nation is maintained and accessed."[28]

Privatization Theory and Public Libraries

Paul Starr wrote that one of the justifying theories for pursuing so much privatization is that it "is desirable for its likely political effect in deflecting and reducing demands on the state." In that sense, privatization is similar to commercialization. Proponents of this theory argue that "[p]rivatizing government enterprises and public services . . . will redirect aspirations into the market and encourage a more entrepreneurial consciousness."[29] How can that kind of ideology, which is the driving force behind most library privatization, be compatible with the contributions libraries make in the service of the public good? While outsourcing and contracting out have a long history in libraries, the encroachment of privatization has some new and very broad implications. It suggests, in fact, that some of the current trends in library management pose a very real threat to publicly funded libraries as we know them.

Definitions of Privatization in the Library Context

In the library context, the definition of *privatization* is extremely controversial since different clauses can be used to either overestimate or underestimate its effects. Essentially, there are three levels of definition. At the first level, library activities are privatized, but management and policy making are not. At the second level, library activities and management are privatized, but policy making is not. At the third level, library activities, management *and* policy making are privatized.

In 1999, the American Library Association's Outsourcing Task Force triggered a whole series of studies and counterstudies when it used the following definition for privatization:

> Privatization is the shifting of policy making and the management of library services or the responsibility for the performance of core library services in their entirety, from the public to the private sector.[30]

This definition, by including aspects of policy and overall management in its vocabulary, fits with the third level of definition noted above. It gives the term a more inclusive scope than does traditional use of the term *outsourcing* or *contracting out*. Following the receipt of the Outsourcing Task Force report in 1999, the ALA affirmed that

> any outsourcing activities in libraries must be compatible with ALA advocacy of policies that support libraries as democratic institutions serving people of all ages, income levels and races, and providing the range of information resources needed to live, learn, govern and work.[31]

The ALA also commissioned a formal study on the impact of outsourcing and privatization on library services and management. In the study, Robert S. Martin and his colleagues took issue with the Outsourcing Task Force's definition in general and specifically with the phrase "performance of core library services." They wondered if the shifting of one core service to the private sector would be sufficient to constitute privatization:

> Our team thought not. Given what the literature review revealed about the probable extent of outsourcing in American libraries, it seemed to us misleading and unhelpful to label the majority of American libraries as "privatized."[32]

They also noted that the Task Force itself had indicated that contracting out core services such as cataloging or selection did not constitute privatization. Accordingly, privatization occurs only when "the responsibility for day to day management of a library or for establishing or altering policies that affect the delivery of service, is delegated to an external commercial agency."[33] Furthermore:

> From at least one perspective . . . "day-to-day management of a library" might be construed as a "specific service" to be contracted out, and from that perspective, a library that contracted out its day-to-day management but retained control over policy could not be construed as "privatized."[34]

For their study Martin and his colleagues operationalized the Task Force definition to read as follows: "Privatization is contracting out for services in a way that shifts control over *policies* for library collections and services from the public to the private sector [italics ours]."[35] As they noted, that definition eliminates the need to define core services and leaves open the possibility of contracting out management. Using the narrow definition, the Martin study found no libraries that had privatized control over policies, and so they claimed that there were no instances of privatization in American public libraries. They managed to minimize the visible amount of privatization in library systems, echoing, in a sense, the way some agencies redraw poverty lines to reduce the number of poor people in given populations.

The Martin study fueled the privatization debate, and the ALA continued to examine the problem of definition. In 2001 Liz Bishoff and Sally G. Reed, members of the ALA Council, proposed the following wording: "[P]rivatization is the shifting of policy making and the management of library services from the public to the private sector."[36] That definition, which restores the term *management of library services*, was implicitly accepted at the 2001 ALA conference,[37] as demonstrated by the adoption of ALA policy 52.7:

> ALA affirms that publicly funded libraries should remain directly accountable to the publics they serve. Therefore, the American Library Association opposes the shifting of policy making and management oversight of library services from the public to the private for-profit sector.[38]

In our opinion, Bishoff and Reed's definition is not clear because it seems to state that privatization occurs only when *both* policy making *and* management oversight are shifted to the private sector. Our reading of the documents convinces us that the intention was that the shifting of policy making *and/or* management oversight would be instances of privatization. The distinction should be clarified in the ALA documents. Our major concern with Bishoff and Reed's definition is that it does not answer the question addressed by Martin and his colleagues of whether contracting out and outsourcing could constitute privatization. Since the phrase "performance of core library services" is left out, those kinds of services, like cataloging and acquisitions, might ipso facto be called contracted out but *not* privatized. Bishoff and Reed wrote that it was their belief "that a more narrow definition of 'privatization' [would] enable the Association to take a stand in support of keeping publicly supported libraries safe from full privatization."[39] Their definition, therefore, was politically based.

Privatization is "the shift from public to private," which is why we agree with Starr and with Tupper and Doern, who identified *any* contracting out of government services as instances of privatization. Therefore, for the purposes of this discussion we have *not* accepted the Bishoff and Reed definition of privatization as "any shifting of policy making and the management of public library services from the public to the private sector." Under that definition, outsourcing is a form of privatization *only* when policy making and management of a function or service are outsourced. We believe that contracting and outsourcing do, in fact, constitute privatization.

Forms of Privatization

Of the various modes of privatization, public libraries are most familiar with the concept of contracting out or outsourcing, though there are quite a few other ways to privatize services. In chapter 4, we established that while libraries have been contracting out some services for decades, other forms of privatization have become more popular only recently. These new forms warrant their own analysis and Ruth Rikowski provides a timely and very useful framework that explains the mechanisms of three main paths to privatization:

1. One possibility is for libraries to be managed completely by the private sector, either by privatization of an existing library or by establishment of a new one with the intention of making a profit. In that scenario, "libraries can be run for profits directly, with up-front charges for core services." Rikowski hypothesizes that this "will not happen in any significant way in the short-term, as not enough money can currently be made out of libraries, but it could happen in the long-term, when the 'market is ripe.'"
2. Another possibility is that companies can make profits "out of running libraries at a lower cost than the price they are contracted to run them." If, say, a company were granted an annual operating fund of $400,000 to run a library but it spent only $300,000, then it would make a profit of $100,000. Practically, that typically means cutting library budgets, especially where staff are concerned. Rikowski notes that this is the U.K. government's "preferred form of privatisation at the current time, as they can then still claim that library services are basically in the 'public' sector."
3. A third option is for private firms to take over and run public-sector capital projects, usually through public–private partnerships whereby a private company participates in "the building of new library buildings or a service-wide ICT [Information and Communication Technology] system."[40]

There is evidence that all of these modes of privatization have occurred and are continuing to occur. We will dissect and consider some examples of each type in this next section.

Libraries Run by the Private Sector

Privatized libraries, for the purposes of this discussion, do not include those special libraries that are run by private firms. Our focus is on privatized libraries that are designed to serve the general public; they may be established with a profit motive (born private) and/or start as public and subsequently become privatized to nonprofit entities. Those established with a profit motive are usually digital libraries that levy up-front charges for services. As an example, Rikowski cites Questia (a company discussed in chapter 4), which provides an online library and offers high school and university students access to its almost 450,000 records for a monthly or annual fee. Other examples of for-profit digital libraries include World eBook Library (part of NetLibrary)[41] and ebrary,[42] both of which market books and other materials in PDF format directly to the general public. Because they provide "library" materials for a fee, these kinds of commercial libraries could challenge any publicly subsidized libraries that provide like services.

Another way in which a library can be privatized is for it to be acquired by a nonprofit foundation that can then find innovative ways of cutting costs (since it is not bound by normal library legislation), such as by replacing public employees with volunteers. Two examples from California illustrate variations of this model.

In 1995, a small branch of the Seal Beach Public Library was sold to the Golden Rain Foundation, a not-for-profit mutual stock cooperative[43] that oversees the management and maintenance of facilities and services at Leisure World (LW), a "guard gated retirement community" that is home to one-third of the population of Seal Beach.[44] Privatization.org, a pro-privatization website, claimed that "this unusual private acquisition of a public library" meant that the library was "saved through privatization."[45] Residents of Leisure World pay a one-time membership fee to the foundation, which covers the cost of facilities, including the LW library, which is no longer part of the Orange County Library System. Because the entire community is privately owned, people who are not LW members cannot use its library, though as residents of the county LW members can use the Orange County libraries.

Privatization.org describes another variation of private-sector operation: One day in 1992, the Welwood Murray Memorial Library, a branch of the Palm Springs Public Library, was closed, and all its books were removed. "A day later, the library started a new life as a private volunteer library, run by a newly incorporated nonprofit foundation." The description from Privatization.org goes on to note that the city's "public librarian had earned almost $70,000 annually to tend the 3,000-book collection" and that the new 8,000-book collection (based completely on donations) was now being run by volunteers.[46] There is no published indication of who may use the library or how satisfied patrons are with the collection and new organizational arrangement.

Issues of library professionalism aside, both of these cases deal with the privatization of small public library branches—though in neither case does it appear to have been done to make a profit. Rather, it seems that the elimination of public funding and its substitution with private money were seen as a positive move in the post–Proposition 13 environment in those California communities.[47] Elizabeth Larson of the libertarian Reason Foundation describes a number of other such instances of privatization and subsequently supports the creation of more private libraries, claiming that "the main advantage of private libraries is their responsiveness to the needs and wants of users." She supports this claim by arguing that popular objections to collection decisions in private libraries "would be felt immediately through lost donations and customers."[48] In her poorly researched polemic, Larson does not address the fact that by their very nature private libraries operating in that way exclude whole groups of potential users, while public libraries, as Schuman states, are "valued for their comprehensiveness, currency, openness and multiplicity of viewpoints."[49]

Creating new or privatized nonprofit libraries such as those described above would not lead to a GATS challenge. Clearly, however, the trend represents an attack on the principle of public tax funding for public libraries. If the trend continues, one can imagine that the idea of "selling" a public library to a foundation might lead to selling a library to a profit-making company. Publicly subsidized libraries might be threatened by trade challenges that could be made on the basis that public libraries have an unfair competitive advantage (in the form of government funding) over private ones.

Companies Profit by Running Libraries at Lower Cost Than Contracted

Partnerships with the private sector take place at all levels of government. The general premise is that any company hoping to obtain a government contract must submit a bid that is lower than those of its competitors. With a winning bid in hand, a company must then find a way to fulfill the terms of the contract without losing money and at the same time position itself to have its contract renewed. As Pat Schuman writes, "The private sector is not always cheaper, except sometimes at the start, when companies lowball their bids to clinch their first contracts."[50] In order to fulfill the contract, the company must cut costs to operate more "efficiently." The best example of a for-profit company that aims to manage libraries at lower cost than contracted is Library Systems & Services (LSSI), a Maryland-based firm that originally managed government and special libraries and that has expanded its market to public libraries.[51] Later in this chapter, we discuss LSSI's operations in greater detail, but here we focus on the subject at hand and how the company runs libraries "at a lower cost than contracted."

When LSSI takes over management of a library, it puts in an LSSI employee as library manager, while the library's original staff either remain city employees or join the LSSI payroll. Staff layoffs are usually forbidden by the contract, but cuts occur through attrition; under one LSSI contract six of thirty-seven employees retired and were not replaced.[52] In a 2004 *Library Journal* article, Norman Oder quoted a former LSSI employee (hired by LSSI as an urban public library manager) as saying "[t]here was a considerable amount of pressure [from LSSI] to look at ways we could generate revenue and not to spend the full budget." Oder goes on to cite the company's cost-cutting measures, which generally involve a combination of replacing MLIS staff with paraprofessionals, relying heavily on volunteers, cutting retirement benefits, and trimming materials budgets.[53] Normal business practice, of course, involves making a profit by spending less than one is paid, and for operating by that rule we do not fault LSSI. We do, however, fault those library boards who believe in running libraries that way. Public libraries are *not* private businesses and should not be run as such.

Private-Sector Firms Take Over and Run Public-Sector Capital Projects

Rikowski's third form of privatization, whereby private sector firms take over and run public sector capital projects, such as building new library branches, is much encouraged by proponents of public–private partnerships (abbreviated as P3, 3P, or PPP). These partnerships involve contracts between for-profit corporations and public agencies. The National Council for Public Private Partnerships (NCPPP), an American PPP advocacy and lobby group, defines the term as follows:

> A Public–Private Partnership is a contractual agreement between a public agency (federal, state or local) and a for-profit corporation. Through this agreement, the skills and assets of each sector (public and private) are shared in delivering a service or facility for the use of the general public. In addition to the sharing of resources, each party shares in the risks and rewards potential in the delivery of the service and/or facility.[54]

Many public libraries are inserting the term "public/private partnership" into their mission statements or lists of goals. For example, the Seattle Public Library lists among its aims:

> Careful stewardship of the public trust, which ensures accountability and makes the most efficient and effective use of funds, both public and private; fosters collaboration, cooperation and co-location where possible with other agencies; and builds public/private partnerships to enhance services to our users.[55]

Public library directors frequently cite successful PPP arrangements, particularly for infrastructure projects in which private contractors design and build new library buildings and turn operations back over to library boards upon completion. The National Council for Public–Private Partnerships describes that as a simple design/build PPP model. However, a number of other PPP models involve operation of the completed infrastructure, such as design/build/operate model, which puts the whole process of designing, building, and operating a structure into the hands of the private sector. Currently, the PPP concept is being expanded to develop partnerships involving dizzyingly varying combinations of public/private financing and private service delivery.[56]

Managing Libraries through Public–Private Partnerships

Using PPPs for public library management and service delivery is increasingly common. In the United Kingdom, the Blair government's "Best Value" initiative was launched in 1997 with the intention to "modernise" local government, calling for "continual improvement of services."[57] One of the direct consequences of the initiative's success was a host of new public–private partnerships for public libraries. The principles of Best Value specifically encourage private-sector involvement in the management of libraries:

> Under best value retaining library services in-house can only be justified where the authority demonstrates that there really are no other more efficient and effective ways of delivering the quality of service required. Library authorities should also explore potential *future* providers and take steps to encourage them—to create a climate for competition that will enable the market to develop.[58]

One of the communities affected by the Best Value initiative was the London Borough of Haringey. In 1999, the government's Best Value inspectors declared the Borough library to have "poor service" with "poor prospects for improvement,"[59] and as a consequence of that verdict the Borough quickly hired Instant Library Ltd. to provide interim management of the council's public libraries.[60] The contract was not a long-term one, however, and in April 2004 the management of the library reverted to the public sector.[61]

As the number of firms providing public library management increases, they will look for more long-term opportunities. Another possibility is that larger companies will want a more involved role in supplying public services. Since the work done at the Haringey libraries was touted as such a success (the borough won the *Municipal Journal*'s 2004 Public Private Partnership of the Year prize),[62] that example could be used by both governments and private companies as evidence that PPPs are effective management strategies.[63]

The market continues to grow and shift. In 2004, Serco, an international public-service-management firm, reported on the launch of a major PPP initiative in Northern Ireland, which consisted of the Belfast Education and Library Board's "looking for a private sector strategic partner to rebuild, refurbish, maintain, service and manage 83 schools, 37 youth clubs and 21 libraries."[64] Clearly, there is no shortage of opportunities for private companies to participate in the public service sector.

In North America, the largest private-sector player in public library management is LSSI, founded in 1981. As we have seen, LSSI originally targeted its management services at corporate and federal-government libraries and contracted with those and with public libraries to provide automation support, technical services, and data entry. In the late 1990s, the company began offering its management services to public and college/school libraries; a number of the contractees are listed on the company website.[65] In June 1997, Riverside County, California, contracted with LSSI to run the Riverside County Library System (RCLS), which consisted of twenty-five branches. While that move was quite a radical one, it is important to note that the administration of the library had always been contracted out; beginning in 1911 the county paid the city of Riverside to run the county library system (services can be contracted out to other service suppliers that are not necessarily in the private sector). The city ran the library until 1997 and when for several reasons the contract ended, the RCLS hurried to find a new service provider. After a request-for-proposal (RFP) process in which vendors were invited to submit bids for the contract to provide services at the RCLS, LSSI was granted the privilege of running the entire system.[66] Martin and his colleagues observed that LSSI faced little competition in its response to the RFP; its contract with Riverside County has since been renewed several times. According to its own website, the RCLS is now the hub of a countywide library network serving other public libraries, schools, and colleges to provide a shared catalogue, facilitate interlibrary loans, offer access to online resources, and help manage acquisitions. LSSI sits on the network's Board of Governors.[67]

In their ALA-backed study of the impact privatization can have on libraries, Martin and his colleagues provided a detailed history of and research findings on the RCLS privatization. As we discussed earlier in this chapter, they defined privatization very narrowly by including in its scope a library's policy making but not its management. They praised the RCLS contract with LSSI and claimed that the outsourcing of library management to LSSI "can not [*sic*] be considered 'privatization' under any reasonable definition of the term because the County retains full and complete control over the assets of the library and over policy matters."[68] Therefore, they identified the RCLS situation as one that exemplifies outsourcing rather than privatization. As described above, the ALA ultimately disagreed with that assessment and broadened its definition of privatization to include management.

The Riverside County Library System contract is considered to be a significant example of privatization, and its existence has generated considerable concern in the library world. The ALA's Outsourcing Task Force addressed the case in its report, which describes the RCLS-LSSI contract as "the first documented instance of the privatization of an entire public library system."[69] Most commentators recognize the case as an example of privatization and side with the ALA-approved Bishoff and Reed definition, which includes in its scope shifting library services management from the public to the private sector.

Meanwhile, the LSSI website markets its library-management services using language that echoes the Martin report:

> When LSSI manages a library, we take full responsibility for developing and implementing the library's programs, technology plans, collection development, staff development, long range planning and the overall day-to-day management of the library. LSSI has also been retained to help conceive, develop and establish new libraries as well as assist in the design and expansion of existing facilities. With creative and skilled management, the libraries we operate are open longer hours, provide more books and materials, are easier to use, provide better customer service and operate more effectively at lower cost per hour. In the public sector, we are accountable to a local authority for the performance of the library. LSSI does not set policies, nor do we acquire any library assets . . . the libraries remain free and open for the public to use.[70]

The clear intent of this statement is to placate organizations like the ALA with a denial of any direct involvement in shaping public library policy. The simple fact that LSSI sits on the RCLS Board of Governors, however, makes the denial difficult to support. LSSI is also careful to describe its agreement with RCLS as a contract without any reference to privatization. The P-word does enter the company lexicon, however. On its website's Achievements page, it boasts that the National Council for Public Private Partnerships "recognized LSSI with its annual Public–Private Partnership Award for the successful management of the Riverside County Library System."[71]

The company is actively marketing its services to a variety of local governments, and, as Norman Oder observes, at "meetings of national city and county associations, the only library exhibitor is often [LSSI], the first company to offer full outsourcing (or privatization, to some) of public libraries. LSSI offers a seductive line: it can do more with less."[72] Oder goes on to explain the company's basic strategy:

> LSSI generally manages the entire library budget, whether it employs all staffers or just senior managers. VP Bob Windrow told the *Dallas Morning News* in

2001 that the company "earns money through streamlining procedures, automation, changing procedures, and staff training." The article doesn't mention that LSSI charges some clients (though not RCLS) general and administrative costs up to 15%, which include handling fees on materials of 5%. Additionally, the difference between the budget and what is spent contributes to profit.

Also, while LSSI can ramp up libraries that have lagged technologically, Windrow's statement sidesteps a key LSSI strategy: saving money on staff. In a proposal to the Dallas PL (DPL) board [in 2003], Windrow acknowledged, according to board minutes, that the company would keep costs down by paying lower salaries and benefits, hiring fewer librarians, and choosing less-educated employees than current DPL staff.[73]

Privatization, Summarized

Privatization involves *any* shift from the public sector to private hands. That shift occurs in public libraries most commonly by outsourcing or contracting out services. While the ALA did not accept the contracting out of specific services as "privatization," we fail to understand why it is not so defined. The ALA did agree, however, that outsourcing management or policy making constitutes privatization, and in this chapter we have focused on examples, most of which entail contracts of some sort. Of the examples used in our discussion, the "born private" commercial digital libraries fall into a different category of privatization. They could be excluded entirely from discussion because they did not originate as public-sector entities. They are included here because, as Rikowski notes, they indicate a "direction in which the whole situation is moving. The environment is being created which will encourage, indeed entice private corporations to see the benefits to be gained from moving into libraries."[74]

The kind of privatization that shifts management from the public to the private sphere is seen by local politicians as an increasingly viable way to solve ongoing management problems or cut personnel costs; some of the most common municipal partnerships are with companies like LSSI that run libraries at a lower-than-contracted cost. As Oder notes, the negative effects of the trend are, with rare exception, not understood by politicians, and the extent to which profits are being made is often ignored. One board chair that Oder cites said, "There are certain things since they [LSSI] are a private company that's not required to be public knowledge. We know the amount of money we pay them for the services we contract for, and we are satisfied."[75] According to Oder, LSSI even requires that contracting libraries agree that in the event of a termination of the LSSI-library partnership, the Library Board and LSSI will issue a joint press release that "will explain the change in the most positive manner possible."[76] Therefore, a library is officially not allowed to give its reasons for canceling or not renewing a contract with LSSI even if that agreement is ending due to a library's dissatisfaction with the company's services or practices.

Given restraints from the private sector and encouragement to privatize from the public sector, the great extent to which public service providers are being urged to engage in public–private partnerships is a cause for concern. Public–private partnerships are touted as a general solution to limited public-sector funding—though it remains to be seen how successful they will be in the long run. As Rikowski argues, "we are being asked to consider a future where library services become a commodity in an information market and where libraries operate in this market place."[77] So far as this trend is concerned, we certainly see no justification for handing over public library operations to the private sector.

COMMERCIALIZATION, PRIVATIZATION, AND THE GATS

This chapter has examined both commercialization and privatization of public libraries. What do these issues have to do with trade agreements? We addressed that question briefly in the chapter's introduction to privatization, citing Allan G. Tupper and Bruce Doern's statement that "privatization includes deregulation, trade liberalization, and the increased contracting out of government services."[78]

However, it is also important to ask whether GATS has an immediate effect on public libraries. Does the promise of new trade agreements measurably induce the types of commercialization and privatization discussed in this chapter? The example of the U.K.'s Best Value Initiative may be just such a response to trade liberalization. According to Rikowski, "Best Value is being used as a mechanism to bring in the GATS—given that the GATS is about bringing in other suppliers, creating a climate of competition, paving the way and enabling the liberalisation of trade in services to take effect."[79] She argues that "the GATS is affecting libraries and information in subtle, seemingly unobtrusive ways" and that librarians acquiesce in the elimination of free public library service by willingly adopting commercialization and privatization measures.[80]

Most obviously, a GATS exemption for services provided under government authority is *not* available for services that are offered on a commercial basis or in competition with private providers. In chapter 4 we examined a number of examples of individual services that are being offered in such a way as to nullify the exemption. Commercialization and privatization put public services into these brackets of competition with the private sector; the more services in libraries are privatized, the more they are managed with a for-profit motive, and the more potential there is for commercial service provision and overlap with services already supplied by the private sector.

Arriving at this conclusion requires a more subtle path, since privatization can come in a variety of forms. One of the most common is outsourcing, which turns a publicly subsidized service into a market for private firms. While there are many examples of government services being outsourced (such as road maintenance and janitorial work), the GATS introduces a range of new problems. Libraries that outsource their services put themselves in a competitive zone in which large companies that provide services to libraries could begin to demand that all library work be outsourced—on the premise that no publicly subsidized library should be providing like services in competition with the private sector. But the GATS problem has the potential to go much deeper, as other foreign service providers may look to the contracts and demand the opportunity to enjoy the same level of treatment.

The issue here is one of a moving target. While libraries are branching out into new service areas to meet the needs of their communities, the private sector is also expanding as it identifies new market opportunities in the exploding information sector. Where these two sides overlap, they create a dangerous zone of competition for libraries. When librarians sign contracts with particular companies, they arouse interest in others who see new market opportunities. The LSSI contracts, for example, piqued the interest of Library Associates, a Los Angeles firm that provides staffing and management services to special libraries.[81] That company responded to a public library RFP, "bid on the contract and now will consider competing in the public library arena."[82] Library Associates came around to the LSSI way of doing business. While the firm focuses on staffing for the information industry, it "has held a multiple year on-going contract to provide temporary professional and support level staffing for a major, multi-branch public library system."[83] As the RFP response indicates, the company is moving into provision of management for public libraries. Private-sector companies such as LSSI and Library Associates have an enormous potential for growth, and as they mature they could argue that public libraries receiving government subsidies have an unfair advantage over private companies whose business enterprise is to provide the same services.

The potential loss of the GATS exemption for services provided under the auspices of governmental authority continues to grow as more and more companies have an increasingly vested interest in taking over more and more library services. The more numerous these companies become in this market, the greater the possibility that publicly funded libraries that do not outsource or privatize could be subject to challenges via trade agreements such as GATS—for no reason other than that their operation uses the public funds to which the private sector wants access.

Many concerns about commercialization and privatization are noted in the various ALA documents that we have cited. Library professionals fear that the basic premise on which they operate—namely, that libraries contribute to the public good and are fundamental to the health of democratic societies—will be demeaned and that with this will come the erosion of the profession. As the zone of competition increases (see figure 2.5), public-sector information services will have an increasingly diminished role. The people not served by the private-sector services will be those who do not have the financial resources to access them. Increasingly, public-sector services will serve only the people at the edges—the marginalized, less affluent members of their communities. Public-sector funding is likely to be threatened as taxpayers who do not use them fail to support public-sector information services. These are valid and important concerns. We hope that librarians will recognize how commercialization and privatization increase the susceptibility of public libraries to threats from GATS.

NOTES

1. Ruth Rikowski, "The Corporate Takeover of Libraries," *Information for Social Change* 14 (Winter 2001–2002), www.libr.org/ISC/articles/14-Ruth_Rikowski.html (accessed 10 July 2005). See also chapter 5 in her book *Globalisation, Information and Libraries: The Implication of the World Trade Organisation's GATS and TRIPS Agreements* (Oxford: Chandos, 2005), which covers the same ground.

2. *The Random House Dictionary of the English Language, Unabridged Edition*, ed. Jess Stein and Laurence Urdang (New York: Random House, 1966).

3. Rikowski, "The Corporate Takeover of Libraries," 7–9.

4. Rikowski, "The Corporate Takeover of Libraries," 7.

5. New York Public Library, *The Library Shop* (New York: NYPL, 2004), www.thelibraryshop.org (accessed 10 July 2005).

6. Museum Stores Association, "Museum Retailers to Get Profit-Enhancing Ideas in Portland, OR, April 17–20, 2004" (Denver, Colo.: MSA, November 4, 2003), www.museumdistrict.com/events/PR_11-4-03MRCE.cfm (accessed 10 July 2005).

7. Rikowski, "The Corporate Takeover of Libraries," 8, 10.

8. Royal Borough of Kensington and Chelsea, "Books for Children," press release (London: RBKC, June 2002), www.rbkc.gov.uk/news/pressrelease/n020619c.asp (accessed 10 July 2005).

9. Multnomah County Library, "Starbucks to Enrich Summer Youth Programming at the Library," news release (Portland, Ore.: Multnomah County Library, 13 March 2003), www.multcolib.org/news/2003/sbsummer.html (accessed 10 July 2005).

10. Multnomah Country Library, "Library and Starbucks Brew Up Partnership," *Entrepreneurial Libraries: Bright Ideas for Today's Librarians*. (Portland, Ore.: Multnomah County Library, 1998), www.multcolib.org/products/entre/espresso.html (accessed 10 July 2005).

11. Seattle Public Library, *Donors Honored by Named Spaces* (Seattle, Wash.: SPL, 2005), www.spl.org/default.asp?pageID=branch_central_naming&branchID=1 (accessed 10 July 2005).

12. GrantsAlert.com, "Foundation Grants: Starbucks Foundation: Power of Literacy" (Tallahassee, Fla.: GrantsAlert.com, 2004), http://grantsalert.com/grants.cfm?id=4&gid=718 (accessed 10 July 2005).

13. Rikowski, "The Corporate Takeover of Libraries," 8, 10.

14. Seattle Public Library, *Donors Honored by Named Spaces.*

15. Providence Public Library, "Knight Memorial Branch Gifts" (Providence: PPL, 2004), www.provlib.org/building/branches/kma/gifts.htm (accessed 10 July 2005).

16. Lesley Ellen Harris, "Micropayments for Libraries, Archives, and Museums," *Copyright and New Media Law Newsletter* 2, no. 3 (1998), http://copyrightlaws.com/newsreps/nrvo2is3.html (accessed 10 July 2005).

17. David Dorman, "Ebrary at Bat," *American Libraries* 33, no. 1 (January 2002): 96–97.

18. Steve Crocker, "The Siren Song of Internet Micropayments," *IMP Magazine on Information Impacts* (April 1999): 22, www.merchantseek.com/article9.htm (accessed 10 July 2005).

19. BitPass, website (Menlo Park, Calif.: BitPass, Inc., 2004), www.bitpass.com (accessed 10 July 2005).

20. Paul Starr, "The Meaning of Privatization," *Yale Law and Policy Review* 6 (1988): 6–41, www.princeton.edu/~starr/meaning.html (accessed 10 July 2005).

21. Allan G. Tupper and Bruce Doern, *Privatization, Public Policy and Public Corporations in Canada* (Halifax, N.S.: Institute for Research on Public Policy, 1988), 1.

22. Peter Bendor-Samuel, "Is 'Contracting' or 'Contracting Out' Just Different Terminology for 'Outsourcing'?" OutsourcingCenter, website (Dallas, Tex.: Everest Partners, 2005), www.outsourcing-faq.com (accessed 10 July 2005).

23. *Online Dictionary of Library and Information Science (ODLIS)*, comp. Joan M. Reitz (Westport, Conn.: Libraries Unlimited, 2004), http://lu.com/odlis/odlis_o.cfm (9 July. 2005).

24. American Library Association Outsourcing Task Force, *Outsourcing & Privatization in American Libraries* (Chicago: ALA, 1999), 3, www.ala.org/ala/oif/iftoolkits/outsourcing/outsourcingamericanlibs.htm (9 July. 2005).

25. As this definition suggests, *contracting out* is a generic term and does not necessarily imply that only the private sector can serve as contractor. For example, one government agency can contract out work to another; that happens frequently in Canada where government departments and agencies contract one-time surveys or ongoing statistical work to the central statistical agency, Statistics Canada, which provides these services on a cost-recovery basis. In another example provided later in this chapter, a county library in Riverside, California, was run by another public library system for a number of years.

26. Public Library Association, *Outsourcing: A Public Library Checklist* (Chicago: ALA, 2000), 6, www.ala.org/ala/pla/plaorg/reportstopla/outsourc.pdf (accessed 8 July 2005).

27. Public Library Association, *Outsourcing: A Public Library Checklist*, 6.

28. Patricia Glass Schuman, "The Selling of the Public Library," *Library Journal* 123, no. 13 (1998): 50–52.

29. Starr, "The Meaning of Privatization," 30.

30. American Library Association Outsourcing Task Force, *Outsourcing & Privatization in American Libraries*, 2.

31. American Library Association, *Outsourcing and Privatization*, website (Chicago: ALA, 2003), www.ala.org/ala/ourassociation/governingdocs/aheadto2010/outsourcing.htm (accessed 10 July 2005).

32. Robert S. Martin, et al., *The Impact of Outsourcing and Privatization on Library Services and Management* (Denton, Tex.: School of Library and Information Studies, Texas Woman's University, 2000), 6, www.ala.org/ala/oif/iftoolkits/outsourcing/outsourcing_doc.pdf (accessed 10 July 2005).

33. American Library Association Outsourcing Task Force, *Outsourcing & Privatization in American Libraries*, 3.

34. Martin, et al., *The Impact of Outsourcing and Privatization on Library Services and Management*, 4.

35. Martin, et al., *The Impact of Outsourcing and Privatization on Library Services and Management*, 4.

36. Liz Bishoff and Sally G. Reed, *ALA Proposal on Outsourcing and Privatization* (Chicago: ALA, 2001), www.ala.org/Template.cfm?Section=outsourcing&Template=/ContentManagement/ContentDisplay.cfm&ContentID=19799 (9 July 2005).

37. American Library Assocation, "Recommendation on Privatization of Publicly Funded Libraries" (Chicago: ALA, 2001), www.ala.org/ala/oif/iftoolkits/outsourcing/recommendation.htm (accessed 10 July 2005).

38. American Library Association, "Privatization of Publicly Funded Libraries (ALA Policy 52.7)," *Outsourcing and Privatization in Libraries* (Chicago: ALA, 2001), www.ala.org/ala/oif/iftoolkits/outsourcing/alapolicy.htm#privatizationpolicy (accessed 10 July 2005).

39. Bishoff and Reed, *ALA Proposal on Outsourcing and Privatization*.

40. Rikowski, "The Corporate Takeover of Libraries," 8.

41. World eBook Library, website (Honolulu: World eBook Library Consortia, 2003), www.netlibrary.net (accessed 10 July 2005).

42. ebrary, website (Palo Alto, Calif.: ebrary, Inc., 2005), http://shop.ebrary.com (accessed 10 July 2005).

43. Leisure World Seal Beach, website (Seal Beach, Calif.: Golden Rain Foundation, 2004), www.lwsb.com (accessed 10 July 2005).

44. Beachcalifornia.com, website, *Leisure World* (Sunset Beach, Calif.: California Travel News, n.d.), www.beachcalifornia.com/seal5.html (accessed 10 July 2005).

45. Privatization.org, *Libraries* (Los Angeles: Reason Public Policy Institute, 2005), www.privatization.org/database/policyissues/libraries_local.html (accessed 10 July 2005).

46. Elizabeth Larson, "Library Renewals: Private Citizens Are Remaking a Public Institution," *Reason* 25, no. 10 (March 1994): 36-40, www.findarticles.com/p/articles/mi_m1568/is_n10_v25/ai_15138944 (accessed 10 July 2005).

47. Proposition 13 was a 1978 ballot referendum in California that put a cap on property taxes, resulting in reduced funding for public services.

48. Larson, "Library Renewals: Private Citizens are Remaking a Public Institution," 40.

49. Schuman, "The Selling of the Public Library," 50.

50. Schuman, "The Selling of the Public Library," 51.

51. Library Systems & Services, website (Germantown, Md: Library Systems and Services, n.d.) www.lssi.com (accessed 10 July 2005).

52. Norman Oder, "LSSI in NJ: One Contract Ends, Efforts Continue," *Library Journal* 129, no. 7 (April 15, 2004): 16–17, http://print.google.com/print/doc?articleid=mlTFUFdiBLG (accessed 10 July 2005).

53. Norman Oder, "When LSSI Comes To Town," *Library Journal* 129, no. 16 (October 1, 2004): 36-40, www.libraryjournal.com/article/CA456252 (accessed 10 July 2005).

54. National Council for Public–Private Partnerships, *How Partnerships Work* (Washington, D.C.: National Council for Public–Private Partnerships, n.d.), www.ncppp.org/howpart/index.html (accessed 10 July. 2005).

55. Seattle Public Library, *Mission Statement* (Seattle: SPL, 2005), www.spl.org/default.asp?pageID=about_mission (accessed 10 July 2005).

56. In the design/build/operate model, the facility's title stays with the public owner unless a transfer occurs. Private partners using this model usually get their revenue from user fees that are charged when the facility is operational. Other PPP models include build/transfer/operate, in which a company is hired to construct a facility, after which it is transferred back to the public owner and then contracted back to the company for operation; and contract services, where public agencies contract with the private sector to supply or maintain particular services or build particular facilities. In addition to these, eleven more models are listed and described in "Types of Public–Private Partnerships," National Council for Public–Private Partnerships, *How Partnerships Work.*

57. Mike Brady, et al., *Introducing Best Value: 1999 IPWEA Overseas Study Tour Group Report* (Sydney, Australia: Institute of Public Works Engineering, 1999), www.ipwea.org.au/upload/best_value.pdf (accessed 10 July 2005).

58. Angela Watson, "Compete," in *Best Returns: Best Value Guidance for Library Authorities in England*, 2nd ed. (London, U.K.: The Library Association, 2001), www.la-hq.org.uk/directory/prof_issues/br5.html (accessed 10 July 2005).

59. United Kingdom Audit Commission, "Rating," *Report: Library Service, Haringey London Borough Council* (London: Audit Commission, 2001), www.audit-commission.gov.uk/reports/BVIR.asp?CategoryID=ENGLISH^576^LOCAL-VIEW^AUTHORITIES^103717&ProdID=E22BDF13-071E-4D82-82A0-C5217ABC97BF (accessed 10 July 2005).

60. Jane Mackenzie, "The Quiet Storm," *Information for Social Change* 16 (Winter 2002/2003), www.libr.org/ISC/articles/16-Mackenzie.html (accessed 10 July 2005).

61. Haringey Council, "Libraries" (Wood Green, U.K.: Haringey Council, 2005), www.haringey.gov.uk/leisure/libraries.htm (24 Mar. 2005).

62. Haringey Council, "Top Award for Haringey Libraries," press release (Wood Green, U.K.: Haringey Council, 2005), www.haringey.gov.uk/pressrelease.htm?id= 16947 (accessed 10 July Mar. 2005).

63. See Rikowski, *Globalisation, Information and Libraries*, 127–129, for discussion of the Haringey case, and 137–145 for other examples.

64. "Northern Ireland Launch £500m PPP Programme," *Industry News* (Hampshire, U.K.: Serco Group plc, 20 May 2004), www.serco.com/media/industrynews/ItemPage.asp?ItemID=2664435 (12 July 2005).

65. Library Systems & Services (LSSI), "Services."

66. Martin, et al., *The Impact of Outsourcing and Privatization on Library Services and Management,* 43.

67. Riverside County Library System, website (Riverside, Calif.: RCPL, July 2004), www.riverside.lib.ca.us/default/index.html (24 Mar. 2005).

68. Martin, et al., *The Impact of Outsourcing and Privatization on Library Services and Management*, 51.

69. American Library Association Outsourcing Task Force, *Outsourcing & Privatization in American Libraries*, 6.

70. Library Systems & Services (LSSI), "Library Management."

71. Library Systems & Services (LSSI), "Achievements."

72. Oder, "When LSSI Comes to Town," 36.

73. Oder, "When LSSI Comes to Town," 37.

74. Rikowski, "The Corporate Takeover of Libraries," 14.

75. Oder, "When LSSI Comes to Town," 39.

76. Oder, "LSSI in NJ: One Contract Ends, Efforts Continue."

77. Rikowski, "The Corporate Takeover of Libraries," 5.

78. Tupper and Doern, *Privatization, Public Policy and Public Corporations in Canada*, 1.

79. Ruth Rikowski, "Library Privatisation: Fact or Fiction?" *Information for Social Change* 17 (Summer 2003), www.libr.org/ISC/articles/17-Rikowski-2.html (accessed 12 July 2005).

80. Rikowski, "The Corporate Takeover of Libraries," 14.

81. Library Associates, "Small Business Profile—Shelf Wealth," *Los Angeles Business Journal,* 15 August 2004, www.libraryassociates.com/index.php4?page= busjourn (accessed 12 July 2005).

82. Norman Oder, "More on LSSI," *Library Journal* 129, no. 6 (1 October 2004) [only in online version], www.libraryjournal.com/article/CA456252 (accessed 12 July 2005).

83. Library Associates, Case Studies, www.libraryassociates.com/index.php4? page=case (accessed 12 July 2005).

6

Avoiding the Negative Impacts of Trade in Services

The two previous chapters outlined a number of ways in which some public library services can be perceived to be either in competition with other service suppliers or operating on a commercial basis, as well as some of the implications that the privatization or commercialization of library space and service can have for public library viability. Under the current WTO agreements on international trade in services (i.e., the GATS), publicly funded libraries cannot be exempted from the GATS disciplines if they either compete with other service suppliers or offer any services on a commercial basis. The fact that many libraries are doing just that (and increasingly so) means they could be subject to international trade challenges. Though publicly funded libraries have not yet been challenged in that way, the potential is a reality. If the WTO were to collapse and take its trade agreements with it, the push by governments and businesses for a globalized trade environment would continue. GATS-like agreements are likely to be a long-term threat to public services—at least until a global reprioritization of values take place. It is best to be both aware of the threats and prepared for possible challenges.

In this chapter we examine some choices librarians have to make with respect to language, funding, and approach to public library service, practices that libraries can avoid in order to prevent or ameliorate the implications of the GATS agreement and other agreements-in-waiting. We look at the means by which libraries can attempt to avoid competing with the private sector while still fulfilling their mandate of public service, and we review the ideology that underlies the market model and the push for commercialization. The increasingly blurred line between public and commercial activity in libraries is given a practical analysis regarding the ways in which librarians choose to define themselves and their patrons in a shift either toward or away from public service. Inherent in the shift are the pros and cons of user fees, and we explore how fees herald a dangerous and unnecessary trend toward competitive and commercial library service. The dangers are compounded by potential threats from the GATS. Fundraising is another possible way for libraries to obtain financial resources. Doing so through Friends of the Library networks or library foundations that operate like charities is far less dangerous than soliciting direct support from the private sector. The chapter concludes with a list of recommendations for librarians willing to take up the public library challenge by limiting a library's vulnerability to a challenge from international trade policies.

HOW ARE LIBRARIES COMPETING WITH OTHER SUPPLIERS?

Public services that fall into a "zone of competition" with private-sector suppliers render a library vulnerable to a challenge from international trade policies. That zone is a moving target: The potential for the private sector to provide services that are not currently offered is of an unknown though seemingly infinite magnitude. Just as good librarians see service gaps for libraries to fill, so, too, do good entrepreneurs.

Because they cannot control the competition, libraries have difficulty avoiding overlapping their services with other service suppliers. Some competition, such as that with bookstores and video outlets, is long-standing, unavoidable, and frankly, not very dangerous. Public libraries have always loaned materials that are also provided by other suppliers. Over the years, libraries and private vendors like bookstores have come to accommodate the existence of the other. And as we explained in chapter 4, avid bookstore customers tend to be avid library users—so the relationship might actually be mutually beneficial.

A GATS challenge arising from retailers because of traditional library lending is unlikely; however, that could change as private-sector suppliers become more internationalized with increased financial resources. Problems are more likely to arise in "nontraditional" service areas such as document delivery, homework help, and information-literacy training, which might already compete with existing or potential private-sector suppliers.

What can libraries do to avoid competition? Imagine your library has decided to reinvent itself by stripping away any services that could *possibly* expose it to trade challenges. First, take away free online reference service and homework help, which are already being offered by the private sector. Second, take out free ESL training because a new college has just opened in your community. Take out children's story time because a company down the road already does that. Then begin to examine the library's collections. A variety of both mainstream and peripheral videos are offered, but they compete with the video retail and rental ventures; consequently, the video collection must be eliminated. Bookstores have many of the same books or can order them; consequently, the library's books must be eliminated.

The lesson here is that GATS threats are a matter of scale. Not every library activity will provoke or even invite a trade challenge; some services are more risky than others. Unfortunately, there is no how-to-secure-your-library-against-international-trade-challenges checklist. A savvy librarian will consult with all of a library's stakeholders to determine what competitive or commercial services are crucial to its operation and will create a policy line between safe and unsafe library practices. Decisions to implement new services or offer old ones on a commercial basis are not to be taken lightly, particularly since the more the public and private sectors explore each other's territory, the more at-risk libraries become.

Arguably, to avoid potential for a trade challenge, libraries should avoid competing "unfairly" in any way. That is, they should not offer free services that are available on a commercial basis. It is, however, an impossible suggestion. Library activities cannot be dictated by latent market forces. That does not mean libraries should begin charging for "competing" services. Charging would make the services less accessible; it would also make public libraries vulnerable to a challenge for providing services on a commercial basis. Any library proposing to levy a fee for access to a service should analyze its potential international-trade consequences. Following this analysis, the library might find it best to either reconsider the fee levy or withdraw its proposal. Fees for service are discussed later in this chapter.

If a library does "compete," it should have justifications and policies for its actions. For example, competition with bookstores has been justified on the grounds that libraries encourage people to read, provide access to older out-of-print materials and a variety of reference works, and serve users who do not or cannot purchase books as quickly as they wish to read them. These arguments are weakened by the fact that library collections also contain multiple copies of popular best-sellers, but librarians can justify the presence of such books inasmuch as people who cannot afford to buy them should also have the opportunity to read them. Many library services are offered on the grounds that people either cannot afford or cannot obtain particular services from the private sector. That is known as "market failure."

Instead of attacking all the library services that libraries do provide, it might be more helpful to examine their basis of unity, which comes down to filling some of the holes left behind by market failure. Approaching the issues from that standpoint is the most constructive way to address the question of where to draw a line of safety. If librarians understand what is most important, they can fight to defend it rather than fearfully dismantling what they have worked so hard to put in place.

How Public Libraries Address Market Failure

Market failure is a term used to describe a situation in which the market fails to serve the public interest because the private sector cannot allocate particular goods and services efficiently. It happens when a particular good or service market is deemed not large or wealthy enough to justify the expense of providing that good or service at a price that will generate profit. Market failure also occurs when goods and services can be shared ("if I use it then you can still use it") or when nonpaying people cannot be kept from using them and more users do not increase the cost. Such good and services are called nonrivalrous and/or nonexcludable. Because there is no way to prevent their free use, the market cannot determine their value or the quantity to be produced and tends to avoid producing such goods.

Where that occurs, governments can allocate the resources themselves and pay for them with public taxes. Street lighting and lighthouses are two clear examples of nonrivalrous and nonexcludable services. These are identified as "public," or "collective," goods, and as such they are a benefit to all who use them—including the broad base of taxpayers, who are the primary funders. In economic language the ability to limit access to those who can pay for the good or service in question is called the *exclusion principle*. Collective goods by their nature cannot be subject to it.[1]

How Do Libraries Fit into This Distinction?

Information per se is theoretically nonrivalrous and not excludable, and information products such as books, though they have an initial price, can be passed around to nonpaying people. Public library services are rivalrous to the extent that there may be limits on the number of patrons who can use library materials at any one time, and they, too, can be excludable to the people who are not members of the library. But these exclusions are minimal, and librarians do their best to maximize access to library materials.

John Jaeger provides two reasons for libraries not being pure public goods. First, "if a significant number of users is added, the cost of providing service to them also increases." The more patrons a library has, the greater its collection and the broader its range of services has to be. Second, it is possible to exclude "nonpayers" from a library. Jaeger argues that public libraries are "merit goods," or goods that the private sector would supply but in insufficient quantity to satisfy the demands of society.[2] Calvin Kent defines these goods and services as those "deemed by society to be so meritorious because of their positive externalities that all should consume them or at least be able to consume them." Free vaccination programs are a perfect example.[3]

When market failure occurs and when there is a public interest in the existence of a good or service, then government often steps in to provide it. Public education is the prime example. Everyone benefits from having an educated population and workforce, even those who have no children in the school system. In Canada, people believe that public-health services provide such great positive externalities to the entire population that they are willing, through their taxes, to fund the entire system.

Publicly funded libraries are justified on similar grounds. As Patricia Glass Schuman writes, "Public libraries, by their very nature are classic 'market failures' . . . they are not profitable activities that a free marketplace will support. Library services are not designed to generate a profit, but rather to provide vital services to the public."[4] The market would not provide free public libraries because purchasing large quantities of material to lend freely to the populace would not be a plausible private enterprise. There is, however, money to be made in some of the services that public libraries provide. Therefore, public libraries exist in an intermediate position; they are not a good example of total market failure.

Meeting Challenges Posed by Private-Sector Competition

In order to avoid being challenged for competing with private-sector service suppliers, public libraries should select the services they do provide with great care. There are "safe" areas where, at present, libraries are not competing with private-sector firms. Some of the ones noted in chapter 4 are the provision of retrospective collections of books that preserve the printed record, educational videos, and some children's and adult programming, such as adult-literacy services, or baby story times. Aspects of almost all other library services are covered at least in part by the private sector. There is an important distinction in how public libraries and private-sector providers operate. Private-sector services are not universally available or likely to continue if unprofitable. Public libraries will always have an important role to play in their communities. Their commitment to meeting nonmarket needs is another reason they should not be subject to the forces of international trade agreements.

If trade challenges are a threat, should libraries eliminate all their potentially competitive services? No! Libraries should continue to provide services as they have done in the past, but in developing "new" services, they should focus in particular on variations in service or niche services that are not offered by private-sector suppliers. They should focus their attention on gaps where market failure occurs. They should also remember that as the zone of competition grows (see figure 2.5), market failure lessens—more businesses find a way to make a profit from librarylike activities, leaving only the marginalized to use public services.

With respect to competition in services that are currently offered, we suggest here, too, that libraries carry on as they have done simply because there might never be a trade challenge to each and every service. There is no justification for considering service discontinuation until trade challenges are actually made. In the case of such a threat to library services, there would be opportunities for governments to appeal the challenges at the WTO. As we described earlier in this book, such appeals are usually not successful, but libraries would at least have a grace period in which to do some targeted advocacy work and build grassroots support—anything to demonstrate how important library services are to the public.

Librarians should avoid complacency while advocating at the local, state/provincial, and federal levels that public libraries be exempted from trade agreements. Libraries should have well-thought-out and conscious reasons for providing their services. If, for example, a particular community has needs that the library could meet, new services to that community would likely be justified, so long as the library did its best to avoid placing that service into a zone of competition with the private sector. The best way to counter potential challenges is to have clear and well-written policies and guidelines about services and—where they exist—their fees. A clear and meticulous planning process will not only help avoid trade challenges but will also serve as a record and evidence of good library practices should a challenge arise. While the WTO is not likely to take such records into account, evidence of best practices can be used as a tool by librarians to support their case for "public" public libraries.

THE COMMERCIALIZATION OF PUBLIC LIBRARY SERVICES

Offering services on a commercial basis can subject publicly subsidized services to trade challenges; public libraries should evaluate the advantages and disadvantages of commercialization carefully. The previous two chapters provided examples of services that libraries currently offer on a commercial basis.

In order to put the commercialization of public-sector services in context, we now turn to a review of the underlying ideology that is shifting library service from the public to the commercial sphere. Two aspects of that trend are relevant to this analysis. First, the choice of words librarians use to describe themselves and their patrons, and second, the arguments for and against implementing public library user fees.

Ideology: The Market Model vs. Public Service

The encroachment of the private sector into public space is occurring in a variety of forms (language and policy, for example) but the forms all share a root in a shifting idea of what constitutes public service. John Buschman, in his text on the manner by which libraries sustain themselves in a changing social and economic environment, contends that principles of economics govern the new rules of public discourse by converting all public questions into economic terms and displacing "an older language of civic values as a framework of public and political choice."[5] Over the past thirty years, the noble tradition of public service has been deprecated—some would say deliberately[6]—with publicly funded institutions and employees accused of waste and inefficiency. The private sector has been suggested as a model of efficiency and good management. Public libraries are urged to operate on a business-based model that "assumes, among other things, that performance can be measured objectively."[7] Management professor Henry Mintzberg argues that measuring the efficiency or productivity of public services is almost impossible:

> Consider the myth of measurement, an ideology embraced with almost religious fervor by the Management movement. What is its effect in government? Things have to be measured, to be sure, especially costs. But how many of the real benefits of government activities lend themselves to such measurement? Some rather simple and directly delivered ones do—especially at the municipal level—such as garbage collection. What about the rest? . . . Many activities are in the public sector precisely because of measurement problems: If everything was so crystal clear and every benefit easily attributable, those activities would have been in the private sector long ago.[8]

It is likely that because the public sector relies on tax funding, it is routinely more closely examined and criticized than any private-sector firm would tolerate. In recent years, various corporate scandals have led many to wonder why management is so easily assumed to be more effective and efficient in the private sector than in the public. The market model ideology continues to be applied to public services, which have been under pressure since the 1980s to perform "more like business." In North America, the public sector has been pushed to spend less, be more efficient, operate with less staff, and so on.

Mintzberg warns that adopting business principles is counterproductive for public services that provide professional services to citizens. He argues that "private sector values are now pervading all of society. But government and other sectors should be careful about what they take from business." He clarifies his argument by saying he is "not against business as business, it is for balance in society":

> Today the prevailing mood supports the privatization of public services. Some of that thinking is probably useful. But a good deal of it is just plain silly. And if we are so prone to scrutinizing what doesn't belong in government, shouldn't we be equally diligent in considering what doesn't belong in business?[9]

The result of multidirectional ideological pressure was that public institutions began to lose their public-service mandate and accept the market model. They began to think of themselves as "businesses," and the people they served gradually became "consumers" or "customers." Public libraries have not been exempt from such pressures. Business-management trends have infused library management literature with the "jargon of the business moment," which has been widely adopted by library leaders.[10]

Language as Message and Symbol

One's choice of words is a political, symbolic, and often strategic act. When librarians talk of those who come to libraries as "customers," they are identifying them differently than they do when calling them "users" or "patrons." A chief librarian who adopts the title chief executive officer (CEO) is also adopting a set of norms and assumptions that accompany business endeavors. In defense of using business language, Darlene Weingand argues that "today's library is in increasingly tight competition for declining resources." She suggests that librarians adopt and master the language of their competitors and that if they fail to do so, libraries will face "a future of declining support and significance."[11] We believe that adopting business language can have a negative impact on the support for and significance of public libraries. That language is inappropriate for use by public-service entities such as libraries.

Corporatespeak has become a recognized term for a quickly evolving cross-sector, business-focused language. It is a strategy being used to fit libraries into the omnipresent market model on the suggestion that they "operate like businesses," and it is a deplorable model to follow. As one commentator on language in information and computer-technology companies writes:

> Business has a language all its own that changes almost daily. It is a language that is limiting, that denies possibility, and that excludes creative thinking. It is also the language with which industry players must grapple in their struggle to make money from new technology.[12]

The "Patron" vs. the "Customer"

Traditionally, librarians use the term *patron* when referring to library users. Lately, however, that word has been frowned upon as not appropriate for a businesslike service because it does not sufficiently reflect the new market model that many envision for libraries. A great deal of the LIS literature today refers to *clients* and *customers*.

We cannot be sure how the term *patron* became the traditional designation for library users. Historically, it describes someone who protects, supports, or sponsors a person or an institution. *Patron* is used outside of libraries too, often with the implication that a person uses a service or facility repetitively (which is certainly what one hopes for in libraries). The *Random House Dictionary of the English Language*'s first definition of *patron* is "a person who is a customer, client or paying guest, especially, a regular one, of a store, hotel, or the like."[13] That definition suggests that *patron*, *customer*, and *client* are synonymous. However, in the library context, the *Online Dictionary of Library and Information Science (ODLIS)*[14] clearly makes a distinction between *patron* and *client*. *Patron* is defined as "any person who uses the resources and services of a library, not necessarily a registered borrower. Synonymous with *user*. Compare with *client*." *Client* is subsequently defined as follows:

> A person who uses the services of a professionally trained expert, or of a professional organization or institution, usually in exchange for payment of a fee. Librarians employed in academic and public libraries usually refer to the people they serve as users or patrons because libraries have traditionally provided most services without charge. Information brokers who operate on a fee-for-service basis can be more appropriately said to serve "clients."

ODLIS defines the word *clientele* as a generic term that would apply to all users as a group: "All the persons who use a library's services and collections on a regular or irregular basis, usually those who live in the district that funds it operations or are members of the institution it serves."

A one-article cross-library debate in *Public Libraries*[15] argues that *patron* is a nineteenth-century term and that its use in the present will convince people that libraries are no longer relevant. That argument is reminiscent of the pressure to drop the word *library* from MLIS faculties. The language certainly will be impoverished if we drop all nineteenth-century terms! Another writer explains that "clients" are business or institutional or research professionals who are not dedicated to the public library as a community-enrichment center; another concludes that since library users pay taxes, they should be called "customers." Yet another suggests that since people use libraries but do not purchase from them, they should be called "users," not "customers." Another argues that the word *users* should be avoided because of its relationship to drug users (an example of perfectly good multipurpose words being captured in one limited context, thus diminishing the richness of the language). An argument in favor of using the term *patron* is that library staff are likely to feel a closer personal connection to "patrons" than to "customers." In all of this discussion, the word *customer* aroused by far the greatest amount of disagreement.

What's Wrong with Customer?

ODLIS does not provide a definition for *customer*, which suggests that the word is inherently unrelated to the library and information science profession. The *Random House Dictionary of the English Language* defines the term as "one who purchases goods from another, a buyer, a patron"; the use of *patron* here is consistent with the dictionary's definition of the word—the act of purchasing a product is central to the meaning of *customer*. Therefore, if one does not buy something, one cannot be a customer. In an editorial in *American Libraries*, Leonard Kniffel writes that while customers want to *buy* something, patrons want to *know* something.[16] John Budd asks if it is really desirable for a library "to place the relationship between itself and the user primarily on material and instrumental grounds," and he claims that where that is done, library users are reduced to economic beings (or consumers) and the offerings of libraries become mere commodities.[17]

With respect to public librarianship, John Buschman argues that the customer metaphor results in customer-driven librarianship, a trend that came to dominate discourse of the field, defining "libraries in economic (vs. democratic) terms."[18] Supporters of customer-driven librarianship argue that "librarians who flinch at the word *customer* are operating out of an outmoded paradigm" that "portrays the library as a 'public good' that 'should' receive public support."[19] Happily, we can transform that statement from an accusation to a statement of purpose by removing the word *outmoded*. Buschman agrees with John Budd's view that the customer service trend is "only a tactical renaming of longstanding professional values." He suggests that in this process "the language in which the essential purpose and framework of service is expressed has taken on economic and business hues." He argues that the evidence does not support the assumption that the business model is the correct way to provide service.[20]

The issues associated with using the term *customer* are not unique to public libraries. Henry Mintzberg refers to the entire public sector:

> I am not a mere customer of my government, thank you. I expect something more than arm's-length trading and something less than the encouragement to consume. When I receive a professional service from government—education, for example—the label *client* seems more appropriate for my role. (General Motors sells automobiles to its *customers*; Ernst and Young provides accounting

services to its *clients*.) In fact a great many of the services I receive from government are professional in nature. But, more important, I am a *citizen* with rights that go far beyond those of customers or even clients.[21]

Mintzberg's brave assertion is being undermined by shifting vocabulary and its accompanying philosophy. Buschman writes that "almost all public institutions and areas of public life have experienced similar effects from the dominance of the new public philosophy," and those effects have accelerated in the past twenty years.[22] Budd reminds us that "the language librarians use to describe their purpose and activities inevitably will define, even if they do not initially reflect, thought."[23]

Given the above definitions and arguments, we urge public librarians to call people in libraries users or patrons but not clients, and certainly not customers. The word *client* implies service in exchange for a fee. The word *clientele*, however, does not have the same implication and is widely used in public-service contexts. It can be used to refer collectively to all the people who come into libraries. The use of *customer* is an acceptance of corporatespeak, which we will discuss later in this chapter.

The Chief Librarian vs. the CEO

Those librarians who have tried to distance themselves from the time-honored and respected title of *librarian* and adopt meaningless nomenclature, such as *information professional* or bizarre constructions such as *cybrarian*, have their roots in special librarians' practice of using titles that they argue fit better in the environments in which they work. One of the biggest problems with using such language in business environments is that it spills over into the public sector, where its presence is completely inappropriate. Heads of public libraries self-identifying as CEOs is a cause of major concern. *Merriam-Webster Online* defines a CEO as "the executive with the chief decision-making authority in an organization or business."[24] Most commonly, the term is associated with the management of corporations, as in the *Wikipedia* definition: "the title generally given to the highest member of day-to-day management in a corporation who usually has the ultimate executive authority within an organization or company," and the word "corporation" (also according to *Wikipedia*) usually refers to a commercial entity.[25]

As a term, *CEO* clearly has corporate and business connotations. Public libraries are *not* businesses. Adopting corporate language to describe the chief librarian results from a failure to recognize and accept that public libraries are not commercial entities and that they should not seek to operate as if they were—which is not to say that they cannot be well managed. The chief librarian who is identified as the CEO is attempting to achieve status in the wider community that she or he perceives would not be offered to a chief librarian or library director or city librarian. But CEOs are everywhere in today's market-focused world—any small company can label its leader the CEO. While CEOs are a dime a dozen, any particular community will have only one chief librarian, city librarian, or library director. Using one of those terms instead of business-centered ones confers status and prestige within the community and ensures recognition that the position is clearly in the public sector.

Why Should Librarians Avoid Corporatespeak?

The broad goal of this chapter is to explore how librarians can avoid the potential negative impacts on public libraries of trade agreements, such as the GATS. Understanding the importance of library exemption from international trade pressures, librarians should emphasize the public and democratic character of the public library and champion clearly and loudly its status as a public service entity. By using corporatespeak, librarians are blurring the line between public and private service, resulting in a kind of self-created identity crisis.

Bonnie Nardi addresses some of the disturbing signs of the identity confusion. Librarians do not know what to call themselves, and, feeling that they should avoid old stereotypes, they give in to the urge to declare themselves technocrats. Nardi criticizes the ALA website for its use of trademark signals and market/military rhetoric: in its @ your library campaign, for example—which, in addition being trademarked, refers to certain people as "critical targets" of advocacy work. According to Nardi, the use of symbols reveals a "puzzling corporate-like mentality that is not in line with [library] services and core values."[26]

Adopting corporate language to describe library patrons, library directors, and other library staff is counterproductive. Those words should be removed from the librarians' lexicon. Latching on to and utilizing what Buschman calls "imitative business language" and corporate buzzwords suggests a certain insecurity about the profession's role and mission.

Some proponents would argue that using corporate language enables them to communicate better with those who control the funding of public agencies (i.e., what is done and who is served will be better explained) and that better understanding will lead to enhanced funding for public libraries. Another view is that language is not just a passive and necessary inheritance. Assuming, instead, that it can be an entirely intentional infringement on public space means it can be challenged head-on. By using public language, we can refuse the kind of "engaging" private-sector-centered language that gives funders agency to treat libraries like businesses.

User Fees and the Librarian's Dilemmas

In addition to using language carefully, librarians must ensure that their activities and strategies comply with the general public's vision of how public institutions operate. That means librarians must operate with care when considering whether to apply fees to the services they provide. The dilemma for librarians who are dealing with ongoing cuts to funding lies in having to choose between trimming their operations and finding alternate sources of funding—including, in particular, fees for services and borrowing privileges. While we noted many examples of services that are provided for a fee in chapter 4, we left the fee-or-free debate for this chapter.

The issue is complex because many libraries are faced with a combination of budget cuts, public pressure to provide enhanced services, and governmental recommendations to operate more "efficiently." While librarians might feel they have little choice in having to charge fees for certain services, the long-term costs of such actions outweigh the short-term benefits.

The imposition of user fees in public libraries has been a controversial issue since the early 1980s, when governments in a number of western countries began to require user fees for a variety of public services. Librarians at that time generally opposed the move, and many are still vocal today. European research found that opposition to proposed user fees in the late 1990s was "so massive that one might talk about an a priori opposition based more on a 'theology of librarianship,' than any willingness to actually discuss . . . user fees."[27]

In recent years, a number of library associations have issued statements and encouraged their members to reject the user-pay model in libraries. The American Library Association's document, *Libraries: An American Value*, states that "free access to the books, ideas, resources, and information in America's libraries is imperative for education, employment, enjoyment, and self-government."[28] In another document, the ALA "opposes the charging of user fees for the provision of information services by all libraries and information services that receive their major support from public funds."[29] At the international level, the UNESCO *Public Library Manifesto* states that "the public library shall in principle be free of charge."[30]

The Dilemmas

In considering whether or not to impose user fees, librarians have routinely faced difficult and troubling decisions. Charging fees discriminates against users who are unable to pay them. However, if a library does not charge fees, it might not be able to provide services that many patrons want and for which user fees would cover some of the associated costs.[31]

Beyond the fundamental dilemma, the idea of imposing user fees always raises related questions about what will and will not be subject to the fees. Traditionally, libraries have charged for overdue books and photocopies, but as Kristine Abelsnes notes in an IFLA paper, "here the user has an alternative: He or she can deliver the books on time or can borrow, take notes or read on site instead of making a photocopy." John Jaeger describes these kinds of fees and rental fees for films and projectors as "fees for convenience or for behavior modification" and makes the distinction between these and the kinds of special fees that may be charged for information-retrieval services, such as online searching.[32]

As explained in chapter 4, libraries often charge fees for new or nontraditional services—that is, for services that they do not consider to be core. There are problems inherent in defining *core*, hence the trade and commercialization implications for those services deemed *not* core. Abelsnes describes the trend to consider charging for what she calls fringe, or supplemental, services and claims that what is included in these services differs widely, "and that in itself should make some alarm bells ring." She cites the lack of consensus on distinguishing between what basic library services should be free and what the other "so called special, value-added or supplemental services [are] for which one can charge," noting that "[s]ome say it is online services, some say it is service to businesses or video rental or urgent action-services [*sic*], others say it is all services that are very expensive for the library."[33]

In examining the research on citizens' attitudes with respect to their willingness to pay for public services, Egholm and Jochumsen found that "the dividing line seems to appear between what has been characterised as 'luxury goods' versus 'necessary services' such as home help to the elderly, day care and public schools."[34] The distinction between luxury and necessary mirrors the distinction made in chapter 4 between core and new services.

Imposing user fees for these services concerns Abelsnes. She identifies the "domino effect," saying that once "you start charging for this, you might as well charge for that." She notes that it can be "extremely difficult to draw the line between charged services and no-charged services" and is concerned that librarians will be under "constant pressure to charge more in order to increase revenue and/or reduce the use of expensive services."[35] In its statement on user fees, the British Columbia Library Association argues that public libraries "that become dependent on user fees can feel pressured to cater to their users and not represent the needs of the greater community. These libraries would then cease to be 'public.'"[36]

Arguments for User Fees

Imposing user fees is considered to be a good idea by those who espouse market models and by librarians or boards who see no other options. Many librarians avoid considering the pros and cons of the arguments; they claim user fees simply aid libraries in times of ever-dwindling budgets and feel they have no choice *but* to charge for particular services. The choice is not a binary one; there are good reasons to oppose user fees and some valid and feasible alternatives to them.

User fees are most simply defined as "the substitution of user charges for tax financing."[37] Economists claim that such fees alter incentives and act to free markets,[38] and Marilyn Gell [Mason] qualified that by saying that fees do this by providing a mechanism "for determining preferences through willingness to pay."[39]

Proponents of fees use five principal arguments to back up their side of the debate. John Jaeger presents both positions of the user-fee debate. The following discussion is based on his presentation.[40]

The first argument is that user fees help libraries avoid redundant work because those who pay for services need or want them. The argument suggests that it is wasteful to provide free services to people who would not use them if they were required to pay for them. In Canada, where there is a public health-care system, citizens probably use doctors more than they would in the United States. There are, however, resulting positive consequences. People can be diagnosed earlier, poor people are healthier, and all citizens have access to the same (formerly very high) level of care. However, funding has not matched increasing costs, pushing Canada's health-care system toward the domain of the private sector. Like doctors, librarians want people to use the service that is publicly available: librarians are professionals trained to help people find information. The more work libraries do to reduce the barriers imposed by their policies, the greater access patrons have to information and hence to the tools they use to participate fully and effectively in their communities.

User fees can regulate online service use (such as databases, which may be particularly expensive). The rationale is that fewer people will use expensive resources if they have to pay for them. The counterargument suggests that librarians do not want to regulate demand. They do want people to be able to use the materials and services that libraries provide, fulfilling information needs, find reading materials, and so on. Regulating access to online resources restricts access instead of facilitating it.

A third argument is that libraries should separate online services from traditional services on the premise that online searching is a convenience rather than an essential service. That argument is becoming moot, however, as a great deal of in-house online searching is now done on public-access computer terminals rather than by librarians acting as intermediaries. The idea is that instead of a regulatory function as in the last argument, online services are seen more as a luxury. The distinctions between core, or traditional, and noncore, or nontraditional, services is arbitrary. The argument can be made that these services are logical extensions of traditional services.

That particular argument evokes questions surrounding international trade agreements like the GATS. If libraries charge for online searching and other nontraditional services, they are operating on a commercial basis; therefore GATS rules apply. If they do not charge for those services, they may be viewed as competing with the private sector; therefore GATS rules also apply. Another factor is that libraries work together as consortia to provide inexpensive access (relative to individual or private-sector subscriptions) to some electronic resources. That may also be subject to trade challenges as libraries are viewed as unfairly competing with private companies.

Libraries have to be clear and careful about the formulation of their library policies and absolutely certain about their justifications for providing access to online searching tools. For what purpose, for what patron group, and by what means are these services being offered by the public library in question?

A fourth argument is that user fees lead to better library management as managers have to be diligent in following funds through library systems and ensuring efficient spending of the public's money. While it may be true that some libraries suffer from poor management or inefficient spending patterns, there is no reason to believe that this is necessarily and singularly tied to public funding. Nor is there a guarantee that a funding model change would result in a proportional shift in management behavior. Because fees alone would never cover all public library costs, management personnel would never be motivated solely by fees. There are many well-managed public libraries. Good management is related to people and library policies rather than to funding models.

John A. Charles argues that a user-pay system is better than reliance on tax revenues because nonusers should not have to support a public service. He suggests that user fees "are especially appropriate in the case of libraries, because the heaviest users are clearly those with the most ability to pay." Charles claims that since people below the poverty line use libraries less than higher-income adults, "broad-based taxation is a regressive way to pay for user-services [*sic*]. Low-income people should not be forced to pay higher rents for luxury services enjoyed by others." Having described public libraries as a luxury service, Charles goes on to argue that "a second advantage of a user fee is that it automatically converts higher patronage into increased revenues." He mentions the Multnomah County library's great increase in per capita book circulation over seven years. He suggests that in any other business, "this would have been an opportunity, not a problem. But the library can't cash in on high demand, because its revenue stream is largely independent of actual use. An appropriate user fee would have brought in more revenue during this period to keep pace with demands."[41]

Charles identifies various ways that user fees could be implemented, including membership fees for library cards and fees for each loan or renewal. While he suggests that it is possible that fees could discourage people from going to the library, he argues that this is not likely because buying books would be more expensive for an individual than an annual or per-use fee to borrow the book. He is suggesting that libraries are simply substitutes for bookstores; he neglects to note that collections often contain many items that are out of print and difficult to purchase (or even find) outside of libraries. He concludes with the argument that libraries "are not truly 'free': someone has to pay. In the long run, switching to user fees will provide better service without the uncertainty caused by once-every-five-year votes."[42] These are standard economic arguments.

Nancy Van House examined the economic functions of public financing and found that the distributional and external benefits of libraries warrant at least partial library-service subsidization by the public sector. However, based partly on the evidence that "lower income groups probably do bear more of the cost of the library [through taxation] than is justified by their use of it" and that "the library is used primarily by middle-income individuals who could afford to pay for its services," she concluded that user "fees are not inconsistent with the library as a publicly supported institution."[43]

The contention that people with low incomes subsidize middle-class library patrons is not a certain argument. Low-income families are less likely to have computers in their homes, and public-access terminals in public libraries may be particularly important to them. For communities in which library use is proportionally less for low-income groups, however, it seems pretty obvious to us that there must be some noneconomic reasons that poor people would not use a free service. Instead of imposing fees across the board, it might be more worthwhile to examine the causes of their lack of use. Imposing user fees on all library patrons does not address that problem. Our response here, again, is that imposing user fees on patrons simply does not facilitate access to library resources and services. As the ALA argues, imposing fees creates economic barriers to information access, and librarians should look for alternatives "that minimize distinctions among users based on their economic status or financial condition."[44]

The actual willingness of users to pay for library services is difficult to determine. In surveys of users and nonusers of public services, many appear willing to pay for some services and not for others. The problem is that the questions posed are usually hypothetical, and that, Egholm and Jochumsen argue, leads to "a degree of insecurity" in interpreting survey results. In their conclusions, however, Egholm and Jochumsen found library patrons to be generally less supportive of user fees than were nonpatrons.[45] Libraries in Alberta and Quebec found that far more people joined their libraries when they dropped their policies to impose user fees.[46] That alone may speak to the point. People may feel as though they are being double-charged for access to their libraries. First they pay taxes, and then they pay additional fees. People are far more willing to borrow books if they don't have to pay for them.

John Jaeger points out that the arguments in favor of user fees tend to be "teleological or 'ends justifying means' kinds of arguments." He argues that while people can "assert that user fees are important because they accomplish something or bring about some good situations for the library and its users," the arguments against user fees are "based on the nature of the public library itself" and center more "on a communitarian understanding of the public library."[47]

Arguments against User Fees

Van House based her justification for user fees on the fact that the public and private (i.e., personal) benefits and the positive externalities of public subsidization of libraries are difficult, perhaps impossible, to measure. Since benefits and externalities cannot be measured, she argued that it is best to keep nonusers from being forced to pay for libraries through taxation and to impose user fees on all library users. The extent to which nonusers might benefit from the use of the library by others in the community is hard to measure, but such benefit is indeed possible to imagine. As we noted in our discussion of market failure, it is widely recognized that all of us—even those of us who do not have children in school or who educate our children privately—benefit from public education. By the same argument, we all (including people who are not library patrons) benefit from public libraries because of what they have to offer in terms of self-education, information, and recreation. People who do use public library materials and services to educate themselves, for example, might be able to find higher paying jobs and thus contribute more to the tax base. Some users may be able to assist in community development or help family members and other individuals because of the information they obtain in the library. By providing a locus in the community for individual development, the community as a whole benefits from the presence of a publicly funded library.

The economic argument on which many base their support of user fees—that poor people are unfairly taxed to support library use by wealthier people and therefore taxation should be replaced by fees for services—does not address such positive externalities. Therefore it is interesting to note that many proponents of library user fees make exemptions for some groups, particularly children, students, or low-income people, because of externalities associated with providing free access to those groups. According to Van House, some economists argue that "use by children and underprivileged adults produces externalities because for these groups any reading at all is educational."[48] While it is a condescending argument, it illustrates how purely economic arguments are often qualified by those who make them. Charles, for example, tempers his argument for user fees by saying that a fee-based system could be made progressive if students and lower-income adults were exempted.[49] He does not indicate how the library would determine which low-income patrons and students would qualify for the exemption. Providing exemptions would require that people ask for them as well as a system of confirming that the exemption is justified. That both stigmatizes patrons needing exemptions and requires bureaucratic record keeping, in effect increasing the cost of saving money. If underprivileged adults and the children of poor taxpayers use the library to any extent, then the economic argument for user fees is void. It might be that use by poor children is sufficient to justify the continuation of taxation as a means of funding, because user fees would be borne most heavily by their parents either directly or through ignominious registration for exemption, but taxation is spread across the whole population.

The most commonly relied-upon argument for not charging user fees is that information has more than financial value. That is, information is not just a commodity. Herbert Schiller explains that librarians are faced with two dramatically different ways to view information. On the one hand, they can regard it as a social good, and on the other hand, they can treat it as a privately produced commodity for sale.[50] As John Budd writes, those who claim that information is only a commodity "emphasize the commodity and ignore the informing quality, the intellectual value of information." He goes on to argue that "[i]nformation as a commodity is removed from information as meaning . . . it becomes nothing more than an object that has a price attached to it."[51] Schiller writes that many librarians resist the information-as-commodity direction and "work valiantly, sometimes successfully, in the democratic tradition, defending the general social good."[52]

The intrinsic benefits of information to society is well documented,[53] specifically the value of public libraries.[54] In her IFLA paper, Abelsnes writes that people who defend the no-charge principles do not suggest that information is without value and therefore should be free. They argue that information has noncommercial value; libraries play a political role in the communities they serve by being an effective means of not only distributing information but also redistributing wealth.[55] She also notes that the problem is not the people who can afford to buy information, literature, and entertainment. Rather the problem is "the great economic differences in the world today" and that libraries "can provide access for all to the world of information and the heritage of literature and the written word. The problem is that we strive to obtain equal access and that even small fees contribute to the opposite."[56]

Another important argument is that by introducing user fees, governments could feel justified in making further cuts to public library budgets. Egholm and Jochumsen suggest that any income gain from user fees would probably be short-term and likely offset by corresponding reductions in budget allocations. The correlation is difficult to prove, however, since governments may give any number of reasons for reducing the amount of money allocated to public libraries; the "decline in library allocations could just as well result from general reductions in public sector allocation."[57] Changes in government could also lead to shifts in political support for libraries; those factors are clearly difficult to isolate. That said, the possibility for a correlation still exists. The scenario could run something like this: A library, faced with a shortfall for its upcoming budget, decides to charge an annual fee for all borrowing cards. Governments, noticing that the library is surviving, may propose further cuts on the grounds that the library is clearly resourceful and creative enough to survive on less funding. As a result the library would have to find ways to meet the challenge of a series of budget cuts when governments make subsequent reductions to cultural spending.

Avoiding fees for library service complies with the precautionary principle. While avoiding fees for services does not encourage government funding of libraries per se, at least governments aren't receiving a message that libraries can make do with whatever funding authorities are willing to give them.

User Fees and the Market Model

The arguments for user fees are more difficult to refute in difficult economic times. The logical end of the movement toward fee-for-service models is the elimination of public libraries. Imposing user fees for public services implies that public revenues are insufficient to cover the costs of providing these services. It is not lack of revenue but political will that directs the funding to and away from specific public services. For example, Jeffrey Donlan points out that the "dead-end investment" in prisons in Colorado is 8 percent of the state budget, while only .03 percent is budgeted for libraries.[58] In addition to politically motivated funding, we have seen unprecedented tax cuts that, our governments argue, are necessary for bringing about economic prosperity. If that is indeed so, then with economic prosperity, government revenues should increase and there ought to be more money for public services.

Judging by governments (particularly Canadian ones) that turn out budget surpluses, should not public services like libraries have access to record-breaking amounts of funding?

A simple analysis of factors in the province of Alberta demonstrates that library spending is a political issue and that library fees are used by the provincial government to off-load its responsibility for supplying public services. There was a population growth of 17.7 percent in Alberta the decade from 1992 to 2002. The total provincial spending on libraries at this time increased by 17.8 percent.[59] Library spending per capita, therefore, was the same at the beginning and end of that decade. At the same time, however, the provincial government was congratulated for a series of budget surpluses. The province had a $7 billion surplus in 2000 and 2001, but it was not reflected in the budget for the following year, which meant Alberta did the lowest per capita spending on culture ("culture" includes libraries) in all of Canada—$57 per capita vs. the national average of $69.[60] While libraries were suffering and most had imposed user fees, and in effect, transferred the balance of care onto the shoulders of library patrons, the Alberta government dropped its general rate for corporate taxes from 15.5 percent to 13 percent in 2002.[61] Shelley Mardiros addressed library service fees in Alberta: "For a mere 0.1 per cent of its anticipated $5.5-billion surplus for the year, Alberta could not only replace the revenue libraries currently raise through user fees, but could redress the underfunding that libraries have endured since 1994 because of provincial funding cut-backs and freezes."[62]

It is often not a simple lack of government money that results in cutbacks in public library funding. Government bodies make a series of decisions based on their priorities at the time. Unfortunately for libraries, priorities tend to be financial rather than social or cultural. Market models often support the political justifications for library budget cuts.

User Fees and International Trade in Services

When publicly subsidized institutions provide services on a commercial basis, they lose the exemption that is available under the GATS for services offered under government authority. The GATS could be replaced by other services agreements, but it is unlikely that the requirements for the public-service exemption would change. International-trade initiatives strive for increasing trade liberalization. The overarching goal is for governments to open their goods and services markets to progressively higher levels of open and free trade. Libraries do not belong in that system, and librarians are responsible for ensuring that public access to information is given the protection it is due.

Charging user fees is an example of "providing services on a commercial basis," which does not necessarily involve a profit motive. Operating on a commercial basis by charging user fees is increasingly suggested as an alternative solution for public library funding challenges. Even before the GATS was a concern, public librarians spoke out against user fees as contrary to the public library's mission, and, as noted above, various library associations have established policy positions in opposition to user fees. Surprisingly, many librarians still believe them to be the best solution to the decline in public funding. By imposing user fees, libraries clearly move themselves into the commercial camp, and the library cannot obtain the exemption for services offered "under the auspices of governmental authority."

FUNDRAISING: AN ALTERNATIVE TO COMMERCIALIZATION?

Faced with budget cuts and driven by the market model, some public library boards and librarians have accepted commercialization as a minimally harmful and logical way to address diminishing funding. However, as we have discussed, that is not a solution librarians should implement—not only because of the GATS implications but also because it supports a growing attack on public-service funding. Library associations have been vocal in their opposition to user fees, as have many individual librarians and library boards. Many of these organizations subsequently turn to other sources of private funding (from corporations, charities, and foundations) to meet their budget needs. While supporting the library no longer rests solely on the shoulders of taxpayers, these fundraising ventures are not entirely risk free. The WTO and other policy setters can interpret libraries' fundraising efforts as illustrative of the need to encourage trade liberalization and justify further cuts to public spending.

The Rise of Fundraising Efforts in Public Libraries

Libraries have participated in a wide variety of fundraising activities ranging from book sales to bake sales. Some libraries have accepted corporate support, including named sponsorships of reading clubs, library activities, and spaces within the library (the named-spaces phenomenon), as well as large-scale corporate giving such as that of the Gates Foundation. Public–private partnerships are widely promoted by businesses, governments, private interest groups, and even some librarians.

More recently, libraries have begun to consider some of the advantages of charity-style fundraising as they develop individual donation and bequest programs. Some libraries have established foundations and/or hired professional fundraisers. There is growing sense of concern that successful fundraising can result in diminished public subsidization. Steve Coffman, who believes that the funding base for public libraries should be diversified, argues that it is a myth to believe that cuts to operating budgets are or would be based on successful fundraising. His argument is that libraries have had their budgets cut regardless of the presence of alternative funding sources and that "cultural and educational institutions have been using plural funding models and successfully combining public and private funds for years without jeopardizing this tax support."[63]

Thomas Hennen disagrees, stating that public libraries "can and do rely on multiple sources of funding, but first, foremost, and always they are a tax-supported public good."[64] He cites the data that indicate widespread public support for tax-funded public libraries and argues that plural funding is a slippery slope: "first plural funding, then 'reasonable user fees.' What's next?"[65] We believe that some of the fundraising alternatives could indeed put libraries in jeopardy of losing public funding. In some cases, increases in library budgets are tied to the raising of private money through fundraising activities. As *Library Journal* editor John Berry unequivocally states, "When city fathers make public money a quid pro quo for private funds, they are pandering to our dislike of taxes and playing politics with essential public services."[66] Rather than focusing on fundraising, we believe, it is far more important for libraries to work to keep the *public* in public libraries by fighting for support through taxation. We recognize, however, that many libraries do turn to alternative funding sources, and librarians might find themselves inadvertently, and sometimes not by their own choice, in a position where their services, ethics, and profession could be compromised. Librarians who engage in fundraising projects need to be aware that some alternative funding sources bear a great number of risks with respect to commercialization, competition, and trade agreements.

A Role for Corporate Donations and Sponsorship?

Many libraries contract with corporate suppliers and create a variety of public–private partnerships. That activity can put libraries in the ludicrous and dangerous position of actually encouraging the growth of corporate competitors and thereby increasing the size of the zone of competition shared by libraries and other service suppliers. Corporate donation and sponsorship, on the other hand, usually operate differently and do not create parallel library service providers in the private sector. However, both have associated risks. The named-spaces phenomenon could be seen as unfairly benefiting one corporation over another.

Corporate donations and sponsorship appear to be based on corporate goodwill and the desire to help public libraries. Donors receive tax deductions, however, and sponsorships are classified as marketing expenses. Both diminish tax revenues. Loss of tax revenue to the public purse is called a tax expenditure, meaning that ultimately the public pays for corporate donations. Most who argue on behalf of corporate donations and sponsorship to supplement public funding cite the Carnegie and Gates examples of philanthropy. Steve Coffman, a sponsorship proponent, says that the Carnegie stipulation that cities tax themselves "at the rate of 10% of the value of the building to maintain the library" shows that "plural funding has already played a major role in public libraries," and the challenge today is how to resurrect philanthropy "to help solve some of current funding problems."[67] Today some historians argue that Carnegie's philanthropy was motivated by egotism rather than altruism. It has been noted that many working class people often could not make use of Carnegie-funded public libraries because their working hours were so extended that they had neither the time nor the leisure to use libraries. Some people outright avoided libraries:

> Carnegie was viewed . . . as a low-wage advocate and the antagonist of the Homestead Mills Strike of 1892 in which over forty workers were killed in a battle with Pinkerton detectives, notorious at this time for working as strikebreakers. While Carnegie's speeches often centered on the benefits to workers of his library philanthropy, labor and its allies viewed his actions as a shrewd policy . . . to expend a trifle of the gains which [were] made off the people in giving them public libraries.[68]

The large Gates Foundation technology donations to public libraries have raised concerns because the recipient library must use the money for technology that accommodates Microsoft products. Sanford Berman argues that "Bill Gates' largesse promotes computers and Microsoft software among recipient libraries. Maybe that is good for some of them, but maybe others, especially those in small communities could actually have better spent some of the $400 million on building repairs and more books and videos."[69] Some would argue that librarians cannot "look gift horses in the mouth," but clearly corporations do not approach libraries with large gifts of money unless it is beneficial to them in some way; as one proponent of private funding stated, sponsors "are trying to market a product and you're not going to get the money if you don't give them some marketing benefit."[70] Leonard Kniffel points out that corporate sponsors, who describe such sponsorships as "cause-related marketing," want a visible role in the organizations they support. Therefore libraries should have written guidelines and sponsorship manuals that guide such contracts with the private sector and protect the reputation and integrity of the library.[71]

There is legitimate concern regarding corporate sponsorships. Sanford Berman remembers the 1993 controversy over McDonald's sponsoring an ALA children's summer reading program. The reading program's materials featured the McDonald's golden arches more prominently than the ALA logo. Furthermore, participating libraries "were pointedly forbidden in the promo instructions to allow fast-food competitors to join in."[72] McDonald's negotiated with ALA to ensure that it would be seen not only a good corporate citizen but also as a better corporate citizen than any other fast-food chain. An act of philanthropy that was not self serving would have promoted the ALA reading programs in McDonald's restaurants and/or donated money with no requirement for aggressive and reciprocal advertising. The Social Responsibilities Round Table (SRRT) of ALA condemned the partnership in a resolution that was subsequently ignored at the 1993 ALA Mid-Winter Council meeting.[73]

The American Library Association continues to support corporate sponsorships as typified by its @ your library campaign. The program's website notes that the library association "seeks sponsors who can help ALA reach the library community and beyond to the millions of people libraries serve" and that the ALA would work with its corporate supporters to develop "effective, targeted, educational marketing communications programs that can help a sponsor achieve its public service goals."[74]

In 1997 the Canadian Library Association issued a position statement on corporate sponsorship declaring that the association "encourages and supports advocacy to maintain and develop public funding as the principal source of support for public, school, academic and government libraries." The statement continued, though, noting that public libraries should explore other avenues of funding, one of which is corporate sponsorships. The statement does outline some of the principles that should be incorporated into the policies and agreements that deal with sponsorships.[75]

Corporate fundraising raises concerns for many librarians. Sanford Berman believes that "teaming up with for-profit business is in its very nature profoundly partisan," favoring political and economic interests over others, and argues that it is "hard . . . to imagine a library with big corporate partners or donors mounting displays, or doing reading lists on topics like classism, corporate power, sweatshops, child labor or corporate welfare."[76] Others argue that the key is moderation and that corporate sponsorships should be allowed for seed money, demonstration projects, or specific capital projects.

Many librarians are interested in corporate sponsorships because they are seen as alternatives to implementing user fees during times of financial hardship. Librarians often overlook the encroachment of the private sector into public space as well as the loss of legitimacy of public libraries (to what extent has the ALA's reputation been affected by its promotion of a fast-food retailer?), but trade threats are more difficult to overlook. Though calls for a GATS challenge regarding corporate sponsorship in libraries are very unlikely, such sponsorships contribute to the overall privatization and commercialization of library spaces. Government funding authorities are beginning to take into account and assume a certain level of private-sector involvement. Therefore, libraries that attempt to dodge private-sector generosity may find themselves falling short on their budgets. However, despite the fact that marketing pockets are deeper than philanthropic pockets (as Leonard Kniffel reminds us),[77] we encourage libraries to avoid corporate sponsorships.

Charitable Giving and Library Foundations

Raising money through various fundraising activities has been viewed as a better alternative to both the user-fee and corporate-sponsorship models. Advice on fundraising began to proliferate in the early 1990s as government spending collapsed. Books[78] and articles[79] appeared quickly and invited librarians to raise additional funds by putting on special events, sending direct mail, soliciting funds from private donors, arranging planned and tribute giving programs, applying for grants, organizing capital project campaigns, and developing telemarketing strategies.[80] More recently the literature has focused on ways to encourage personal donations of money; there are many recommendations for libraries to establish library foundations and hire full-time fundraisers. Andrew Richard Albanese explains that where fundraising was "once the domain of Friends groups and local board members generous with their checkbooks," fundraising is now a professional activity in many libraries.[81] Library foundations are "independent nonprofit organizations established according to the relevant state and federal regulations." They are autonomous organizations with greater political independence than public libraries and "typically have a single purpose: to raise private funds for the support of the library, often including support for library building projects."[82] Libraries establish foundations in order to attract tax-deductible gifts for capital campaigns or asset bequests, or to have an ongoing funding source.[83] A quick search of the Internet shows that many library foundations have been established by public libraries. While some foundations look for corporate donors, most concentrate on obtaining donations from individuals. Foundations might, in fact, be a positive alternative to other fundraising methods—Albanese argues that foundations of this sort actually bolster "the library's image and reach."[84] The downside is that shift of funding responsibility from governments to librarians and library boards. The more successful these alternative fundraising ventures are, the more it will appear that public libraries need not be priorities for government funding.

What Are the GATS Implication of Fundraising?

The two issues of greatest concern with respect to the GATS that affect public libraries are the commercialization of public-sector services and competition with other service suppliers. User fees are an example of commercialization that should be avoided. On the surface, fundraising does not appear to create problems vis-à-vis the GATS. Corporate fundraising, however, can present problems. As noted with the McDonald's example, if a donor is provided with exclusive rights within a publicly subsidized institution, then there is a possibility that competitors of the donor could claim that the publicly funded library is unfairly favoring one business over the other. That is not a simple business contract but a promotional advantage. As the SRRT resolution states, the summer reading program agreement represented an "advertising windfall for McDonald's."[85]

Corporate sponsorships should be avoided. Charitable fundraising from individuals does not present the same problems.

Hazards of Fundraising

The foremost argument against fundraising is that it can undermine tax support. Albanese believes that the question of whether local lawmakers would slash public funds if libraries are too successful at fundraising is a valid concern, but his view is that library administrators are realists who recognize that libraries must develop partnerships and that any philosophical concerns about fundraising in public libraries must be put aside.[86] John Berry, on the other hand, argues that rather than adding resources to the public library, private fundraising can have the opposite effect and can "undermine the case for tax support upon which public libraries must depend."[87] According to Berry, drawing a line can be difficult when making decisions to take private funding. When, for example, "the mayor tells the trustees that the city cannot increase the library budget until the library starts a foundation to raise private money, he comes very close to crossing the line." That negotiation, "which has occurred in dozens of cities . . . rarely results in increased resources for that library."[88] Sanford Berman argues that private-sector support might affect necessary increases in the library budget "predicated on local public funders' perception that the library seems to be pretty good at finding these extra revenue sources."[89]

John Berry identifies another problem, which is that "when a public service is supported and sustained with private philanthropy, it weakens its argument for being an essential public service." He continues:

> In hard times, libraries are more heavily used. They offer information and recreation that can help every citizen get through difficulties more easily and effectively. That is still a job for government. It is a job that can be enhanced with

private support, but private funding is not dependable enough to be given total responsibility for that important work. Don't let government off the hook.[90]

Thomas Hennen takes note of Steve Coffman's observation that successful fundraising is particularly difficult in small communities and argues that 95 percent of the libraries in the United States are in communities too small to do effective fundraising. Yet under Coffman's plural-funding model, Hennen argues, "libraries will be punished for failing to do the impossible; and even in major urban areas there are communities that have less fundraising potential than others."[91] Expecting all public libraries to supplement diminished public funding through fundraising is clearly an example of optimism overriding reality.

Herbert Schiller writes that there are two dramatically different ways to view information. On the one hand, one can regard it as a social good, and on the other hand, one can treat it as a privately produced commodity for sale.[92] He notes that under the pressure of the latter view, "the public library system, a long-standing custodian of the idea and practice of information as a social good, is tottering."[93] John Buschman presents a valid summation. He states that the potential of democracy is realized through independent institutions, such as libraries, that are widespread, equitably funded, and accessibly organized—connected in a meaningful way to their communities, able to meet the needs of fully informed participants and acting as a space apart from the commodification that characterizes so much of the culture.[94]

RECOMMENDATIONS

Following is a summary of the recommendations of the previous three chapters.

Adhering to best practices *and* acting as library advocates involves meeting the myriad challenges libraries face. Businesses profit by privatizing public space, governments are succumbing to pressure to make libraries financially self-sustaining, international agreements like the GATS have the potential to destroy the entire foundations of these institutions, and the public needs public libraries as much as ever.

Librarians who address these complex challenges have responsibilities. The first is to offer high-quality services and ensure that they are meeting the needs of their patrons. To that end, librarians must continue to provide services that have always been in their repertoire, and when they develop new services and collections, they should do so with clear and appropriate policies in place for documenting that community needs are being met by the implementation of these services. Excellent quality of service is the best guarantee that libraries will not be perceived by members of a progressively commodified society as outdated or replaceable. If libraries provide the best services, people will demand access to them.

The public requires a guarantee that it have free and universal access to library services and collections. If librarians assume that information is not a commodity but something more (or as Sandra Braman says, "a constitutive force in society"), the tone is set for treating libraries as public goods rather than commodified spaces. Avoiding commodified language, commercialization, privatization, and user fees are important components of both building and preserving public space.

The second responsibility is to discourage the trend toward privatization and commercialization. Public library funding is threatened by the increasing reliance on the market model, and librarians must actively counter this trend. As more companies take on librarylike activities, the zone of competition increases, and public-sector information services become marginalized and increasingly subject to the GATS disciplines.

The third responsibility librarians have is to ensure that libraries be adequately funded. It is impossible to maintain high levels of service if libraries do not have fundamental operating expenses funded, but the corollary is also true: Without a good track record for management, meeting community needs, and advocacy, funders will be reluctant to see libraries as a funding priority. It is vital that librarians continue to request public funding while advocating library protections in regional, national, and—now, particularly—international codes. It will be a difficult task. The push for public funding meets only local resistance, and pushing for broad library exceptions in the GATS and other agreements will be met with international resistance. It is important to note that at this time, neither the GATS public-services exemption nor lack of 10.C commitments guarantees any security for public libraries.

Finally, librarians must work to ensure that their country does not make a 10.C commitment, if it has not already done so. (See chapter 3 for a description of the GATS classifications.)

We realize that this is a great deal of responsibility for librarians who probably already feel overwhelmed in their jobs, considering the current climate of budget cutbacks and pressure from the private sector to outsource and privatize services. We hope, however, that these same librarians can fall back on knowing how important libraries are to the communities they serve and how different our society would be without them. Guaranteed free and universal access to a service is a rare treasure these days; and because librarians are recognized leaders in the push for public space and discourse, we offer them our most sincere support and encouragement.

Recommendations for Avoiding GATS Challenges

- Continue to provide services that are currently provided in your library.
- Have documented reasons for providing services currently provided and develop policies and guidelines for the services that justify their provision.
- Limit commercialization, and avoid user fees.
- When providing new services, avoid competing with other service suppliers.
- Discourage privatization.
- Engage in advocacy for public libraries.
- Monitor trade developments.
- Above all, avoid complacency.

NOTES

1. Thelma Freides, "The Federal Information Controversy from an Economic Perspective," *College and Research Libraries* 47 (1986): 429.
2. John Jaeger, "User Fees, Community Goods, and the Public Library," *Public Library Quarterly* 17 no. 2 (1999): 56–57.
3. Calvin A. Kent, "The Privatizing of Government Information: Economic Considerations," *Government Publications Review* 16 (1989): 120.
4. Patricia Glass Schuman, "The Selling of the Public Library," *Library Journal* 123, no. 13 (1998): 50–52.
5. John E. Buschman, *Dismantling the Public Sphere: Situating and Sustaining Librarianship in the Age of the New Public Philosophy* (Westport, Conn.: Libraries Unlimited, 2003), 16.
6. Lewis Lapham, "Tentacles of Rage," *Harper's Magazine* 309, no. 1852 (September 2004): 31–41.
7. John E. Buschman, "Staying Public: The Real Crisis in Librarianship," *American Libraries* 35, no.7 (August 2004): 41.
8. Henry Mintzberg, "Managing Government: Governing Management," *Harvard Business Review* 74, no. 3 (May–June 1996): 79.
9. Mintzberg, "Managing Government: Governing Management," 83.
10. See Chapter 5 "Co-opted or Rolling Over?" in Buschman, *Dismantling the Public Sphere.*
11. Darlene E. Weingand, *Customer Service Excellence* (Chicago: ALA, 1997), 3.
12. Jeff Leiper, "Corporatespeak: Deconstructing the New Language of Business," *Writer's Block* (Winter 2001), www.writersblock.ca/winter2001/essay.htm (accessed

10 July 2005).

13. *Random House Dictionary of the English Language,* Unabridged Edition (New York: Random House, 1966).

14. *Online Dictionary of Library and Information Science* (*ODLIS*), comp. Joan M. Reitz (Westport, Conn.: Libraries Unlimited, 2004), http://lu.com/odlis/odlis_o.cfm (accessed 9 July 2005).

15. For arguments on terminology, see the essays in Hampton Auld, ed., "Patrons, Customers, Users, Clients: Who Are They and What Difference Does It Make What We Call Them?" *Public Libraries* 43 no. 2 (March/April 2004), 81–87.

16. Leonard Kniffel, "Libraries Aren't Bookstores, and Patrons Aren't Customers," Editorial, *American Libraries* 28, no. 7 (August 1997): 38.

17. John M. Budd, "A Critique of Customer and Commodity," *College and Research Libraries* 58, no. 4 (July 1997): 314, 316.

18. Buschman, *Dismantling the Public Sphere*, 117.

19. Weingand, *Customer Service Excellence*, 3.

20. Buschman, *Dismantling the Public Sphere*, 117.

21. Mintzberg, "Managing Government: Governing Management," 77.

22. Buschman, *Dismantling the Public Sphere*, 118.

23. Budd, "A Critique of Customer and Commodity," 330.

24. *Merriam-Webster Online* (Springfield, Mass.: Merriam-Webster Inc., 2004), www.m-w.com/dictionary.htm (accessed 10 July 2005).

25. *Wikipedia: The Free Encyclopedia* (St. Petersburg, Fla.: Wikimedia Foundation, 2005), http://en.wikipedia.org/wiki/Main_Page (accessed 10 July 2005).

26. Bonnie A. Nardi, "The *Genius Loci* of the Library," PowerPoint presentation 2003, www.simmons.edu/gslis/alumni/Nardi_2003_Presentation.ppt (accessed 10 July 2005).

27. Charlotte Egholm and Henrik Jochumsen, "Perspectives Concerning User Fees in Pubic Libraries," *Information Management* 21, no. 6 (2000): 299.

28. American Library Association, *Libraries: An American Value* (Chicago: ALA, 1999), www.ala.org/ala/oif/statementspols/americanvalue/librariesamerican.htm (accessed 10 July 2005).

29. American Library Association, *Access to Electronic Information Services and Networks* (Chicago: ALA, 2004), www.ala.org/alaorg/oif/electacc.html (accessed 10 July 2005).

30. UNESCO and IFLA, *Public Library Manifesto* (Paris: UNESCO, 1994), www.ifla.org/VII/s8/unesco/eng.htm (accessed 10 July 2005).

31. Kristine Abelsnes, "Fees for Library Services" *IFLANET Social Responsibilities Discussion Group Paper* (Paris: IFLA, 1998), www.ifla.org/VII/dg/srdg/srdg1.htm (accessed 10 July 2005).

32. Jaeger, "User Fees, Community Goods, and the Public Library," 51.

33. Abelsnes, "Fees for Library Services."

34. Egholm and Jochumsen, "Perspectives Concerning User Fees in Pubic Libraries," 300–301.

35. Abelsnes, "Fees for Library Services."

36. British Columbia Library Association, *Statement and Guidelines on Public Library User Fees* (Vancouver: BCLA, 1995), www.bcla.bc.ca/default.aspx (accessed 10 July 2005).

37. Lennart Lundqvist, "Privatization: Towards a Concept of Comparative Policy Analysis," *Journal of Public Policy* 8 (1988): 11.

38. David L. Weimer and Aidan R. Vining, *Policy Analysis: Concept and Practice*. 2nd ed. (Englewood Cliffs, N.J.: Prentice-Hall, 1991), 148.

39. Marilyn Killibrew Gell, "User Fees I: The Economic Argument," in *Key Papers in the Economics of Information,* ed. Donald W. King, Nancy K. Roderer, and Harold A. Olsen (White Plains, N.Y.: Knowledge Industry Publications for the American Society for Information Science, 1983), 158.

40. Jaeger, "User Fees, Community Goods, and the Public Library."

41. John A. Charles, "Check Out Library Fees," *Cascade Commentaries* No. 2002–13 (Portland, Ore.: Cascade Policy Institute, 2002), 1–2, www.cascadepolicy.org/pdf/fiscal/2002_13.pdf (accessed 10 July 2005).

42. Charles, "Check Out Library Fees."

43. Nancy A. Van House, *Public Library User Fees: The Use and Finance of Public Libraries* (Westport, Conn.: Greenwood Press, 1983), 47, 105–106.

44. American Library Association, *Economic Barriers to Information Access: An Interpretation of the Library Bill of Rights*, (Chicago: ALA, 1993), www.ala.org/ala/oif/statementspols/statementsif/interpretations/economicbarriers.pdf (accessed 10 July 2005).

45. Egholm and Jochumsen, "Perspectives Concerning User Fees in Pubic Libraries," 300–301.

46. Shelley Mardiros, "Spreading the Word: Banff's Very Public Library," *Alberta Views* 4, no. 1 (January/February 2001): 37–39, www.albertaviews.ab.ca/janfeb01/janfeb01social2.pdf (accessed 10 July. 2005).

47. Jaeger, "User Fees, Community Goods, and the Public Library," 53–56.

48. Van House, *Public Library User Fees*, 30.

49. Charles, "Check Out Library Fees."

50. Herbert Schiller, *Information Inequality: The Deepening Social Crisis in America* (New York: Routledge, 1996), 34–37.

51. Budd, "A Critique of Customer and Commodity," 316–317.

52. Schiller, *Information Inequality*, 37.

53. See for example, Fritz Machlup, "Uses, Value, and Benefits of Knowledge," in *Key Papers in the Economics of Information*, ed. Donald W. King, Nancy K. Roderer, and Harold A. Olsen (White Plains, N.Y.: Knowledge Industry Publications for the American Society for Information Science, 1983), 245–264.

54. See for example Leslie Fitch and Jody Warner, *Dividends: The Value of Public Libraries in Canada* (Toronto: Book and Periodical Council, 1997), www.nald.ca/fulltext/dividend/cover.htm (accessed 10 July 2005); Charles Oppenheim, "The Value of Library and Information Services: And How to Beat the Economists at Their Own Game" *State Librarian* 34 (July 1986): 24–26.

55. Abelsnes, "Fees for Library Services."

56. Abelsnes, "Fees for Library Services."

57. Egholm and Jochumsen, "Perspectives Concerning User Fees in Pubic Libraries," 300.

58. Jeffrey Donlan, "We Must Protect State Library Funding," *Library Journal* 128, no. 12 (July 2003): 50.

59. Alberta, Alberta Community Development, "Library Statistics Year 2004," *Building Strong Communities* (Edmonton: Government of Alberta, 2004), www.cd.gov.ab.ca/building_communities/public_library/statistics/statistics/index.asp (accessed 10 July 2005).

60. Statistics Canada, "Government Expenditures on Culture 2001/02," *The Daily*, 7 January 2004, www.statcan.ca/Daily/English/040107/d040107a.htm (accessed 10 July 2005).

61. BDO Dunwoody LLP, "2001 Alberta Budget Report," *BDO Federal and Provincial Budget Reports*, 24 April 2003, www.bdo.ca/en/library/publications/taxpub/budgetreports/al0401.cfm (accessed 10 July 2005).

62. Mardiros, "Spreading the Word: Banff's Very Public Library."

63. Steven Coffman, "Saving Ourselves: Plural Funding for Public Libraries," *American Libraries* 35, no. 2 (February 2004): 39.

64. Thomas J. Hennen, "Restore Our Destiny: Full—Not Plural—Funding," *American Libraries* 35, no. 7 (August 2004): 43.

65. Hennen, "Restore Our Destiny," 45.

66. John N. Berry, "Don't Let Government off the Hook," *Library Journal* 127, no. 8 (1 May 2002): 8.

67. Coffman, "Saving Ourselves: Plural Funding for Public Libraries," 39.

68. Ann C. Sparanese, "Service to the Labor Community: A Public Library Perspective," *Library Trends* 51, no. 1 (Summer 2002): 24.

69. Beverly Goldberg, "What Price Partnerships? Public Librarians Linda Mielke and Sanford Berman Draw Their Bottom Lines over Private-Sector Fundraising," *American Libraries* 29, no. 2 (February 1998): 43–46.

70. Cited in Leonard Kniffel, "Corporate Sponsorship: The New Direction in Fundraising," *American Libraries* 26, no. 10 (1995): 1024.

71. Kniffel, "Corporate Sponsorship," 1025.

72. Goldberg, "What Price Partnerships?" 44.

73. This example is discussed in Elaine Harger, "Institutionalizing Silence within ALA?" *Progressive Librarian* 14 (Spring 1998): 1–4, www.libr.org/PL/14_Editorial.html (accessed 10 July 2005).

74. American Library Association, *@ your library—The Campaign for America's Libraries* (Chicago: ALA, 2005), www.ala.org/ala/development/majorfundraising/campaignforlibraries/campaignamericas.htm (accessed 10 July 2005).

75. Canadian Library Association, *Corporate Sponsorship Agreement in Libraries,* Position Statement Approved by Executive Council, 21 June 1997 (Ottawa, CLA, 1997), www.cla.ca/about/sponsor.htm (accessed 10 July 2005).

76. Goldberg, "What Price Partnerships?" 44.

77. Kniffel, "Corporate Sponsorship: The New Direction in Fundraising," 1023.

78. See for example Adam Corson-Finnerty and Ann Blanchard, *Fundraising and Friend-Raising on the Web: A Handbook for Libraries and Other Nonprofit*

Organizations (Chicago: ALA Editions, 1998); James Swan, *Fundraising for the Small Public Library* (New York: Neal Schuman, 1990).

79. See for example James Swan, "Alternate Funding Sources: Grass Roots Fundraising," *Bottom Line* 3, no. 3 (1989): 31-32; Kathryn Covier Hannah, "Alternative Funding for Libraries: A Plan for Success," *Bottom Line* 10, no. 4 (1997): 169–175.

80. Hannah, "Alternative Funding for Libraries: A Plan for Success," 169.

81. Andrew Richard Albanese, "Foundations for the Future," *Library Journal* 127, no. 8 (1 January 2002): 40.

82. Wisconsin Dept. of Public Instruction, "Trustee Essential 24: Library Friends and Library Foundations," in *Trustee Essentials: A Handbook for Wisconsin Public Library Trustees* (Madison, Wis.: Dept. of Public Instruction, 2002), www.dpi.state.wi.us/dltcl/pld/te24.html (accessed 10 July 2005).

83. Library Funding Associates, website (Brentwood, Tenn.: Library Funding Associates, 2005), www.libraryfunding.com (20 March 2005). This private firm provides advice to libraries on fundraising.

84. Albanese, "Foundations for the Future," 41.

85. Harger, "Editorial: Institutionalizing Silence within ALA?"

86. Albanese, "Foundations for the Future," 41.

87. Berry, "Don't Let Government Off the Hook," 8.

88. Berry, "Don't Let Government Off the Hook," 8.

89. Goldberg, "What Price Partnerships?" 46.

90. Berry, "Don't Let Government Off the Hook," 8.

91. Hennen, "Restore Our Destiny: Full—Not Plural—Funding," 43.

92. Schiller, *Information Inequality*, 34–37.

93. Schiller, *Information Inequality*, 35.

94. Buschman, *Dismantling the Public Sphere*, 8.

7

Advocacy for Public Libraries

Librarianship through its professional associations can more actively engage with GATS issues. Librarians have the ability to participate in a program of effective advocacy geared toward educating the public about the dangers of GATS[1] through their associations. Coalitions can be built with other public service sectors that are faced with the same issues. Librarianship, as a public service, is not alone in addressing these issues. Many other public services, such as education,[2] health care,[3] and social services,[4] have an equal potential to be affected.

BARRIERS TO EFFECTIVE ADVOCACY

More effective advocacy initiatives will be addressed by identifying some of the barriers that have been encountered to date. The first barrier is the uncertainty factor, which arises from difficulties in making confident predictions about the real dangers posed by GATS. The second related barrier is the complacency factor. It arises from the environment of uncertainty and can be exacerbated by a degree of organizational inertia. The third barrier to more effective advocacy in this area is the overload factor, which arises from the reality that library associations are already engaged in numerous policy issues and working with limited resources. The library community needs larger numbers of advocacy staff, more participation by its members in these efforts, and greater resources for accomplishing these ends. But as nonprofits, the library associations work with limited resources, and their advocacy efforts are limited. The more visible issues get immediate attention, especially those that have a direct, obvious, and immediate bearing on the work of librarians.

Rather than think of these three factors as separate and distinct, they should be understood as highly interdependent and overlapping.

The Uncertainty Factor

It is hard to effectively address an issue that is incomprehensible. By design, the international trade regime is confusing, and equally by design it is fully accessible only to the most specialized trade lawyers and lobbyists. It is difficult to make accurate predictions about the impact of a services agreement that has no precedent and few analogues. The GATS agenda is ongoing and not always transparent. At the root, there is an underlying tension in reconciling the trade-liberalization objectives of the GATS with the public policies needed to ensure an ongoing and vital role for public-sector libraries. The text of the GATS agreement does not help ameliorate that uncertainty. While on its face GATS purports to protect public services by providing an exception for services offered under the auspices of a governmental authority, we have seen that the exemption is extremely limited and may not be effective in the case of public library services. That the interrelationships and overlaps between services provided by the public and private sectors are constantly in flux only adds to the uncertainty. It is sometimes unclear when a service or potential service is in the expanding zone of competition depicted in figures 2.3, 2.4, and 2.5.

Another factor leading to uncertainty is that GATS is still in an early stage of development, so there is a lack of solid authority on how a particular service might fare in the face of a challenge. As indicated in chapter 2, there is no direct GATS panel decision on point with respect to the scope of the public-services exemption. While we were able to identify and discuss some early precedents that help us appreciate how broad the scope of the agreement really is, it is important to recall that the GATS agreement itself is nothing but a framework. The ongoing process of negotiations leading to the preparation of schedules of commitments is constantly a moving target. To make the situation worse, so much of what occurs in the scope of negotiations is not visible to the public. GATS suffers from serious transparency problems. The visibility of GATS is different from that of the typical legislative process, the traditional subject of the advocacy work of the associations. While there is always some uncertainty in the legislative process (the maneuvering behind the scenes), it is relatively open and transparent. If a bill is pending in Congress or Parliament, our associations will know about it and be ready to respond effectively. But in the case of GATS or other international-trade negotiations, such crucial information is usually hidden from public view.

Consequently, the question of how international trade agreements affect library service initially seems remote. Many leaders in the library profession and its associations, as well as library trustees and library board members, have difficulty grasping the connection between international trade and library services. In contrast with the more obvious issues of library funding, intellectual freedom, and copyright legislation, the area of international trade agreements does not directly register for many as a "library issue."

The Complacency Factor

Not only do international-trade issues seem remote to the concerns of the library profession, but to date there have also been no direct challenges to public library services based on GATS. Thus one might question what the GATS opponents are so worried about. That tendency is certainly apparent in the rhetoric of GATS proponents who attempt to marginalize GATS critics. As discussed in chapter 2, a recent WTO Report entitled *GATS—Fact and Fiction* characterizes many criticisms of GATS as implausible scare stories:

> It is claimed for example that the right to maintain public services and the power to enforce health and safety standards are under threat, though both are explicitly safeguarded under the GATS. How have serious people come to believe what is, on the face of it, out of the question? Why should any Government, let alone over 140 Governments, agree to allow themselves to be forced, or force each other, to surrender or compromise powers which are important to them, and to all of us?[5]

The counterarguments help promote the complacency factor. In a December 2001 comment in *American Libraries*, Emily Sheketoff (executive director of ALA's Washington office), Rick Weingarten, (director of ALA's office for information technology policy) and Miriam Nisbet (legislative counsel to ALA's office of government relations) responded to a piece by Canadian librarian activist and GATS critic Fiona Hunt:

> Although Fiona Hunt was partially correct in her article written for the September 2001 issue of the *Library Journal*, we believe that her argument falters when she critiques the World Trade Organization General Agreement on Trade in Services (GATS). In addition to all the domestic policy concerns that are confronting libraries these days, we must add a growing list of international issues—including trade negotiations. Ms. Hunt argues that GATS threatens to treat libraries as government subsidized commercial enterprises. This is highly unlikely. To see why, we just need to look at the exact language of GATS.[6]

Sheketoff, Weingarten, and Nesbitt then discuss the public services exemption, which they seem quite confident protects library services.

> [T]he agreement exempts from coverage "a service supplied in the exercise of government authority." On the face of it, that would seem to spare public libraries. The problem comes about because the agreement removes from the exemption services "supplied on a commercial basis" and "in competition with one or more service suppliers." The purpose of this clause is to deal with countries that have nationalized banks and telecommunication companies. What it clearly does not do is extend GATS coverage to normal government services like police, education, libraries, and roads—all of which have commercial analogs (private schools, private security services, and the like). But, these government functions are not, in the words of the agreement, "supplied on a commercial basis." Their services are not for sale.[7]

Hunt had argued that libraries were in more immediate danger because of the limited scope of the public services exemption. She also asked, "What can librarians do?"

> They can start where they usually do—by reading up on the facts, forming an opinion, and voicing it. Also, they can disseminate information to their service populations:
>
> - Acquire materials about the WTO in general and the GATS in particular.
> - Set up displays and offer reading lists to patrons.
> - Invite speakers to lecture on international trade agreements and their effect on local economies.
> - Lobby local library associations to make a public statement about the GATS and other such agreements.[8]

Library trustees and board members can support library staff in these efforts.

Rebutting Sheketoff, Weingarten, and Nisbett, Hunt responded that she was "alarmed and disappointed by the apparent complacency demonstrated in the ALA office's response [to her article]" and urged ALA "to take a closer look at the implications for libraries embodied by the WTO's General Agreement on Trade in Services (GATS)." She argued that while the "ALA office correctly points out the ambiguous nature of the clauses in the GATS concerning exemption of government services and identifies these clauses as confusing," they still failed "to address the exact nature of the confusion and to recognize its potential impact on libraries."[9]

The Overload Factor

In reviewing the websites from various library associations, one can readily appreciate how thoroughly engaged they already are in advocacy work on a variety of policy issues.[10] Library funding, copyright, and intellectual-freedom issues continue to be central to the policy agendas of the associations. Now, in an era of globalization, the additional layer of international issues must also be considered. Unfortunately, the budgets and staffing levels for our associations' advocacy work can never keep up with the additional issues that need to be addressed. The overload factor can be addressed by expanding the volunteer base in individual associations, as well as by avoiding a duplication of effort through stronger coalition work.

A THREE-POINT PROGRAM FOR MORE EFFECTIVE ADVOCACY WORK

Specific steps can be taken toward more effective advocacy programs. It is a three-point initiative. The first is to view international trade agreements as a component of broader information policy so that GATS-type issues are less isolated, and become better integrated with issues, such as funding, that are already front and center on librarians' advocacy agendas. This is addressed at length in chapter 8.

The second point addresses internal education. Before we can make effective external presentations on these issues, the associations need to better inform their members (including trustees and library boards) about the importance of international trade matters and how they relate to the provision of library services. In recent years there has been increased activity in this area, as evinced by special sections in library associations' websites, as well as GATS-related programming at library conferences.[11] While these resources and activities could be enhanced and better coordinated, it does appear as if there has been increased awareness in the past few years.

The third point is to emphasize the importance of coalition work in this area. At the first level of coalition building, library associations have been joining in various joint submissions on international issues. In the past two years, library associations in the United States have sent in various submissions on the FTAA[12] and other free trade agreements.[13] More recently there has been a series of submissions from IFLA and other library associations, including the American Association of Law Libraries, the American Library Association, the Association of Research Libraries, the Medical Library Association, and the Special Libraries Association, on the issue of the WIPO development agenda.[14] The attention given to the WIPO development agenda by the library community demonstrates that when international issues are linked with other, more readily recognizable "library issues" such as copyright, they get a stronger response from the associations than international trade issues.

Joint submissions can often make a more powerful impact than individual letters. In addition to increasing the level of unity between different organizations, they make clear to elected policymakers that the authors represent the views of substantial numbers of constituents. These coalitions must be extended beyond the library community. As libraries are not unique among public services that are challenged by GATS issues, there is no reason to think that effective advocacy should be limited to the library associations standing alone. Other sectors that are situated similarly to librarianship with respect to GATS challenges need to be identified, and their associations then need to be approached with a view toward joint work. The areas of education, social services, and public health come immediately to mind. In Canada, progress has already been made in joining library associations with other groups in the educational sector. The Canadian Library Association, Canadian Association of Law Libraries, and Canadian Association of Research Libraries are part of the broader Copyright Forum, which includes other associations in the education sector.[15] While additional work must be done to expand the nature of the coalition in terms of both membership and issue areas, there is already positive movement in that direction.

What is the particular role that could be played by the library sector in such coalitions? In his presentation to the 2000 IFLA Conference in Jerusalem, Canadian trade lawyer Steven Shrybman pointed directly to the information-dissemination role that could be played by the library community:

> It seems to me that there is a particular role for librarians to play as well, and not just as the defenders of public libraries, although without your determined intervention I fear the era of such public institutions, which emerged only a little more than a century ago, will not survive very much longer. But there is another and equally important service you can provide, which would be to provide effective public access to the complex, obscure and often secretive reports, submissions, studies, and negotiating texts which comprise the record of contemporary trade negotiations and dispute resolution. There is great need to find ways to reveal this vital information which far too often has been shrouded from public view.[16]

NOTES

1. For a review of the work of individual library associations on the issue to date, see chapter 6 in Ruth Rikowski, *Globalisation, Information and Libraries: The Implications of the World Trade Organisations's GATS and TRIPS Agreements* (Oxford: Chandos Publishing, 2005), 161–84. Rikowski credits the British Columbia Library Association with being the first group to raise the issue and then reviews the contributions of IFLA, the Canadian Library Association, the American Library Association, EBLIDA, and others.

2. See Jim Grieshaber-Otto and Matthew Sanger, *Perilous Lessons: The Impact of the WTO Services Agreement (GATS) on Canada's Public Education System* (Ottawa:

Canadian Centre for Policy Alternatives, 2002); and Canadian Federation of Students, "How the GATS Threatens Post-Secondary Education," *Fact Sheet* 7, no. 4 (February 2001), www.cfs-fcee.ca/html/english/research/factsheets/fs-7(4)-gats.pdf (accessed 8 July 2005).

3. See Matthew Sanger, *Reckless Abandon: Canada, the GATS and the Future of Health Care* (Ottawa: Canadian Centre for Policy Alternatives, 2001). Executive Summary available online at www.policyalternatives.ca/documents/National_Office_Pubs/reckless_abandon_summary.pdf (accessed 8 July 2005).

4. See Andrew Jackson and Matthew Sanger, *When Worlds Collide: Implications of International Trade and Investment Agreements for Non-Profit Social Services*. (Ottawa: Canadian Centre for Policy Alternatives, 2002). Introduction available online at www.policyalternatives.ca/documents/National_Office_Pubs/wwc_tc_intro.pdf (accessed 8 July 2005).

5. World Trade Organization, *GATS—Fact and Fiction* (Geneva: WTO, 2001), 2, www.wto.org/english/tratop_e/serv_e/gatsfacts1004_e.pdf (accessed 8 July 2005).

6. Emily Sheketoff, Rick Weingarten, and Miriam Nisbet, "Washington Office Responds to WTO Article," *American Libraries*. 32, no. 11 (December 2001): 12. See the ALA's "Resolution on Protecting the Interests of America's Libraries Under the WTO General Agreement on Trade in Services," CD #20.7 (Chicago: ALA, 2001–2002), www.libr.org/GATS/GATSresol.pdf 98 July 2005) Compare the ALA statement with the Canadian Library Association's 1999 Statement, *Canadian Library Association Perspective on the World Trade Organization Meetings* (Ottawa: CLA, 1999) www.cla.ca/about/wto.htm (accessed 8 July 2005), and *The IFLA Position on the World Trade Organization* (The Hague: IFLA, 2001, latest revision 22 December 2002). www.ifla.org/III/clm/p1/wto-ifla.htm (accessed 8 July 2005).

7. Sheketoff, Weingarten, and Nisbet, "Washington Office Responds to WTO Article."

8. Fiona Hunt, "Why the World Trade Organization Is a Threat to Libraries," *American Libraries* 32, no. 8 (September 2001): 32–33.

9. Fiona Hunt, "Hunt's Response to the ALA Washington Office Letter, Unpublished by *American Libraries*," Libr.org: Supporting Progressive Librarians since 1998 (website) (n.d.), http://libr.org/GATS/Hunt-Sheketoff.html (accessed 8 July 2005).

10. For examples of policy issues being considered at various associations, see American Library Association, *Links to Washington, Office Issues* (Washington: ALA, 2005), www.ala.org/ala/washoff/WOissues/issues.htm; American Association of Law Libraries, *Washington Affairs* (Washington: Georgetown University Law Library, 2005), www.ll.georgetown.edu/aallwash; Special Libraries Association, *About Us—Advocacy* (Alexandria Va: SLA, 2005), www.sla.org/content/SLA/advocacy; Canadian Library Association, *Library Issues—CLA Briefs* (Ottawa: CLA, 2005), www.cla.ca/issues/clabrief.htm; European Bureau of Library, Information and Documentation Associations, *EBLIDA Position Papers* (The Hague: EBLIDA, 2005) www.eblida.org/position/index.htm; International Federation of Library Associations and Institutions Committee on Copyright and other Legal Matters (CLM), *The IFLA Position on the Geneva Declaration on the Future of WIPO* (The Hague: IFLA, 2005), www.ifla.org/III/clm/copyr.htm; Medical

Library Association, Government Relations, *Information Issues and Policy* (Chicago: MLA, 2005), www.mlanet.org/government/ (all websites accessed 8 July 2005).

11. For example, see Canadian Library Association WTO/GATS Working Group, *WTO/GATS/FTAA Related Resources* (Ottawa: CLA, 2001), www.cla.ca/resources/gats_resources.htm; British Columbia Library Association, BCLA Information Policy Committee, *Globalization, GATS and the WTO* (Vancouver: BCLA, n.d.), www.vcn.bc.ca/bcla-ip/globalization/; Libr.org website, *The GATS and Libraries* (last updated March 2004), www.libr.org/GATS; *and* International Responsibilities Task Force of the American Library Association's Social Responsibilities Roundtable, *Libraries and the World Trade Organization*. (last modified April 28, 2005), www.pitt.edu/~ttwiss/irtf/wto.html (all websites accessed 8 July 2005).

12. See American Association of Law Libraries, "Comments of the American Library Association, Association of Research Libraries, American Association of Law Libraries, Medical Library Association, and Special Libraries Association on the Second Draft Consolidated Texts of the Free Trade Area of the Americas Agreement," *Washington Affairs,* 31 January 2003, www.ll.georgetown.edu/aallwash/lt01312003.html; "Supplemental Comments of the American Association of Law Libraries, the American Library Association, the Association of Research Libraries and the Special Libraries Association on the Second Draft Consolidated Texts of the Free Trade Area of the Americas Agreement," *Washington Affairs,* 28 February 2003, www.ll.georgetown.edu/aallwash/lt02282003.html (websites accessed 8 July 2005).

13. See for example the joint submission from American Association of Law Libraries, the American Library Association, the Association of Research Libraries, the Medical Library Association, the Special Libraries Association and the Digital Future Coalition regarding bilateral trade agreements in: American Association of Law Libraries, "RE: U.S.–Chile and U.S.–Singapore Free Trade Agreements," *Washington Affairs* 19 June 2003, www.ll.georgetown.edu/aallwash/lt06192003.html (accessed 8 July 2005).

14. See International Federation of Library Associations and Institutions Committee on Copyright and other Legal Matters (CLM), *The IFLA Position on the Geneva Declaration on the Future of WIPO*; American Association of Law Libraries, *Library-Related Principles for the International Development Agenda of the World Intellectual Property Organization* (Washington: Georgetown University Law Library, 2005), www.ll.georgetown.edu/aallwash/Principles012605.pdf (all websites accessed 8 July 2005).

15. Other member organizations include the Association of Canadian Community Colleges, the Canadian Association of University Teachers, the Canadian Federation for the Humanities and the Social Sciences, Canadian Historical Association, the Canadian Museums Association, the Canadian Home and School Federation, the Canadian School Boards Association, the Canadian Teachers' Federation, and the Copyright Consortium of the Council of Ministers of Education. While the Copyright Forum is, as its title suggests, interested in Copyright related issues, the internationalization of copyright, and its subsumption within the WTO through TRIPS helps the strong interrelationship between international intellectual property and international service issues.

16. Steve Shrybman, "Information, Commodification and the World Trade Organization" (paper presented at IFLA 2000 Conference, Jerusalem 13–18 August 2000), www.ifla.org/IV/ifla66/papers/176-148e.htm (accessed 8 July 2005).

8

International Trade Policy as Information Policy

Over the past twenty years, broad public policies of budget and tax cuts, restructuring, a push for privatization, and growing support for corporate welfare have had an impact on libraries and librarians.[1] These activities reflect a new public philosophy that harnesses public institutions to work toward economically productive ends, a process described by John Buschman in his book *Dismantling the Public Sphere*.[2] Those policies can have an impact on local institutions such as schools, libraries, and museums. Some policies, such as government support for technological advances and access to technology, can be helpful, while others, such as budget cuts and restructuring programs, can be crippling.

A useful way to discuss information policy is to distinguish manifest (direct) policy from that which is latent—more tangential but having unanticipated consequences for information creation, dissemination, access, or use. The distinction can highlight the extent to which latent policies exist. Information policy can originate from many sources; the ones most important to a discussion about libraries are the interrelated national and international policies that strongly influence the development and implementation of local information policy. Of particular interest is the role of international-trade regimes such as the World Trade Organization, which, one might argue, makes trade policy, not information policy. However, WTO agreements can have enormous effects on both manifest and latent information policy. Before describing some of these effects, however, we must describe exactly what we mean by the term *information policy*.

WHAT IS INFORMATION POLICY?

Information policy is a term employed in a variety of contexts, but how exactly is it defined? Using the term implies that we know what we mean when we use the words *information* and *policy*, but many writers have argued that the terms are ambiguous and have multiple connotations. Sandra Braman addresses the ambiguity of the word *information*, explaining that it can be treated as a resource, a commodity, a perception, or as a constitutive force in society.[3] The term *policy* is just as multifaceted. According to Mairéad Browne, it can describe many different realities or potentialities, including theories and models, expressions of general purpose or desired state of affairs, fields of activity, specific governmental proposals or decisions, and a variety of processes.[4] Therefore, Browne concludes, the boundaries of information policy are porous and lack clear consensus.

Though people seeking to map such boundaries face a range of definitional dilemmas, Browne contends that a definition will emerge as information policy scholars and practitioners themselves assign what belongs to the field of information policy.[5] By that argument, information policy follows a historical trend: Just as governments developed agricultural policy to address the growing complexity of agricultural societies and industrial policies were a consequence of an emerging industrial-based society, so, too, do information policies grow out of a burgeoning information society.

The field is still to be defined, though it must be addressed as a concept. One way writers have chosen to address information is to identify its life cycle, enabling the examination of the full sequence of its creation, dissemination, and use through to its ultimate disposition and preservation. Information policy is arguably any policy that affects the life cycle. Defining information policy as any policy that affects the creation, dissemination, use, disposition, or preservation of information has the benefit of uniting many information-related fields that are usually classified individually and separately. Policies relating to government information, privacy, freedom of information, broadcasting, telecommunications, the Internet, censorship and intellectual freedom, intellectual property, and information and computer technology are all included in the domain. Film policy and publishing policy, generally considered to be more closely related to cultural policy, also have their places in the information life cycle. Sometimes, information-policy definitions try to incorporate organizational-level and workplace policy; however, Browne argues that the term *information policy* should be reserved for *public* policy.[6] In this book, the focus is on public policy, with the recognition that public policy ultimately has a downstream effect on organizational policymaking.

All public policy can be categorized as "manifest" or "latent." As Sandra Braman defines these terms, manifest policy is "visibly pertinent to the issue area," while latent policy exists but is not visible.[7] Manifest information policies can be easily identified: copyright, freedom of information, and privacy laws, as well as government policy directives and administrative actions, such as those concerned with national information-technology access and those by which government agencies limit their own information collection and dissemination.[8]

Latent information policies, on the other hand, can emerge from any number of government initiatives and their sources, and effects on the information life cycle are often difficult to anticipate because their target is not necessarily the control of information in and of itself. Regulatory instruments regarding financial or commercial disclosure, for example, are designed to control commercial behavior; "right-to-know" laws guarantee workers' rights to know about hazards in their work environment (requiring, for example, the labeling of chemical containers); product information requirements such as food labeling designed to protect consumers, and so on. All such controls affect our access to information, though their purpose is not information control per se. Other latent policies are more subtle in their impact. For example, government budget cuts can affect the size and administration of government agencies and reduce their capacity to collect and disseminate information. Furthermore, government restructuring and privatization can limit access to government information. Public agencies that are transferred to the private sector are no longer subject to the same freedom of information legislation,[9] and governmentwide cost-recovery and restraint initiatives can raise the costs of obtaining information.[10] Cuts to education budgets can result in lower school library budgets and decreased library collections. Municipal financing changes can reduce the amount of money available to school and public libraries.[11] Dominant government ideology, such as neoconservatism and neoliberalism, can result in policies that affect information as well.[12] Hastily enacted legislation can have unintended consequences. For example, though the 2001 USA PATRIOT Act was designed to control terrorism, its implementation has raised concerns about patron privacy in libraries and bookstores, for patron records may be subject to surveillance. That, too, is an information-policy issue.[13] None of those initiatives were implemented for the purpose of targeting information. They had other goals. Their cumulative effect on information, however, and specifically on libraries, proves that latent information policies are worth examining and, indeed, trying to anticipate.

LIBRARIES AND INFORMATION POLICY

A few examples of information policy in libraries may help highlight how manifest and latent policies affect the structure and delivery of library services and collections.

Copyright Policy

According to those who draft and promote copyright laws, copyright policies are designed to encourage creativity, protecting rights holders by limiting the ways in which works can be reproduced, distributed, and stored. Because copyright law relates to information-transfer activity, libraries are affected by copyright as increased restrictions (such as those reflected in the Digital Millenium Copyright Act and its subsequent Amendments) continue to limit access to information in terms of time and scope. The effect is to create increased restrictions on the patrons' use of library collections and information resources. Copyright policy controls information, and it is a clear example of manifest policy.

Privacy Policies

Many countries have enacted specific and all-encompassing privacy laws, though in the United States such legislation has been slow to develop. There, as Joel Reidenberg describes it, "[i]nformation privacy is protected only through an amalgam of narrowly targeted rules."[14] In Canada, privacy legislation was enacted beginning in 1983 at the federal, provincial, and municipal levels, and personal information held by Canadian governments has been protected from disclosure.

Contemporary privacy policies such as the European Union Privacy Directives[15] and Canada's Personal Information Protection and Electronic Documents Act (PIPEDA)[16] have new requirements for the protection of privacy of electronic data. Under PIPEDA, individuals have the right to control the collection, use, and disclosure of personal information by both public and private organizations in the course of any commercial activity. For the moment, because PIPEDA is a federal act, it applies only to those information transactions that fall under federal jurisdiction—namely trade and commerce—and not activities that fall under other jurisdictions. Provincial versions of PIPEDA, however, are being passed. As a consequence of this limited application, different kinds of libraries are affected in different ways. While special libraries that exist in commercial settings are subject to PIPEDA, public libraries, though subject to provincial and municipal privacy legislation, are not commercial entities and so do not have to comply with PIPEDA rules—unless, for example, they want to *sell* their patron membership list.

Privacy policies are usually based on privacy legislation and are clearly manifest information policies. However, even here one can have latent policy. For example, the Canadian central statistical agency, Statistics Canada, refused to release all census records from 1902 onward; not even allowing them to be transferred to the National Archives. The refusal was based on the 1906

Statistics Act, which guarantees secrecy to future census respondents. The move has been a bane to social scientists, historians and, of course, the many librarians who help genealogists.[17] Another example of latent information policy is the USA PATRIOT Act. Though it ostensibly targets terrorists, its effect in public libraries has been to expand the possibilities for government agencies demanding patron information, and increasing the potential legal repercussions on library staff.[18] These trends are well documented by the American Library Association.[19]

Policies Pertaining to Government Information

Policies that governments make about the dissemination of their own information have direct effects on public libraries. As governments have been converting their information holdings to electronic formats since the early 1980s,[20] access to the documents has improved for some but become more limited for others. Librarians who seek to assist users in accessing government information and services must provide more electronic access points and must train staff to locate the information, provide information-literacy education, and lead users through the electronic-access procedures. Even when libraries receive government information free of charge through depository programs, government guidelines require that they provide access,[21] and libraries are expected to bear the costs of doing so.[22] Meanwhile, there is pressure within government to eliminate depository programs or substantially cut the funding needed to sustain them. For example, in February 2005 the U.S. Superintendent of Documents announced plans to limit distribution of print documents to depository libraries.[23]

These examples are manifest information policy, but many government policies can be categorized as latent information policy, in that they are not visibly pertinent to the issue area of information yet have effects on the information life cycle just the same. One example is the funding of public services.

Funding for Public Libraries

Government policies regarding the funding of public libraries are not always recognized as information policy, yet these obviously have effects on information access. Government budget cuts are not usually targeted at "information" per se; however, diminished public funding for public libraries results in changes to the amount and format of materials that a library can purchase.[24] Though budget cuts are not aimed at access to information, that is, in fact, exactly what they hit; therefore, the cuts can be identified as latent information policy. Public funding for libraries might also be undermined by government outsourcing and privatization policies, which, again, are not directed at information but at how government services are provided. As we discussed in chapter 5, privatization contributes to the private sector's competition with public libraries. As the International Federation of Library Associations and Institutions says, "[T]he eventual outcome of permitting the private sector to compete with libraries and educational institutions will be to undermine their tax-supported status."[25] Accordingly, privatization policies that affect public library services can also be categorized as latent information policy.

WHO MAKES INFORMATION POLICY?

National governments are important sources of information policy. The term "national information policy" is used to identify broad-reaching policy initiatives that are made by governments;[26] in the 1970s and 1980s there was a great deal of discussion about national scientific and technical information policy,[27] and more recently, new foci, such as national information technology policy and "networked society" policy, have been emerging.[28] Organizations often try to target national policy makers with the intention of having a say in the direction of national policy development and implementation. In the United States, for example, the National Commission on Libraries and Information Science (NCLIS) is one of the key government bodies seeking to influence the national policies that relate to the nation's library and information needs, despite attempts by the government to cut its funding.[29]

While these national initiatives are important, they do not comprise the totality of a nation's information policies, and no one national policy can account for all aspects of the information life cycle. Ian Rowlands argues that there is actually no such thing as a single information policy. Instead, policies address specific issues, and Rowlands emphasizes that "there are neither 'good' nor 'bad' policies, but maybe there can be effective compromises between competing interests."[30] Therefore, instead of treating "national information policy" as a single unit, it is more useful and inclusive to think of it as the sum of policies that affect a nation's information supply.

International Influences on Information Policy

When broad information policies emerge at the national level, they are often influenced by international trends and intergovernmental agreements. Comparing the range of information policies in a variety of countries reveals that those policies tend to converge around particular issues. Colin Bennett has shown that there is a good deal of policy learning that goes on as countries tackle similar problems. He argues that this policy learning shows up in interdependent domestic policy and reflects external policy developments, and "[i]nternational organizations or regimes, multinational corporations, transnational policy communities, bilateral negotiations, etc.,"[31] can all exert pressure on domestic information-policy initiatives.

Canada's PIPEDA legislation was modeled after the Organisation for Economic Cooperation and Development (OECD) guidelines on privacy.[32] In another domain, international standards created by the International Telecommunications Union can force developments in national IT policy. Regional policy initiatives, such as those of the European Union, the North American Free Trade Agreement (NAFTA), and other treaty agreements also influence policy development. The World Trade Organization is another influence on policy.

TRADE POLICY AS INFORMATION POLICY

Information policy can have a variety of effects on libraries. Both manifest and latent policy can force changes in the internal policies of libraries and require that they adapt to changing conditions. Global trade policies potentially have an impact on both libraries and the information that libraries contain or to which they provide access.

How does trade policy translate into latent information policy? Information itself has been seen as a tradable commodity at least since Marc Porat's 1977 groundbreaking study identifying an information economy.[33] Once information was identified as a commodity, it became subject to the same policy trends and directives that were already being applied to tradable goods and services. And once information is identified as a commodity provided by service providers, it is automatically subject to WTO agreements on trade goods *and* services.

Other WTO agreements can also be identified as relating to information policy. The most obvious of these is the Trade-Related Aspects of Intellectual Property (TRIPS) agreement, which extends the boundaries of intellectual property while limiting public access to information. Another area of concern is that of cultural products and services, including libraries, which are not afforded any particular protection under WTO agreements. They are incorporated into discussions of noncultural goods (like refrigerators) and services (like insurance). Many people have argued that there should be special trade exemptions for "culture" to acknowledge its noncommercial-but-essential value to society; however, that has not happened to any remarkable extent, as we will discuss later.

Trade-Related Aspects of Intellectual Property Rights

The TRIPS agreement, which came into effect in 1995, is described by the WTO as "an attempt to narrow the gap in the way these rights are protected around the world, and to bring them under common international rules."[34] The agreement continues the Berne and Paris conventions on copyright and intellectual property but adds new or higher standards. For example, it adds rental rights to copyright rules, thereby enabling authors of computer programs and producers of sound recordings to prohibit the public and commercial rental of their works. It also enables performers to prevent unauthorized recordings, production, and broadcast of live performances. Like national copyright legislation, the TRIPS agreement is clearly manifest information policy.

Licensing Provisions of TRIPS

Of interest to libraries are the provisions regarding licensing. Many public library systems, either alone or within consortia, have signed license agreements with a variety of electronic service providers. Licensed databases are covered by copyright because they are "compilations of data or other material, whether in machine readable or other form, which by reason of the selection or arrangement of their contents constitute intellectual creations shall be protected as such."[35] Licensing itself is covered by TRIPS: "The owner of a copyright, patent, or other form of intellectual property right can issue a license for someone else to produce or copy the protected trademark, work, invention, design, etc."[36] However Article 40 of the agreement states that "some licensing practices . . . may have adverse effects on trade and may impede the transfer and dissemination of technology."[37] According to Keith Maskus, these clauses reflect the concerns of developing countries that "stronger patents, trademarks and trade secrets protection could permit rights holders to impose abusive licensing conditions, thereby inhibiting the effective transfer of technology."[38] Patent holders, for example, are allowed to license the production of new drugs at such a high price that those in the developing countries cannot afford them, and the restrictive license provisions often prevent local producers from making less expensive or generic versions.

The implications of TRIPS on libraries is not clear. However, one of the possible access points is the mention of anticompetitive practices in Article 40, section 2, on "coercive package licensing." That kind of licensing negatively impacts many libraries; perhaps librarians could challenge the kinds of licenses that aggregators impose, namely, that they often require that libraries buy—for a very high price, and even though library patrons would likely require a fraction of the available content—the publisher's entire repertoire of text, abstracts, and indexes. At issue are the excessive pricing of materials deemed "essential" and libraries' subsequently being unable to afford them. Under Article 40, could libraries turn the tables by challenging the aggregators for their "coercive package licensing" and hence their restrictions on competition? In a proposal to the Experts Meeting on the WIPO Development Agenda in February 2005,[39] James Love, director of the Consumer Project on Technology, recommended that an Advisory Committee on the Control of Anticompetitive Practices (ACCAP) be established. One of its tasks would be to "collect and disseminate information about state practice on addressing problems relating to excessive pricing of essential knowledge goods, including education materials, essential software, library reference materials and scientific databases."[40] The possible room for maneuver in the opposite direction, where a trade agreement might actually lend itself in support of public libraries, is an unusual circumstance that librarians could use to their advantage.

Effects of TRIPS on National Copyright Legislation

Most of the time TRIPS is more likely to hurt than help libraries, for the full weight of national treatment and dispute resolution using trade sanctions can be applied to member countries that do not conform to the agreement. TRIPS can be used to alter national copyright laws, some of which have been written to protect the public's right to access information. Libraries have fought hard to have fair use, fair dealing, and other such provisions incorporated into national copyright laws. As the IFLA's position statement on the WTO explains, however, there is "little assurance that the balance between the public interest and rights of content owner . . . will be considered by the WTO in any intellectual property disputes that come before it."[41] Steven Shrybman confirms that and argues that the TRIPS agreement "is likely to be as important to the content of library services as the GATS will be to determining the role of public-sector libraries as content providers."[42] Clearly, the TRIPS is an example of manifest information policy that public libraries should monitor.

Cultural Issues

The implementation of WTO agreements has raised a number of concerns for cultural sectors in many countries. In addition to the potential for GATS challenges to cultural service providers such as public libraries, museums, and archives, another problem stems from the products of cultural industries (books, films, recordings, etc.) being categorized as "goods" and falling under the GATT agreement. Any public funding or support for cultural industries could be grounds for a challenge. Critics argue that cultural products represent and enhance cultural diversity and should be exempted from trade agreements. Nevertheless, WTO treats cultural products as "goods" and has rejected counterarguments, making only a limited "cultural exception" available under GATT. Because the WTO focus is so steadfastly and clearly on expediting trade, other areas of human social life are ignored in the decision-making process.

The 1997 resolution of the Canada–United States magazine dispute provides a good example of the singular focus of trade agreements. Over the course of several decades, Canada had implemented a number of measures to protect its magazine industry and thereby ensure that Canadian cultural content would be available on magazine stands. In response to those measures, American objections were made specifically against the Canadian legislation:

(a) It prohibited the importation of certain periodicals (based not on their content but on how they were published).
(b) It imposed a tax on "split-run" periodicals—foreign publications that were sold in Canada with Canadian advertising but very little Canadian content, and
(c) It gave preferential postage rates for Canadian periodicals.

Large U.S. magazine publishing interests (specifically Time-Warner Inc.) claimed that the protective Canadian policies violated the national-treatment principle of the GATT and managed to persuade the U.S. government to bring the case before the WTO. In March 1997, the WTO dispute panel sided with the United States.[43] In its appeal to the panel decision, Canada argued that it was protecting cultural interests. The United States countered that cultural interest was irrelevant in this case. In June 1997, the Appellate Body agreed.[44] Following this ruling, Canadian Heritage issued a press release listing the measures it would take to comply with the WTO ruling:

- remove the existing custom tariff prohibiting the importation of "split-run" magazines ("Canadian" editions of foreign magazines);
- eliminate the excise tax on "split-runs" distributed in Canada;
- restructure the administration of the postal subsidy program to conform to the rules on subsidies by making payments directly to magazine publishers; and
- harmonize the commercial postal rate for domestic and foreign publications.[45]

In discussing the case, Steven Shrybman noted that the WTO "demonstrated a stunning ability to keep its focus on trade policy objectives, no matter how skewed its reasoning might appear in the larger view."[46]

In the initial rounds of negotiation for the GATS agreement, the European Union fought hard for continuation of the "cultural exception" that was available under the GATT. That exception covered certain cultural products (particularly films), and it maintains a general exception for measures designed "to protect national treasures of artistic, historic or archaeological value" (Article XX.f). All other cultural goods—except for developed films and home-recorded videos—are subject to the GATT disciplines within the current WTO agreements.[47]

The extent to which governments should protect national identity and cultural diversity is the basis for an ongoing debate. Concerned nations have argued individually and collectively for exceptions both to protect cultural products and cultural diversity and to develop a separate set of rules to govern the trade in cultural products.[48] In 2001, Canada and the European Union issued a joint statement that called for the WTO to support "sustainable development and other broad social goals, including the right of each WTO Member to promote cultural diversity."[49] UNESCO supported that with its call for general acknowledgment that "cultural goods and services (books, music, multimedia games, films, and audiovisuals) are different from other goods and services, and deserve different and/or exceptional treatment that sets them apart from standardised mass consumption." UNESCO's view was that this requires "a differential treatment in international trade agreements and possibly effective strong regulatory frameworks to redefine cultural policies focusing on the promotion and development of cultural industries."[50]

In November 2001, UNESCO adopted the Universal Declaration on Cultural Diversity, which Director-General Koïchiro Matsuura described as "a determining instrument to humanise globalisation."[51] While the declaration is not binding for UN member countries and does not override WTO requirements, its passage indicates, at least, a level of concern. Following adoption of the declaration, considerable support developed for a proposed UN convention on cultural diversity that would be a binding treaty. Championed by sixty European and developing countries led by Canada and France, but opposed by the United States, the convention "would take cultural goods, such as films, plays, and music, out of the realm of trade negotiations. It would exempt them from free-trade rules, allow governments to protect and support their cultural industries, and enshrine the 'cultural exception' that European nations have defended in international law."[52] Finally, on 20 October 2005, the UNESCO General Conference approved the Convention on the Protection and Promotion of the Diversity of Cultural Expressions. In December,

Canada became the first state to ratify the convention, which will enter into force three months after its ratification by thirty states.[53]

There is no evidence that the WTO is either interested in differential treatment for particular products or supportive of such regulatory frameworks. As Fiona Hunt points out, the WTO rejects cultural diversity as a legitimate policy objective.[54]

The international diversity of cultures and the different material they produce relate directly to the nature of library collections. Public libraries aim to provide collections as culturally diverse as their clientele. If one result of WTO agreements and its complete lack of support for cultural diversity is increasingly homogenous collections, libraries will be devalued, impoverished, and unable to serve their communities of patrons and their increasingly diverse information needs. The requirements for national treatment in the WTO agreements have made it very difficult to ensure diversity of content and preservation of cultural differences in products of cultural industries. By no means does this mean that all the deals have been set in stone; it only indicates the urgency of our involvement in such issues.

CONCLUSION

A major problem with the WTO with regard to information policy is its focus on trade to the exclusion of all other considerations. It is unlikely that the original GATS and TRIPS negotiators considered social and cultural issues; it is clear that they did not consider libraries. The potential effect of the agreements on libraries was unanticipated. When governments agree to abide by World Trade Organization decisions, some of the consequences for information access are not necessarily obvious to negotiators who focus on trade liberalization. Librarians and library associations, however, recognize that both manifest and latent public policies, including those under the auspices of WTO agreements, have many consequences; the full range of information "creation, dissemination, access, use, and preservation" can be put on a chopping block by an unintentional and unfortunate lack of foresight.

This chapter has introduced the scope and importance of the information policy field as well as some of its relationships to public libraries. Librarians developing or responding to information policies at the local level need to be aware of some of the manifest and latent policy shifts taking place at national and international levels, because the shifts will undoubtedly change the roles and responsiveness of library systems. As the WTO becomes a more far-reaching authority in our economic system, librarians have an opportunity (as well as a responsibility) to become advocates on behalf of publicly funded libraries. Librarians can do many things to try to influence the direction of information policies; we discuss that in some detail in chapter 7.

So long as the negotiators of WTO agreements are representatives of their respective nations, we can remind them of the long-term implications of trade policy on information policy, cultural diversity, and public libraries.

NOTES

1. An earlier version of this chapter was published as Kirsti Nilsen, "Information Policy and Global Trade Policy as Forces for Change in Public Educational Institutions and Research Libraries," in *Global Issues in 21st Century Research Librarianship*, ed. Sigrun Klara Hannesdottir, NORDINFO Publication 48 (Helsinki: NORDINFO, 2002), 17–35.
2. John Buschman, *Dismantling the Public Sphere: Situating and Sustaining Librarianship in the Age of the New Public Philosophy* (Westport, Conn.: Libraries Unlimited, 2002).
3. Sandra Braman, "Defining Information: An Approach for Policymakers," *Telecommunications Policy* 13, no. 3 (1989): 233–242.
4. Mairéad Browne, "The Field of Information Policy: 1. Fundamental Concepts," *Journal of Information Science* 23, no. 4 (1997): 261–275.
5. Browne, "The Field of Information Policy: 1," 270.
6. Browne, "The Field of Information Policy: 1," 269.
7. Sandra Braman, "The Unique Characteristics of Information Policy and Their U.S. Consequences," in *Information Literacies for the Twenty-First Century,* ed. Virgil L. P. Blake and Renee Tjoumas, 47–77 (Boston: G. K. Hall, 1990).
8. Examples of these policies are listed online: American Library Association, *Less Access To Less Information* (Washington: ALA, 2005), www.ala.org/ala/washoff/WOissues/governmentinfo/lessacc.htm (accessed 10 July 2005).
9. See for example Alasdair Roberts, "Less Government, More Secrecy: Reinvention and the Weakening of Freedom of Information Law," *Public Administration Review* 60, no. 4 (2000): 308–320.
10. See for example Kirsti Nilsen, *The Impact of Information Policy: Measuring the Effects of the Commercialization of Canadian Government Statistics* (Westport, Conn.: Ablex / Greenwood Publishing Group, 2001).
11. For a European example, see Ole Harbro, "The Development of Public Libraries in Denmark since 1964," *Advances in Librarianship* 25 (2001): 214.
12. Nilsen, *The Impact of Information Policy*, 193–94.
13. See Herbert N. Foerstel, *Refuge of a Scoundrel: The Patriot Act in Libraries* (Westport, Conn.: Libraries Unlimited, 2004); and Robin Rice, "The USA Patriot Act and American Libraries," *Information for Social Change* no. 16 (2002/2003), http://libr.org/ISC/articles/16-Rice.html (accessed 10 July 2005).

14. Joel Reidenberg, "Privacy Wrongs in Search of Remedies" (Fordham School of Law, Pub-Law Research Paper No. 25), *Hastings Law Journal* 54 (2003), http://papers.ssrn.com/sol3/papers.cfm?abstract_id=434585 (accessed 10 July 2005). An anonymous reader of the manuscript for this book stated, "I would disagree that U.S. has patchworked privacy laws. We have pretty serious privacy laws both for consumers and students. One consideration is who is requesting the information . . . the government, i.e., in search warrant or FISA warrant, or private entities."

15. Council of Europe, *Directive on the Protection of Individuals with Regard to the Processing of Personal Data and on the Free Movement of Such Data* (95/46/EC); *Directive Concerning the Processing of Personal Data and the Protection of Privacy* (97/66/EC) (Brussels: European Union, 1995; 1997).

16. *Personal Information Protection and Electronic Documents Act, Statutes of Canada* 2000, c. 5. Unofficial version available at http://laws.justice.gc.ca/en/p-8.6/text.html (accessed 6 July 2005).

17. Post 1901 Census Project (Campbellville, Ont.: Global, Everything for the Family Historian, 2006), http://globalgenealogy.com/Census (accessed 30 March 2006). After negotiation among government ministers, a special 1906 census of Alberta, Manitoba, and Saskatchewan was released. Finally, on 29 June 2005, the government passed Bill S-18, An Act to Amend the Statistics Act, clarifying the Statistics Act; also see Shawn Murphy, "Campaign for Release of Historic Census Records Finally Over," news release, 29 June 2005, www.shawnmurphymp.ca/news/142 (accessed 4 July 2005).

18. Foerstel, *Refuge of a Scoundrel: The Patriot Act in Libraries*, 60–64.

19. American Library Association, *FBI in Your Library* (Washington, D.C.: ALA, 2005), www.ala.org/Template.cfm?Section=Intellectual_Freedom_Issues&Template=/ContentManagement/ContentDisplay.cfm&ContentID=21662 (10 July 2005); Cynthia Murphy, "Research on Library Patron Privacy Policies with Regard to the USA PATRIOT ACT: An Annotated Bibliography," Library Patron Privacy and the USA Patriot Act, n.d., http://xauen.nudio.net/patriot/main.html (accessed 6 July 2005).

20. See for example Kirsti Nilsen, "Canadian Government Electronic Information Policy," *Government Information Quarterly* 10, no.2 (1993): 201–218.

21. Federal Depository Library Program, "Depository Library Public Service Guidelines for Government Information in Electronic Formats," *Administrative Notes* 19, no. 11 (1998), FDLP Desktop, www.access.gpo.gov/su_docs/fdlp/mgt/pseguide.html (accessed 10 July 2005).

22. Elizabeth Dolan and Liwen Vaughan, *Electronic Access to Canadian Federal Government Information: How Prepared Are the Depository Libraries?* Report to Depository Services Program, Canadian Government Publishing, Public Works and Government Services Canada (Ottawa: Depository Services Program, 1997), http://dsp-psd.communication.gc.ca/Rapports/DV/rep1-e.html (accessed 10 July 2005).

23. American Library Association, "Call for Oversight on GPO Initiatives," *Washington Office Newsline* 14, no. 6, 27 January 2005, www.ala.org/ala/washoff/washnews/2005ab/006jan27.htm (accessed 10 July 2005).

24. Online Computer Library Center, "Worldwide Education and Library Spending," in *2003 Environmental Scan: A Report to the OCLC Membership* (Dublin, Ohio: OCLC, 2004), www.oclc.org/membership/escan/downloads/economic.pdf (accessed 10 July 2005).

25. International Federation of Library Associations and Institutions, *The IFLA Position on WTO Treaty Negotiations* (The Hague: IFLA, 2002), www.ifla.org/III/clm/p1/pos-wto.htm (accessed 8 July 2005).

26. See for example Victor Montviloff, *National Information Policies: A Handbook on the Formulation, Approval, Implementation and Operation of a National Policy on Information* (Paris: UNESCO, 1990).

27. See for example Michael Hill, *National Information Policies: A Review of the Situation in Seventeen Industrialized Countries, with Particular Reference to Scientific and Technical Information* (The Hague: UNESCO, 1989).

28. See for example *Digital Denmark: Conversion to the Networked Society* (Copenhagen: Forskningsministeriet [Ministry of Science, Technology and Innovation], 2000), www.detdigitaledanmark.dk/english (10 July 2005).

29. U.S. National Commission on Libraries and Information Science, *Highlights of the Year 2002* (Washington, D.C.: NCLIS, 2002), www.nclis.gov/about/highlights/bowker02.html (accessed 10 July 2005).

30. Ian Rowlands, "Understanding Information Policy: Concepts, Frameworks and Research Tools," *Journal of Information Science* 22, no. 1 (1996): 14–15.

31. Colin J. Bennett, "How States Utilize Foreign Evidence," *Journal of Public Policy* 11, no. 1 (1991): 31–32.

32. Organisation for Economic Cooperation and Development, *Guidelines on the Protection of Privacy and Transborder Flows of Personal Data* (Paris: OECD, 1981).

33. Marc Porat, *The Information Economy, Definition and Measurement* (Washington, D.C.: U.S. Dept. of Commerce, 1977).

34. World Trade Organization, "Intellectual Property: Protection and Enforcement," *Understanding the WTO—The Agreements* (Geneva: WTO, n.d.), www.wto.org/english/thewto_e/whatis_e/tif_e/agrm7_e.htm (accessed 10 July 2005).

35. World Trade Organization, "Part II—Standards Concerning the Availability, Scope and Use of Intellectual Property Rights; Section 1 Copyright and Related Rights, Article 10, Computer Programs and Compilations of Data," *TRIPS: Agreement on Trade-Related Aspects of Intellectual Property Rights* (Geneva: WTO, n.d.), www.wto.org/english/tratop_e/trips_e/t_agm3_e.htm#1 (accessed 10 July 2005).

36. World Trade Organization, "Curbing Anti-Competitive Licensing Contracts," *Understanding the WTO—The Agreements;* "Intellectual Property: Protection and Enforcement," *Understanding the WTO—The Agreements* (Geneva: WTO, n.d.).

37. World Trade Organization, "Part II—Standards Concerning the Availability, Scope and Use of Intellectual Property Rights, Section 8, Control of Anti-Competitive Practices in Contractural Licenses, Article 40," *TRIPS: Agreement on Trade-Related Aspects of Intellectual Property Rights*.

38. Keith E. Maskus, "A Road Map for the TRIPs Ahead," in *Intellectual Property Rights in the Global Economy* (Washington, D.C.: Institute for International Economics, 2000), 24, www.iie.com/publications/chapters_preview/99/2iie2822.pdf (accessed 10 July 2005).

39. Martin Khor, "Offsetting IPRs' Adverse Effects on Access to Knowledge," Choike.Org: A Portal on Southern Civil Societies (Montevideo, Uruguay: Third World Institute, n.d.), www.choike.org/nuevo_eng/informes/2630.html (accessed 10 July 2005).

40. James Love, "Proposal on Issues Related to the Control of Anticompetitive Practices in Contractual Licenses, 23 January 2005" (Washington, D.C.: Consumer Project on Technology, 2005), www.cptech.org/a2k/anticompetitive.doc (accessed 10 July 2005).

41. International Federation of Library Associations and Institutions, *The IFLA Position on the World Trade Organization* (The Hague: IFLA, 2001), http://www.ifla.org/III/clm/p1/wto-ifla.htm (accessed 10 July 2005).

42. Steven Shrybman, "Public Sector Libraries and the GATS: Executive Summary," in *An Assessment of the Impact of the General Agreement on Trade in Services on Policy, Programs and Law Concerning Public Sector Libraries* (Ottawa: Canadian Library Association, 2001), ii, www.cla.ca/resources/execsummarygats.pdf (accessed 10 July 2005).

43. World Trade Organization, *Canada—Certain Measures Concerning Periodicals, Report of the Panel* WT/DS31/R, 14 March 1997 (Geneva: WTO, 1997), www.worldtradelaw.net/reports/wtopanels/canada-periodicals(panel).pdf (accessed 10 July 2005).

44. World Trade Organization, Appellate Body, *Canada—Certain Measures Concerning Periodicals, Report of the Appellate Body*, AB-1997-2, WT/DS31/AB/R, Adopted by Dispute Settlement Body, 30 July 1997 (Geneva: WTO, 1997), www.worldtradelaw.net/reports/wtoab/canada-periodicals(ab).pdf (accessed 10 July 2005).

45. Canada, Dept. of Canadian Heritage, "New Advertising Services Measure to Promote Canadian Culture," news release, 29 July 1998, www.canadianheritage.gc.ca/newsroom/news_e.cfm?Action=Display&code=8NR064E (accessed 10 July 2005).

46. Steven Shrybman, "Information, Commodification and the World Trade Organization" (paper presented at IFLA 2000 Conference, Jerusalem, 13–18 August 2000), www.ifla.org/IV/ifla66/papers/176-148e.htm (accessed 8 July 2005).

47. UNESCO, "Questions and Answers," *Culture, Trade and Globalization* (Paris: UNESCO, n.d.), www.unesco.org/culture/industries/trade (accessed 10 July 2005).

48. A recent example is in response to Google's move to digitze the content of libraries (see chapter 4). French cultural officials argue that this initiative could result in "the crushing domination of the U.S. in shaping the worldview of future generations," and France is spearheading a project to make European literary works available online; "France to Develop Google Rival," *BBC News World Edition*, 17 March 2005, http://new.bbc.uk/2/hi/europe/4358871.stm (accessed 23 June 2005).

49. Canada Europa Mundi (website), Canada–EU Joint Statement on the World Trade Organization (WTO), June 2001 (Ottawa: Dept. of Foreign Affairs and International Trade), Related Documents. Statements, www.dfait-maeci.gc.ca/canada-europa/mundi/canada-eu-c-1-en.asp (accessed 17 March, 2006).

50. UNESCO, "Questions and Answers."

51. UNESCO, "General Conference Adopts Universal Declaration on Cultural Diversity," *News Release* No. 2001-120 (Paris: UNESCO, 2001), www.unesco.org/bpi/eng/unescopress/2001/01-120e.shtml (10 July 2005).

52. Peter Ford, "Global Pushback against 'Titanic' Culture: A Proposed UN Treaty Would Protect Nations' Arts," *The Christian Science Monitor*, 20 October 2003, www.csmonitor.com/2003/1020/p01s03-wogi.html (accessed 10 July 2005).

53. UNESCO. Convention on the Protection and Promotion of the Diversity of Cultural Expressions.Paris: UNESCO, 2005. http://portal.unesco.org/culture/en/ev.phpURL_ID=11281&URL_DO=DO_TOPIC&URL_SECTION=201.html (accessed 17 March 2006).

54. Fiona Hunt, "The WTO and the Threat to Libraries," *Progressive Librarian* 18 (Summer 2001), www.libr.org/PL/18_Hunt.html (accessed 10 July 2005).

Appendix A

Pertinent Sections of the GATS Agreement

The articles and sections referred to in this book are included here, along with other articles or sections of interest. Note that some articles and sections and all clarifying footnotes have been removed from the selection below. For the full text of the GATS agreement, see www.wto.org/english/docs_e/legal_e/26-gats.pdf, or www.wto.org/english/docs_e/legal_e/26-gats.doc.

The selection below includes selected parts of the following articles:

Article I	Scope and Definition
Article II	Most-Favoured-Nation Treatment
Article III	Transparency
Article III *bis*	Disclosure of Confidential Information
Article IV	Increasing Participation of Developing Countries
Article V	Economic Integration
Article V *bis*	Labour Markets Integration Agreements
Article VI	Domestic Regulation
Article VII	Recognition
Article VIII	Monopolies and Exclusive Service Suppliers
Article IX	Business Practices
Article XIII	Government Procurement
Article XIV	General Exceptions
Article XV	Subsidies
Article XVI	Market Access
Article XVII	National Treatment
Article XVIII	Additional Commitments
Article XIX	Negotiation of Specific Commitments
Article XX	Schedules of Specific Commitments

ARTICLE I SCOPE AND DEFINITION

1. This Agreement applies to measures by Members affecting trade in services.
2. For the purposes of this Agreement, trade in services is defined as the supply of a service:
   (a) from the territory of one Member into the territory of any other Member;
   (b) in the territory of one Member to the service consumer of any other Member;
   (c) by a service supplier of one Member, through commercial presence in the territory of any other Member;
   (d) by a service supplier of one Member, through presence of natural persons of a Member in the territory of any other Member.
3. For the purposes of this Agreement:
   (a) "measures by Members" means measures taken by:
      (i) central, regional or local governments and authorities; and
      (ii) non-governmental bodies in the exercise of powers delegated by central, regional or local governments or authorities;

   In fulfilling its obligations and commitments under the Agreement, each Member shall take such reasonable measures as may be available to it to ensure their observance by regional and local governments and authorities and non-governmental bodies within its territory;

   (b) "services" includes any service in any sector except services supplied in the exercise of governmental authority;
   (c) "a service supplied in the exercise of governmental authority" means any service which is supplied neither on a commercial basis, nor in competition with one or more service suppliers.

ARTICLE II MOST-FAVOURED-NATION TREATMENT

1. With respect to any measure covered by this Agreement, each Member shall accord immediately and unconditionally to services and service suppliers of any other Member treatment no less favourable than that it accords to like services and service suppliers of any other country.
2. A Member may maintain a measure inconsistent with paragraph 1 provided that such a measure is listed in, and meets the conditions of, the Annex on Article II Exemptions.
3. The provisions of this Agreement shall not be so construed as to prevent any Member from conferring or according advantages to adjacent countries in order to facilitate exchanges limited to contiguous frontier zones of services that are both locally produced and consumed.

ARTICLE III TRANSPARENCY

1. Each Member shall publish promptly and, except in emergency situations, at the latest by the time of their entry into force, all relevant measures of general application which pertain to or affect the operation of this Agreement. International agreements pertaining to or affecting trade in services to which a Member is a signatory shall also be published.
2. Where publication as referred to in paragraph 1 is not practicable, such information shall be made otherwise publicly available.
3. Each Member shall promptly and at least annually inform the Council for Trade in Services of the introduction of any new, or any changes to existing, laws, regulations or administrative guidelines which significantly affect trade in services covered by its specific commitments under this Agreement.
4. Each Member shall respond promptly to all requests by any other Member for specific information on any of its measures of general application or international agreements within the meaning of paragraph 1. Each Member shall also establish one or more enquiry points to provide specific information to other Members, upon request, on all such matters as well as those subject to the notification requirement in paragraph 3. Such enquiry points shall be established within two years from the date of entry into force of the Agreement Establishing the WTO (referred to in this Agreement as the "WTO Agreement"). Appropriate flexibility with respect to the time-limit within which such enquiry points are to be established may be

agreed upon for individual developing country Members. Enquiry points need not be depositories of laws and regulations.

5. Any Member may notify to the Council for Trade in Services any measure, taken by any other Member, which it considers affects the operation of this Agreement.

ARTICLE III *BIS* DISCLOSURE OF CONFIDENTIAL INFORMATION

Nothing in this Agreement shall require any Member to provide confidential information, the disclosure of which would impede law enforcement, or otherwise be contrary to the public interest, or which would prejudice legitimate commercial interests of particular enterprises, public or private.

ARTICLE IV INCREASING PARTICIPATION OF DEVELOPING COUNTRIES

1. The increasing participation of developing country Members in world trade shall be facilitated through negotiated specific commitments, by different Members pursuant to Parts III and IV of this Agreement, relating to:
   (a) the strengthening of their domestic services capacity and its efficiency and competitiveness, *inter alia* through access to technology on a commercial basis;
   (b) the improvement of their access to distribution channels and information networks; and
   (c) the liberalization of market access in sectors and modes of supply of export interest to them.
2. Developed country Members, and to the extent possible other Members, shall establish contact points within two years from the date of entry into force of the WTO Agreement to facilitate the access of developing country Members' service suppliers to information, related to their respective markets, concerning:
   (a) commercial and technical aspects of the supply of services;
   (b) registration, recognition and obtaining of professional qualifications; and
   (c) the availability of services technology.
3. Special priority shall be given to the least-developed country Members in the implementation of paragraphs 1 and 2. Particular account shall be taken of the serious difficulty of the least-developed countries in accepting negotiated specific commitments in view of their special economic situation and their development, trade and financial needs.

ARTICLE V ECONOMIC INTEGRATION

1. This Agreement shall not prevent any of its Members from being a party to or entering into an agreement liberalizing trade in services between or among the parties to such an agreement, provided that such an agreement:
   (a) has substantial sectoral coverage, and
   (b) provides for the absence or elimination of substantially all discrimination, in the sense of Article XVII, between or among the parties, in the sectors covered under subparagraph (a), through:
      (i) elimination of existing discriminatory measures, and/or
      (ii) prohibition of new or more discriminatory measures,
4. Any agreement referred to in paragraph 1 shall be designed to facilitate trade between the parties to the agreement and shall not in respect of any Member outside the agreement raise the overall level of barriers to trade in services within the respective sectors or subsectors compared to the level applicable prior to such an agreement.
6. A service supplier of any other Member that is a juridical person constituted under the laws of a party to an agreement referred to in paragraph 1 shall be entitled to treatment granted under such agreement, provided that it engages in substantive business operations in the territory of the parties to such agreement.
8. A Member which is a party to any agreement referred to in paragraph 1 may not seek compensation for trade benefits that may accrue to any other Member from such agreement.

ARTICLE V *BIS* LABOUR MARKETS INTEGRATION AGREEMENTS

This Agreement shall not prevent any of its Members from being a party to an agreement establishing full integration of the labour markets between or among the parties to such an agreement, provided that such an agreement:

(a) exempts citizens of parties to the agreement from requirements concerning residency and work permits;

ARTICLE VI DOMESTIC REGULATION

1. In sectors where specific commitments are undertaken, each Member shall ensure that all measures of general application affecting trade in

services are administered in a reasonable, objective and impartial manner.

4. With a view to ensuring that measures relating to qualification requirements and procedures, technical standards and licensing requirements do not constitute unnecessary barriers to trade in services, the Council for Trade in Services shall, through appropriate bodies it may establish, develop any necessary disciplines. Such disciplines shall aim to ensure that such requirements are, *inter alia*:
   (a) based on objective and transparent criteria, such as competence and the ability to supply the service;
   (b) not more burdensome than necessary to ensure the quality of the service;
   (c) in the case of licensing procedures, not in themselves a restriction on the supply of the service.

. . .

5.
   (a) In sectors in which a Member has undertaken specific commitments, pending the entry into force of disciplines developed in these sectors pursuant to paragraph 4, the Member shall not apply licensing and qualification requirements and technical standards that nullify or impair such specific commitments in a manner which:
      (i) does not comply with the criteria outlined in subparagraphs 4(a), (b) or (c); and
      (ii) could not reasonably have been expected of that Member at the time the specific commitments in those sectors were made.
   (b) In determining whether a Member is in conformity with the obligation under paragraph 5(a), account shall be taken of international standards of relevant international organizations applied by that Member.

6. In sectors where specific commitments regarding professional services are undertaken, each Member shall provide for adequate procedures to verify the competence of professionals of any other Member.

ARTICLE VII RECOGNITION

1. For the purposes of the fulfilment, in whole or in part, of its standards or criteria for the authorization, licensing or certification of services suppliers, and subject to the requirements of paragraph 3, a Member may recognize the education or experience obtained, requirements met, or licenses or certifications granted in a particular country. Such recognition, which may be achieved through harmonization or otherwise,

may be based upon an agreement or arrangement with the country concerned or may be accorded autonomously.

2. A Member that is a party to an agreement or arrangement of the type referred to in paragraph 1, whether existing or future, shall afford adequate opportunity for other interested Members to negotiate their accession to such an agreement or arrangement or to negotiate comparable ones with it. Where a Member accords recognition autonomously, it shall afford adequate opportunity for any other Member to demonstrate that education, experience, licenses, or certifications obtained or requirements met in that other Member's territory should be recognized.
3. A Member shall not accord recognition in a manner which would constitute a means of discrimination between countries in the application of its standards or criteria for the authorization, licensing or certification of services suppliers, or a disguised restriction on trade in services.
5. Wherever appropriate, recognition should be based on multilaterally agreed criteria. In appropriate cases, Members shall work in cooperation with relevant intergovernmental and non-governmental organizations towards the establishment and adoption of common international standards and criteria for recognition and common international standards for the practice of relevant services trades and professions.

ARTICLE VIII MONOPOLIES AND EXCLUSIVE SERVICE SUPPLIERS

1. Each Member shall ensure that any monopoly supplier of a service in its territory does not, in the supply of the monopoly service in the relevant market, act in a manner inconsistent with that Member's obligations under Article II and specific commitments.
2. Where a Member's monopoly supplier competes, either directly or through an affiliated company, in the supply of a service outside the scope of its monopoly rights and which is subject to that Member's specific commitments, the Member shall ensure that such a supplier does not abuse its monopoly position to act in its territory in a manner inconsistent with such commitments.
5. The provisions of this Article shall also apply to cases of exclusive service suppliers, where a Member, formally or in effect, (*a*) authorizes or establishes a small number of service suppliers and (*b*) substantially prevents competition among those suppliers in its territory.

ARTICLE IX BUSINESS PRACTICES

1. Members recognize that certain business practices of service suppliers, other than those falling under Article VIII, may restrain competition and thereby restrict trade in services.

ARTICLE XIII GOVERNMENT PROCUREMENT

1. Articles II, XVI and XVII shall not apply to laws, regulations or requirements governing the procurement by governmental agencies of services purchased for governmental purposes and not with a view to commercial resale or with a view to use in the supply of services for commercial sale.

ARTICLE XIV GENERAL EXCEPTIONS

Subject to the requirement that such measures are not applied in a manner which would constitute a means of arbitrary or unjustifiable discrimination between countries where like conditions prevail, or a disguised restriction on trade in services, nothing in this Agreement shall be construed to prevent the adoption or enforcement by any Member of measures:

(c) necessary to secure compliance with laws or regulations which are not inconsistent with the provisions of this Agreement including those relating to:
  (i) the prevention of deceptive and fraudulent practices or to deal with the effects of a default on services contracts;
  (ii) the protection of the privacy of individuals in relation to the processing and dissemination of personal data and the protection of confidentiality of individual records and accounts;

ARTICLE XV SUBSIDIES

1. Members recognize that, in certain circumstances, subsidies may have distortive effects on trade in services. Members shall enter into negotiations with a view to developing the necessary multilateral disciplines to avoid such trade-distortive effects. The negotiations shall also address the appropriateness of countervailing procedures. Such negotia-

tions shall recognize the role of subsidies in relation to the development programmes of developing countries and take into account the needs of Members, particularly developing country Members, for flexibility in this area. For the purpose of such negotiations, Members shall exchange information concerning all subsidies related to trade in services that they provide to their domestic service suppliers.

2. Any Member which considers that it is adversely affected by a subsidy of another Member may request consultations with that Member on such matters. Such requests shall be accorded sympathetic consideration.

ARTICLE XVI MARKET ACCESS

1. With respect to market access through the modes of supply identified in Article I, each Member shall accord services and service suppliers of any other Member treatment no less favourable than that provided for under the terms, limitations and conditions agreed and specified in its Schedule.
2. In sectors where market-access commitments are undertaken, the measures which a Member shall not maintain or adopt either on the basis of a regional subdivision or on the basis of its entire territory, unless otherwise specified in its Schedule, are defined as:
   (a) limitations on the number of service suppliers whether in the form of numerical quotas, monopolies, exclusive service suppliers or the requirements of an economic needs test;
   (b) limitations on the total value of service transactions or assets in the form of numerical quotas or the requirement of an economic needs test;
   (c) limitations on the total number of service operations or on the total quantity of service output expressed in terms of designated numerical units in the form of quotas or the requirement of an economic needs test;
   (d) limitations on the total number of natural persons that may be employed in a particular service sector or that a service supplier may employ and who are necessary for, and directly related to, the supply of a specific service in the form of numerical quotas or the requirement of an economic needs test;
   (e) measures which restrict or require specific types of legal entity or joint venture through which a service supplier may supply a service; and
   (f) limitations on the participation of foreign capital in terms of maximum percentage limit on foreign shareholding or the total value of individual or aggregate foreign investment.

ARTICLE XVII NATIONAL TREATMENT

1. In the sectors inscribed in its Schedule, and subject to any conditions and qualifications set out therein, each Member shall accord to services and service suppliers of any other Member, in respect of all measures affecting the supply of services, treatment no less favourable than that it accords to its own like services and service suppliers.
2. A Member may meet the requirement of paragraph 1 by according to services and service suppliers of any other Member, either formally identical treatment or formally different treatment to that it accords to its own like services and service suppliers.
3. Formally identical or formally different treatment shall be considered to be less favourable if it modifies the conditions of competition in favour of services or service suppliers of the Member compared to like services or service suppliers of any other Member.

ARTICLE XVIII ADDITIONAL COMMITMENTS

Members may negotiate commitments with respect to measures affecting trade in services not subject to scheduling under Articles XVI or XVII, including those regarding qualifications, standards or licensing matters. Such commitments shall be inscribed in a Member's Schedule.

ARTICLE XIX NEGOTIATION OF SPECIFIC COMMITMENTS

1. In pursuance of the objectives of this Agreement, Members shall enter into successive rounds of negotiations, beginning not later than five years from the date of entry into force of the WTO Agreement and periodically thereafter, with a view to achieving a progressively higher level of liberalization. Such negotiations shall be directed to the reduction or elimination of the adverse effects on trade in services of measures as a means of providing effective market access. This process shall take place with a view to promoting the interests of all participants on a mutually advantageous basis and to securing an overall balance of rights and obligations.
2. The process of liberalization shall take place with due respect for national policy objectives and the level of development of individual

Members, both overall and in individual sectors. There shall be appropriate flexibility for individual developing country Members for opening fewer sectors, liberalizing fewer types of transactions, progressively extending market access in line with their development situation and, when making access to their markets available to foreign service suppliers, attaching to such access conditions aimed at achieving the objectives referred to in Article IV.

3. For each round, negotiating guidelines and procedures shall be established. For the purposes of establishing such guidelines, the Council for Trade in Services shall carry out an assessment of trade in services in overall terms and on a sectoral basis with reference to the objectives of this Agreement, including those set out in paragraph 1 of Article IV. Negotiating guidelines shall establish modalities for the treatment of liberalization undertaken autonomously by Members since previous negotiations, as well as for the special treatment for least-developed country Members under the provisions of paragraph 3 of Article IV.
4. The process of progressive liberalization shall be advanced in each such round through bilateral, plurilateral or multilateral negotiations directed towards increasing the general level of specific commitments undertaken by Members under this Agreement.

ARTICLE XX SCHEDULES OF SPECIFIC COMMITMENTS

1. Each Member shall set out in a schedule the specific commitments it undertakes under Part III of this Agreement. With respect to sectors where such commitments are undertaken, each Schedule shall specify:
   (a) terms, limitations and conditions on market access;
   (b) conditions and qualifications on national treatment;
   (c) undertakings relating to additional commitments;
   (d) where appropriate the time-frame for implementation of such commitments; and
   (e) the date of entry into force of such commitments.
2. Measures inconsistent with both Articles XVI and XVII shall be inscribed in the column relating to Article XVI. In this case the inscription will be considered to provide a condition or qualification to Article XVII as well.
3. Schedules of specific commitments shall be annexed to this Agreement and shall form an integral part thereof.

ARTICLE XXI MODIFICATION OF SCHEDULES

. . .

1.

(a) A Member (referred to in this Article as the "modifying Member") may modify or withdraw any commitment in its Schedule, at any time after three years have elapsed from the date on which that commitment entered into force, in accordance with the provisions of this Article.

(b) A modifying Member shall notify its intent to modify or withdraw a commitment pursuant to this Article to the Council for Trade in Services no later than three months before the intended date of implementation of the modification or withdrawal.

2.

(a) At the request of any Member the benefits of which under this Agreement may be affected (referred to in this Article as an "affected Member") by a proposed modification or withdrawal notified under subparagraph 1(b), the modifying Member shall enter into negotiations with a view to reaching agreement on any necessary compensatory adjustment. In such negotiations and agreement, the Members concerned shall endeavour to maintain a general level of mutually advantageous commitments not less favourable to trade than that provided for in Schedules of specific commitments prior to such negotiations.

(b) Compensatory adjustments shall be made on a most-favoured-nation basis.

3.

(a) If agreement is not reached between the modifying Member and any affected Member before the end of the period provided for negotiations, such affected Member may refer the matter to arbitration. Any affected Member that wishes to enforce a right that it may have to compensation must participate in the arbitration.

(b) If no affected Member has requested arbitration, the modifying Member shall be free to implement the proposed modification or withdrawal.

4.

(a) The modifying Member may not modify or withdraw its commitment until it has made compensatory adjustments in conformity with the findings of the arbitration.

(b) If the modifying Member implements its proposed modification or withdrawal and does not comply with the findings of the arbitration, any affected Member that participated in the arbitration may modify or withdraw substantially equivalent benefits in conformity with those findings. Notwithstanding Article II, such a modification or withdrawal may be implemented solely with respect to the modifying Member.

ARTICLE XXIII DISPUTE SETTLEMENT AND ENFORCEMENT

1. If any Member should consider that any other Member fails to carry out its obligations or specific commitments under this Agreement, it may with a view to reaching a mutually satisfactory resolution of the matter have recourse to the DSU.
2. If the DSB considers that the circumstances are serious enough to justify such action, it may authorize a Member or Members to suspend the application to any other Member or Members of obligations and specific commitments in accordance with Article 22 of the DSU.
3. If any Member considers that any benefit it could reasonably have expected to accrue to it under a specific commitment of another Member under Part III of this Agreement is being nullified or impaired as a result of the application of any measure which does not conflict with the provisions of this Agreement, it may have recourse to the DSU. If the measure is determined by the DSB to have nullified or impaired such a benefit, the Member affected shall be entitled to a mutually satisfactory adjustment on the basis of paragraph 2 of Article XXI, which may include the modification or withdrawal of the measure. In the event an agreement cannot be reached between the Members concerned, Article 22 of the DSU shall apply.

ARTICLE XXVIII DEFINITIONS

For the purpose of this Agreement:

(a) "measure" means any measure by a Member, whether in the form of a law, regulation, rule, procedure, decision, administrative action, or any other form;
(b) "supply of a service" includes the production, distribution, marketing, sale and delivery of a service;
(c) "measures by Members affecting trade in services" include measures in respect of

(i) the purchase, payment or use of a service;
(ii) the access to and use of, in connection with the supply of a service, services which are required by those Members to be offered to the public generally;
(iii) the presence, including commercial presence, of persons of a Member for the supply of a service in the territory of another Member;

(d) "commercial presence" means any type of business or professional establishment, including through
(i) the constitution, acquisition or maintenance of a juridical person, or
(ii) the creation or maintenance of a branch or a representative office,
within the territory of a Member for the purpose of supplying a service;

(e) "sector" of a service means,
(i) with reference to a specific commitment, one or more, or all, subsectors of that service, as specified in a Member's Schedule,
(ii) otherwise, the whole of that service sector, including all of its subsectors;

(f) "service of another Member" means a service which is supplied,
(i) from or in the territory of that other Member, or in the case of maritime transport, by a vessel registered under the laws of that other Member, or by a person of that other Member which supplies the service through the operation of a vessel and/or its use in whole or in part; or
(ii) in the case of the supply of a service through commercial presence or through the presence of natural persons, by a service supplier of that other Member;

(g) "service supplier" means any person that supplies a service;

(h) "monopoly supplier of a service" means any person, public or private, which in the relevant market of the territory of a Member is authorized or established formally or in effect by that Member as the sole supplier of that service;

(i) "service consumer" means any person that receives or uses a service;

(j) "person" means either a natural person or a juridical person;

(k) "natural person of another Member" means a natural person who resides in the territory of that other Member or any other Member, and who under the law of that other Member:
(i) is a national of that other Member; or
(ii) has the right of permanent residence in that other Member, in the case of a Member which:
1. does not have nationals; or
2. accords substantially the same treatment to its permanent residents as it does to its nationals in respect of measures affecting trade in services, as notified in its acceptance of or accession

to the WTO Agreement, provided that no Member is obligated to accord to such permanent residents treatment more favourable than would be accorded by that other Member to such permanent residents. Such notification shall include the assurance to assume, with respect to those permanent residents, in accordance with its laws and regulations, the same responsibilities that other Member bears with respect to its nationals;

(l) "juridical person" means any legal entity duly constituted or otherwise organized under applicable law, whether for profit or otherwise, and whether privately-owned or governmentally-owned, including any corporation, trust, partnership, joint venture, sole proprietorship or association;

(m) "juridical person of another Member" means a juridical person which is either:

   (i) constituted or otherwise organized under the law of that other Member, and is engaged in substantive business operations in the territory of that Member or any other Member; or

   (ii) in the case of the supply of a service through commercial presence, owned or controlled by:

      1. natural persons of that Member; or
      2. juridical persons of that other Member identified under subparagraph (i);

(n) a juridical person is:

   (i) "owned" by persons of a Member if more than 50 per cent of the equity interest in it is beneficially owned by persons of that Member;

   (ii) "controlled" by persons of a Member if such persons have the power to name a majority of its directors or otherwise to legally direct its actions;

   (iii) "affiliated" with another person when it controls, or is controlled by, that other person; or when it and the other person are both controlled by the same person;

(o) "direct taxes" comprise all taxes on total income, on total capital or on elements of income or of capital, including taxes on gains from the alienation of property, taxes on estates, inheritances and gifts, and taxes on the total amounts of wages or salaries paid by enterprises, as well as taxes on capital appreciation.

ARTICLE XXIX ANNEXES

The Annexes to this Agreement are an integral part of this Agreement.

ANNEX ON ARTICLE II EXEMPTIONS

Scope

1. This Annex specifies the conditions under which a Member, at the entry into force of this Agreement, is exempted from its obligations under paragraph 1 of Article II.
6. In principle, such exemptions should not exceed a period of 10 years. In any event, they shall be subject to negotiation in subsequent trade liberalizing rounds.

ANNEX ON MOVEMENT OF NATURAL PERSONS SUPPLYING SERVICES UNDER THE AGREEMENT

1. This Annex applies to measures affecting natural persons who are service suppliers of a Member, and natural persons of a Member who are employed by a service supplier of a Member, in respect of the supply of a service.
2. The Agreement shall not apply to measures affecting natural persons seeking access to the employment market of a Member, nor shall it apply to measures regarding citizenship, residence or employment on a permanent basis.
3. In accordance with Parts III and IV of the Agreement, Members may negotiate specific commitments applying to the movement of all categories of natural persons supplying services under the Agreement. Natural persons covered by a specific commitment shall be allowed to supply the service in accordance with the terms of that commitment.
4. The Agreement shall not prevent a Member from applying measures to regulate the entry of natural persons into, or their temporary stay in, its territory, including those measures necessary to protect the integrity of, and to ensure the orderly movement of natural persons across, its borders, provided that such measures are not applied in such a manner as to nullify or impair the benefits accruing to any Member under the terms of a specific commitment.

ANNEX ON TELECOMMUNICATIONS

1. Objectives

   Recognizing the specificities of the telecommunications services sector and, in particular, its dual role as a distinct sector of economic activity and as the underlying transport means for other economic activities, the Members have agreed to the following Annex with the objective of elaborating upon the provisions of the Agreement with respect to measures affecting access to and use of public telecommunications transport networks and services. Accordingly, this Annex provides notes and supplementary provisions to the Agreement.

2. Scope
   (a) This Annex shall apply to all measures of a Member that affect access to and use of public telecommunications transport networks and services.
   (b) This Annex shall not apply to measures affecting the cable or broadcast distribution of radio or television programming.
   (c) Nothing in this Annex shall be construed:
      (i) to require a Member to authorize a service supplier of any other Member to establish, construct, acquire, lease, operate, or supply telecommunications transport networks or services, other than as provided for in its Schedule; or
      (ii) to require a Member (or to require a Member to oblige service suppliers under its jurisdiction) to establish, construct, acquire, lease, operate or supply telecommunications transport networks or services not offered to the public generally.
3. Definitions

   For the purposes of this Annex:
   (a) "Telecommunications" means the transmission and reception of signals by any electromagnetic means.
   (b) "Public telecommunications transport service" means any telecommunications transport service required, explicitly or in effect, by a Member to be offered to the public generally. Such services may include, *inter alia*, telegraph, telephone, telex, and data transmission typically involving the real-time transmission of customer-supplied information between two or more points without any end-to-end change in the form or content of the customer's information.
   (c) "Public telecommunications transport network" means the public telecommunications infrastructure which permits telecommunications between and among defined network termination points.
   (d) "Intra-corporate communications" means telecommunications through which a company communicates within the company or with or among its subsidiaries, branches and, subject to a Member's domestic laws and regulations, affiliates. For these purposes, "subsidiaries", "branches" and, where applicable, "affiliates" shall be as defined by each Member. "Intra-corporate communications" in this Annex excludes commercial or non-commercial services that are supplied to companies that are not related subsidiaries, branches or affiliates, or that are offered to customers or potential customers.

(e) Any reference to a paragraph or subparagraph of this Annex includes all subdivisions thereof.

4. Transparency
In the application of Article III of the Agreement, each Member shall ensure that relevant information on conditions affecting access to and use of public telecommunications transport networks and services is publicly available, including: tariffs and other terms and conditions of service; specifications of technical interfaces with such networks and services; information on bodies responsible for the preparation and adoption of standards affecting such access and use; conditions applying to attachment of terminal or other equipment; and notifications, registration or licensing requirements, if any.

5. Access to and use of Public Telecommunications Transport Networks and Services
   (a) Each Member shall ensure that any service supplier of any other Member is accorded access to and use of public telecommunications transport networks and services on reasonable and non-discriminatory terms and conditions, for the supply of a service included in its Schedule. This obligation shall be applied, *inter alia*, through paragraphs (b) through (f).
   (b) Each Member shall ensure that service suppliers of any other Member have access to and use of any public telecommunications transport network or service offered within or across the border of that Member, including private leased circuits, and to this end shall ensure, subject to paragraphs (e) and (f), that such suppliers are permitted:
      (i) to purchase or lease and attach terminal or other equipment which interfaces with the network and which is necessary to supply a supplier's services;
      (ii) to interconnect private leased or owned circuits with public telecommunications transport networks and services or with circuits leased or owned by another service supplier; and
      (iii) to use operating protocols of the service supplier's choice in the supply of any service, other than as necessary to ensure the availability of telecommunications transport networks and services to the public generally.
   (c) Each Member shall ensure that service suppliers of any other Member may use public telecommunications transport networks and services for the movement of information within and across borders, including for intra-corporate communications of such service suppliers, and for access to information contained in data bases or oth-

erwise stored in machine-readable form in the territory of any Member. Any new or amended measures of a Member significantly affecting such use shall be notified and shall be subject to consultation, in accordance with relevant provisions of the Agreement.

(d) Notwithstanding the preceding paragraph, a Member may take such measures as are necessary to ensure the security and confidentiality of messages, subject to the requirement that such measures are not applied in a manner which would constitute a means of arbitrary or unjustifiable discrimination or a disguised restriction on trade in services.

(e) Each Member shall ensure that no condition is imposed on access to and use of public telecommunications transport networks and services other than as necessary:

(i) to safeguard the public service responsibilities of suppliers of public telecommunications transport networks and services, in particular their ability to make their networks or services available to the public generally;

(ii) to protect the technical integrity of public telecommunications transport networks or services; or

(iii) to ensure that service suppliers of any other Member do not supply services unless permitted pursuant to commitments in the Member's Schedule.

(f) Provided that they satisfy the criteria set out in paragraph (e), conditions for access to and use of public telecommunications transport networks and services may include:

(i) restrictions on resale or shared use of such services;

(ii) a requirement to use specified technical interfaces, including interface protocols, for inter-connection with such networks and services;

(iii) requirements, where necessary, for the inter-operability of such services and to encourage the achievement of the goals set out in paragraph 7(a);

(iv) type approval of terminal or other equipment which interfaces with the network and technical requirements relating to the attachment of such equipment to such networks;

(v) restrictions on inter-connection of private leased or owned circuits with such networks or services, or with circuits leased or owned by another service supplier; or

(vi) notification, registration and licensing.

Appendix B

Pertinent Sections of the WTO Dispute Settlement Understanding (DSU)

The articles and sections referred to in this book are included here, as well as additional sections of interest. Note that several sections and all clarifying footnotes have been removed from the selection below. See the full text of the DSU (i.e., Annex 2 of the WTO Agreement) at www.wto.org/english/docs_e/legal_e/28-dsu.pdf, or at www.wto.org/english/docs_e/legal_e/28-dsu.doc.

UNDERSTANDING ON RULES AND PROCEDURES GOVERNING THE SETTLEMENT OF DISPUTES

Article 1 Coverage and Application

1. The rules and procedures of this Understanding shall apply to disputes brought pursuant to the consultation and dispute settlement provisions of the agreements listed in Appendix 1 to this Understanding (referred to in this Understanding as the "covered agreements"). The rules and procedures of this Understanding shall also apply to consultations and the settlement of disputes between Members concerning their rights and obligations under the provisions of the Agreement Establishing the World Trade Organization (referred to in this Understanding as the "WTO Agreement") and of this Understanding taken in isolation or in combination with any other covered agreement.

Article 2 Administration

1. The Dispute Settlement Body is hereby established to administer these rules and procedures and, except as otherwise provided in a covered

agreement, the consultation and dispute settlement provisions of the covered agreements. Accordingly, the DSB shall have the authority to establish panels, adopt panel and Appellate Body reports, maintain surveillance of implementation of rulings and recommendations, and authorize suspension of concessions and other obligations under the covered agreements. With respect to disputes arising under a covered agreement which is a Plurilateral Trade Agreement, the term "Member" as used herein shall refer only to those Members that are parties to the relevant Plurilateral Trade Agreement. Where the DSB administers the dispute settlement provisions of a Plurilateral Trade Agreement, only those Members that are parties to that Agreement may participate in decisions or actions taken by the DSB with respect to that dispute.

Article 3 General Provisions

. . .

2. The dispute settlement system of the WTO is a central element in providing security and predictability to the multilateral trading system. The Members recognize that it serves to preserve the rights and obligations of Members under the covered agreements, and to clarify the existing provisions of those agreements in accordance with customary rules of interpretation of public international law. Recommendations and rulings of the DSB cannot add to or diminish the rights and obligations provided in the covered agreements.

Article 4 Consultations

2. Each Member undertakes to accord sympathetic consideration to and afford adequate opportunity for consultation regarding any representations made by another Member concerning measures affecting the operation of any covered agreement taken within the territory of the former.
4. All such requests for consultations shall be notified to the DSB and the relevant Councils and Committees by the Member which requests consultations. Any request for consultations shall be submitted in writing and shall give the reasons for the request, including identification of the measures at issue and an indication of the legal basis for the complaint.
5. In the course of consultations in accordance with the provisions of a covered agreement, before resorting to further action under this Understanding, Members should attempt to obtain satisfactory adjustment of the matter.
6. Consultations shall be confidential, and without prejudice to the rights of any Member in any further proceedings.

Article 6 Establishment of Panels

2. The request for the establishment of a panel shall be made in writing. It shall indicate whether consultations were held, identify the specific measures at issue and provide a brief summary of the legal basis of the complaint sufficient to present the problem clearly. In case the applicant requests the establishment of a panel with other than standard terms of reference, the written request shall include the proposed text of special terms of reference.

Article 8 Composition of Panels

1. Panels shall be composed of well-qualified governmental and/or non-governmental individuals, including persons who have served on or presented a case to a panel, served as a representative of a Member or of a contracting party to GATT 1947 or as a representative to the Council or Committee of any covered agreement or its predecessor agreement, or in the Secretariat, taught or published on international trade law or policy, or served as a senior trade policy official of a Member.
2. Panel members should be selected with a view to ensuring the independence of the members, a sufficiently diverse background and a wide spectrum of experience.
3. Citizens of Members whose governments are parties to the dispute or third parties as defined in paragraph 2 of Article 10 shall not serve on a panel concerned with that dispute, unless the parties to the dispute agree otherwise.
4. To assist in the selection of panelists, the Secretariat shall maintain an indicative list of governmental and non-governmental individuals possessing the qualifications outlined in paragraph 1, from which panelists may be drawn as appropriate.
5. Panels shall be composed of three panelists unless the parties to the dispute agree, within 10 days from the establishment of the panel, to a panel composed of five panelists. Members shall be informed promptly of the composition of the panel.
6. The Secretariat shall propose nominations for the panel to the parties to the dispute. The parties to the dispute shall not oppose nominations except for compelling reasons.
9. Panelists shall serve in their individual capacities and not as government representatives, nor as representatives of any organization. Members shall therefore not give them instructions nor seek to influence them as individuals with regard to matters before a panel.

Article 11 Function of Panels

The function of panels is to assist the DSB in discharging its responsibilities under this Understanding and the covered agreements. Accordingly, a panel should make an objective assessment of the matter before it, including an objective assessment of the facts of the case and the applicability of and conformity with the relevant covered agreements, and make such other findings as will assist the DSB in making the recommendations or in giving the rulings provided for in the covered agreements. Panels should consult regularly with the parties to the dispute and give them adequate opportunity to develop a mutually satisfactory solution.

Article 14 Confidentiality

1. Panel deliberations shall be confidential.
2. The reports of panels shall be drafted without the presence of the parties to the dispute in the light of the information provided and the statements made.
3. Opinions expressed in the panel report by individual panelists shall be anonymous.

Article 16 Adoption of Panel Reports

1. In order to provide sufficient time for the Members to consider panel reports, the reports shall not be considered for adoption by the DSB until 20 days after the date they have been circulated to the Members.
2. Members having objections to a panel report shall give written reasons to explain their objections for circulation at least 10 days prior to the DSB meeting at which the panel report will be considered.
3. The parties to a dispute shall have the right to participate fully in the consideration of the panel report by the DSB, and their views shall be fully recorded.
4. Within 60 days after the date of circulation of a panel report to the Members, the report shall be adopted at a DSB meeting unless a party to the dispute formally notifies the DSB of its decision to appeal or the DSB decides by consensus not to adopt the report. If a party has notified its decision to appeal, the report by the panel shall not be considered for adoption by the DSB until after completion of the appeal. This adoption procedure is without prejudice to the right of Members to express their views on a panel report.

Article 17 Appellate Review

1. A standing Appellate Body shall be established by the DSB. The Appellate Body shall hear appeals from panel cases.
3. The Appellate Body shall comprise persons of recognized authority, with demonstrated expertise in law, international trade and the subject matter of the covered agreements generally. They shall be unaffiliated with any government. The Appellate Body membership shall be broadly representative of membership in the WTO. All persons serving on the Appellate Body shall be available at all times and on short notice, and shall stay abreast of dispute settlement activities and other relevant activities of the WTO. They shall not participate in the consideration of any disputes that would create a direct or indirect conflict of interest.
4. Only parties to the dispute, not third parties, may appeal a panel report. Third parties which have notified the DSB of a substantial interest in the matter pursuant to paragraph 2 of Article 10 may make written submissions to, and be given an opportunity to be heard by, the Appellate Body.
6. An appeal shall be limited to issues of law covered in the panel report and legal interpretations developed by the panel.
10. The proceedings of the Appellate Body shall be confidential. The reports of the Appellate Body shall be drafted without the presence of the parties to the dispute and in the light of the information provided and the statements made.
11. Opinions expressed in the Appellate Body report by individuals serving on the Appellate Body shall be anonymous.
13. The Appellate Body may uphold, modify or reverse the legal findings and conclusions of the panel.
14. An Appellate Body report shall be adopted by the DSB and unconditionally accepted by the parties to the dispute unless the DSB decides by consensus not to adopt the [report].

Article 19 Panel and Appellate Body Recommendations

1. Where a panel or the Appellate Body concludes that a measure is inconsistent with a covered agreement, it shall recommend that the Member concerned bring the measure into conformity with that agreement. In addition to its recommendations, the panel or Appellate Body may suggest ways in which the Member concerned could implement the recommendations.

Article 21 Surveillance of Implementation of Recommendations and Rulings

1. Prompt compliance with recommendations or rulings of the DSB is essential in order to ensure effective resolution of disputes to the benefit of all Members.
3. At a DSB meeting held within 30 days after the date of adoption of the panel or Appellate Body report, the Member concerned shall inform the DSB of its intentions in respect of implementation of the recommendations and rulings of the DSB. If it is impracticable to comply immediately with the recommendations and rulings, the Member concerned shall have a reasonable period of time in which to do so. The reasonable period of time shall be:
   (a) the period of time proposed by the Member concerned, provided that such period is approved by the DSB; or, in the absence of such approval,
   (b) a period of time mutually agreed by the parties to the dispute within 45 days after the date of adoption of the recommendations and rulings; or, in the absence of such agreement,
   (c) a period of time determined through binding arbitration within 90 days after the date of adoption of the recommendations and rulings. In such arbitration, a guideline for the arbitrator should be that the reasonable period of time to implement panel or Appellate Body recommendations should not exceed 15 months from the date of adoption of a panel or Appellate Body report. However, that time may be shorter or longer, depending upon the particular circumstances.
6. The DSB shall keep under surveillance the implementation of adopted recommendations or rulings. The issue of implementation of the recommendations or rulings may be raised at the DSB by any Member at any time following their adoption. Unless the DSB decides otherwise, the issue of implementation of the recommendations or rulings shall be placed on the agenda of the DSB meeting after six months following the date of establishment of the reasonable period of time pursuant to paragraph 3 and shall remain on the DSB's agenda until the issue is resolved. At least 10 days prior to each such DSB meeting, the Member concerned shall provide the DSB with a status report in writing of its progress in the implementation of the recommendations or rulings.

Article 22 Compensation and the Suspension of Concessions

1. Compensation and the suspension of concessions or other obligations are temporary measures available in the event that the recommendations

and rulings are not implemented within a reasonable period of time. However, neither compensation nor the suspension of concessions or other obligations is preferred to full implementation of a recommendation to bring a measure into conformity with the covered agreements. Compensation is voluntary and, if granted, shall be consistent with the covered agreements.

2. If the Member concerned fails to bring the measure found to be inconsistent with a covered agreement into compliance therewith or otherwise comply with the recommendations and rulings within the reasonable period of time determined pursuant to paragraph 3 of Article 21, such Member shall, if so requested, and no later than the expiry of the reasonable period of time, enter into negotiations with any party having invoked the dispute settlement procedures, with a view to developing mutually acceptable compensation. If no satisfactory compensation has been agreed within 20 days after the date of expiry of the reasonable period of time, any party having invoked the dispute settlement procedures may request authorization from the DSB to suspend the application to the Member concerned of concessions or other obligations under the covered agreements.
3. In considering what concessions or other obligations to suspend, the complaining party shall apply the following principles and procedures:
   (a) the general principle is that the complaining party should first seek to suspend concessions or other obligations with respect to the same sector(s) as that in which the panel or Appellate Body has found a violation or other nullification or impairment;
   (b) if that party considers that it is not practicable or effective to suspend concessions or other obligations with respect to the same sector(s), it may seek to suspend concessions or other obligations in other sectors under the same agreement;
   (c) if that party considers that it is not practicable or effective to suspend concessions or other obligations with respect to other sectors under the same agreement, and that the circumstances are serious enough, it may seek to suspend concessions or other obligations under another covered agreement;
   (d) in applying the above principles, that party shall take into account:
      (i) the trade in the sector or under the agreement under which the panel or Appellate Body has found a violation or other nullification or impairment, and the importance of such trade to that party;
      (ii) the broader economic elements related to the nullification or impairment and the broader economic consequences of the suspension of concessions or other obligations;
   (e) if that party decides to request authorization to suspend concessions or other obligations pursuant to subparagraphs (b) or (c), it shall

state the reasons therefor in its request. At the same time as the request is forwarded to the DSB, it also shall be forwarded to the relevant Councils and also, in the case of a request pursuant to subparagraph (b), the relevant sectoral bodies;

(f) for purposes of this paragraph, "sector" means:
   (i) with respect to goods, all goods;
   (ii) with respect to services, a principal sector as identified in the current "Services Sectoral Classification List" which identifies such sectors;
   (iii) with respect to trade-related intellectual property rights, each of the categories of intellectual property rights covered in Section 1, or Section 2, or Section 3, or Section 4, or Section 5, or Section 6, or Section 7 of Part II, or the obligations under Part III, or Part IV of the Agreement on TRIPS;

(g) for purposes of this paragraph, "agreement" means:
   (i) with respect to goods, the agreements listed in Annex 1A of the WTO Agreement, taken as a whole as well as the Plurilateral Trade Agreements in so far as the relevant parties to the dispute are parties to these agreements;
   (ii) with respect to services, the GATS;
   (iii) with respect to intellectual property rights, the Agreement on TRIPS.

4. The level of the suspension of concessions or other obligations authorized by the DSB shall be equivalent to the level of the nullification or impairment.
5. The DSB shall not authorize suspension of concessions or other obligations if a covered agreement prohibits such suspension.
6. When the situation described in paragraph 2 occurs, the DSB, upon request, shall grant authorization to suspend concessions or other obligations within 30 days of the expiry of the reasonable period of time unless the DSB decides by consensus to reject the request. However, if the Member concerned objects to the level of suspension proposed, or claims that the principles and procedures set forth in paragraph 3 have not been followed where a complaining party has requested authorization to suspend concessions or other obligations pursuant to paragraph 3(b) or (c), the matter shall be referred to arbitration. Such arbitration shall be carried out by the original panel, if members are available, or by an arbitrator appointed by the Director-General and shall be completed within 60 days after the date of expiry of the reasonable period of time. Concessions or other obligations shall not be suspended during the course of the arbitration.

7. The arbitrator acting pursuant to paragraph 6 shall not examine the nature of the concessions or other obligations to be suspended but shall determine whether the level of such suspension is equivalent to the level of nullification or impairment. The arbitrator may also determine if the proposed suspension of concessions or other obligations is allowed under the covered agreement. However, if the matter referred to arbitration includes a claim that the principles and procedures set forth in paragraph 3 have not been followed, the arbitrator shall examine that claim. In the event the arbitrator determines that those principles and procedures have not been followed, the complaining party shall apply them consistent with paragraph 3. The parties shall accept the arbitrator's decision as final and the parties concerned shall not seek a second arbitration. The DSB shall be informed promptly of the decision of the arbitrator and shall upon request, grant authorization to suspend concessions or other obligations where the request is consistent with the decision of the arbitrator, unless the DSB decides by consensus to reject the request.
8. The suspension of concessions or other obligations shall be temporary and shall only be applied until such time as the measure found to be inconsistent with a covered agreement has been removed, or the Member that must implement recommendations or rulings provides a solution to the nullification or impairment of benefits, or a mutually satisfactory solution is reached. In accordance with paragraph 6 of Article 21, the DSB shall continue to keep under surveillance the implementation of adopted recommendations or rulings, including those cases where compensation has been provided or concessions or other obligations have been suspended but the recommendations to bring a measure into conformity with the covered agreements have not been implemented.
9. The dispute settlement provisions of the covered agreements may be invoked in respect of measures affecting their observance taken by regional or local governments or authorities within the territory of a Member. When the DSB has ruled that a provision of a covered agreement has not been observed, the responsible Member shall take such reasonable measures as may be available to it to ensure its observance. The provisions of the covered agreements and this Understanding relating to compensation and suspension of concessions or other obligations apply in cases where it has not been possible to secure such observance.

Article 23 Strengthening of the Multilateral System

1. When Members seek the redress of a violation of obligations or other nullification or impairment of benefits under the covered agreements or

an impediment to the attainment of any objective of the covered agreements, they shall have recourse to, and abide by, the rules and procedures of this Understanding.

2. In such cases, Members shall:
   (a) not make a determination to the effect that a violation has occurred, that benefits have been nullified or impaired or that the attainment of any objective of the covered agreements has been impeded, except through recourse to dispute settlement in accordance with the rules and procedures of this Understanding, and shall make any such determination consistent with the findings contained in the panel or Appellate Body report adopted by the DSB or an arbitration award rendered under this Understanding;
   (b) follow the procedures set forth in Article 21 to determine the reasonable period of time for the Member concerned to implement the recommendations and rulings; and
   (c) follow the procedures set forth in Article 22 to determine the level of suspension of concessions or other obligations and obtain DSB authorization in accordance with those procedures before suspending concessions or other obligations under the covered agreements in response to the failure of the Member concerned to implement the recommendations and rulings within that reasonable period of time.

Appendix C

The IFLA Position on the World Trade Organization (2001)

INTRODUCTION

1. The World Trade Organization (WTO), with a growing membership of over 140 countries, oversees a variety of treaties governing international trade. The WTO treaties with the most significant implications for libraries and the information sector are the General Agreement on Trade in Services (GATS) and the Agreement on Trade-Related Aspects of Intellectual Property Rights (TRIPS).
2. Libraries are a public good. They are unique social organizations dedicated to providing the broadest range of information and ideas to the public, regardless of age, religion, physical and mental health, social status, race, gender or language. The long-established library traditions of intellectual freedom and equitable access to information and cultural expression form the basis for ensuring that library goals are achieved.
3. Libraries of all types form an interrelated network, which serves the citizenry, from the great national, state and research institutions to public and school libraries. The well being of libraries is essential in ensuring access to the full range of human expression and providing individuals with the skills necessary to access and use this content.
4. There is growing evidence that WTO decisions, directly or indirectly, may adversely affect the operations and future development of library services, especially in not-for-profit institutions.

BACKGROUND

5. It is important to recognize that the WTO, and the international trade authorities of its members, are engaged in shaping policy and applications of this policy on an ongoing basis. While the infrequent Ministerial Conferences with their attendant protests are the most visible manifestation of the negotiations, the process is continuous, with decisions often reached without public scrutiny. What makes the WTO unique is that it has a binding dispute mechanism as part of its operations with the strongest enforcement procedures of any international agreement. IFLA urges its members to inform themselves on the WTO and their national trade policy deliberations and to promote the library and related issues when possible. Awareness of international trade issues is a necessary component of effective advocacy in shaping national policy, programmes and law as they relate to library service.

SPECIFIC CONCERNS

Not-for-Profit Libraries

6. The GATS Agreement has the potential to open up all aspects of a national economy to foreign competition including public sector services such as libraries. Corporations can be set up in any Member State and compete against public services. In such instances, the foreign corporation can challenge government support for public sector service and could claim national treatment; i.e. the same level of subsidy received from the government by the public sector agency. Sub-Central governments (state/provincial, regional and municipal governments and their management boards) are included in any agreements, which cover the Member State.
7. The GATS Agreement does not apply to "services supplied in the exercise of government authority." Critics have argued that the WTO will interpret this clause very narrowly. The GATS agreement itself states "a service supplied in the exercise of government authority means any service, which is supplied neither on a commercial basis, nor in competition with one or more service providers." With the advent of for profit on-line content providers targeting individual users of education services and public libraries, the potential for GATS challenges to traditional library service is increasing. While the concept of allowing "competition" appears benign, the eventual outcome of such challenges will be the undermining of the tax-supported status of public sector libraries at the na-

tional, regional and local levels. Without tax support, the library's role as a democratic institution, making available the widest range of material reflecting the diversity of society, will be compromised.

8. In their submissions to the GATS negotiations, individual countries make commitments on service sectors which would then be subject to GATS requirements. At the commencement of the second round of GATS negotiations in 2001, thirteen members had made a commitment to open negotiations on "libraries, archives, museums and other cultural services." (1) Given that specific library services will fall under other GATS categories such as communications ("on-line information and data retrieval; electronic data interchange"), even if they have not listed library service, it is probable that many more countries will be entering into GATS negotiations, which will directly affect libraries.
9. IFLA encourages its members to promote awareness of library values and concerns in the context of GATS to the trade negotiators in their country. The potentially far-reaching implications of trade liberalization in services for not-for-profit libraries should be openly debated. Negotiators should be strongly encouraged to ensure that government support for traditional library service is not exposed to a GATS challenge.

Intellectual Property

10. The TRIPS Agreement applies the enforcement apparatus of the WTO to the Bern and other conventions established under the World Intellectual Property Organization (WIPO). TRIPS has the potential to directly and indirectly shape national copyright policy and law. In one instance to date, a WTO dispute panel has found a permitted use in a national copyright law in violation of international trade treaty commitments. Ranging from fair use and similar fair practices to preservation copying by libraries, permitted uses lay out the rights of users of copyrighted content. There is little assurance that the balance between the public interest and rights of content owners sought in national copyright policy debate will be considered by the WTO in any intellectual property disputes which come before it. WTO dispute panels are "likely to resolve competing claims to intellectual property with little regard for the non-commercial values upon which a reasonable balance of private rights and public interest depends."(2)
11. The regulatory weight of the WTO has the potential to have a chilling effect on the development of national copyright law by providing

those advocating fewer permitted uses and extended protection a "trump card" to derail advocacy efforts on behalf of users. IFLA urges its members to work to ensure that the interests of libraries and library users are not marginalized through the application of the WTO regime to domestic copyright legislation.

Cultural Diversity

12. Publicly funded libraries are part of the cultural sector. They are involved in encouraging the development and promotion of cultural works, particularly literature, and the preservation and dissemination of those works. Libraries should be part of protections proposed for culture and should support and be part of any possible separate treaty which allows special consideration for cultural goods and services in international trade.
13. IFLA will work with national and international cultural groups to create alliances for achieving recognition and protection for the development of regional and domestic cultural products. The objective of such an alliance is the creation of cultural diversity and the encouragement of multiple voices rather than homogenized and globalized cultural works, which dominate by virtue of financial or corporate strength.
14. While supporting the right of WTO Member States to promote and nurture national culture, IFLA opposes any obstacles to the free flow across international borders of legally produced information and cultural content normally collected or distributed by libraries. IFLA opposes tariffs or other duties or taxes on the importation of print on paper or digital content. Such measures have the potential to stifle intellectual freedom.

CONCLUSION

15. As an active international alliance of library and information associations, libraries and information services, and concerned individuals, IFLA is strategically positioned to advocate at the WTO on behalf of libraries and information services and to ensure that its members are informed in order to be able to advocate effectively at the national level.
16. In order to ensure a strong public sector, IFLA and its members will continue to build links and work with library and information, archive,

museum, education and other organizations in furthering awareness of the implications of international trade treaties for the public sector.

NOTES

1. Bolivia, Central African Republic, Ecuador, Gambia, Guinea-Bissau, Hong Kong, Iceland, Japan, New Caledonia, Sierra Leone, Singapore, USA, Venezuela.
2. Steven Shrybman, "Information, Commodification and the World Trade Organization," IFLA Jerusalem Conference, Aug. 2000. Approved by the Governing Board of IFLA, at its meeting in Boston, USA, 25th August 2001.

INTERNATIONAL FEDERATION OF LIBRARY
ASSOCIATIONS AND INSTITUTIONS (IFLA)
P O Box 95312
2509 CH THE HAGUE
Netherlands
September 2001

Source: http://www.ifla.org/III/clm/p1/wto-ifla.htm (accessed 17 October 2005)

Appendix D

Canadian Library Association Letter to Department of Foreign Affairs and International Trade

This letter from Wendy Newman, then president of the Canadian Library Association (CLA), to Paul Robertson, director of the Services Trade Policy Division (EBS) of the Department of Foreign Affairs and International Trade, October 23, 2002, outlined CLA's concerns about the possible impact the General Agreement on Trade in Services might have on library operations in Canada.

October 23, 2002
Mr Paul Robertson
Director
Services Trade Policy Division (EBS)
Department of Foreign Affairs and International Trade
125 Sussex Drive
Ottawa, Ontario, K1A 0G2

Dear Mr Robertson:

Last February, the Canadian Library Association wrote to the Minister of International Trade, outlining for him CLA's concerns about the possible impact the General Agreement on Trade in Services might have on library operations in Canada. These concerns had been discussed with you in a preliminary fashion at a meeting held on December 10th, 2001. The purpose of this letter is to provide you with more specific information about each of the five library services that we believe are threatened by the GATS:

1. digital publication of scholarly research;
2. video services;

3. provision of Internet access;
4. document delivery services; and
5. virtual reference and information services.

Before examining each of these services in turn, we would like to make a few general comments that provide the context for our concern.

CONTEXT

First, with the advent of new information and communication technologies in the last 15 years, libraries have expanded the scope of their activities beyond the acquiring, lending, conserving and holding for reference of print-based materials. To continue to provide society with free and convenient access to information and to assist in the strengthening of Canada's knowledge-based economy, libraries have had to invest in new media equipment and training, with all the ramifications that such an investment entails in their operations.

Second, libraries, in CLA's reading of section 3 of Article 1 of the GATS, can be defined as non-governmental bodies exercising powers delegated by central, regional or local governments or authorities. The services provided by these bodies come under the terms of the Agreement unless it can be shown that they are supplied "neither on a commercial basis, nor in competition with one or more commercial service suppliers". As not-for-profit bodies, libraries meet the first condition for exemption; they do not, however, necessarily meet the second condition. Indeed, there is a whole range of not-for-profit institutions, many of them established as a result of the exercise of government authority, that supply services that can be viewed as being in competition with commercial service suppliers. For example, Crown corporations, established for good policy reasons to fill a gap not provided for by market forces, necessarily wind up 'competing' at the margin with for-profit service suppliers.

Third, CLA recognizes that it is certainly not the Government of Canada's intention to offer up library services as a sector for trade liberalization. However, it certainly is the Government's intention to open the doors to international trade for Canada's vibrant information and communication technologies sector. And characteristic of this sector is the fact that its applications can be found cutting across nearly all other sectors of society. What, from a not-for-profit perspective, may be viewed as an integral part of contemporary library services (where no commitments have been made) can quite legitimately be viewed, from a commercial perspective, as a market niche for special applications of information and communication technology (where commitments have been made). In this dynamic area, other signatories to the GATS will expect reciprocal rights.

Finally, other signatories may view certain measures taken by Canadian government authorities, or by non-governmental bodies acting with delegated authority, as unfairly affecting the trade in competitively provided services. These measures may vary from direct financial assistance for the introduction and provision of a service to covering the indirect costs of supplying a service, and to tax treatment that favours not-for-profit organizations.

With the above comments as context, what follows is a description of five services that are now considered to be part of overall library services. Of course, not all libraries offer these extended services. Depending on its size and the community it serves, a particular library may be more or less affected by these developments.

In summary, what is of great concern to CLA is that these services extend beyond the strict definition of library and archive services provided by the World Trade Organization. According to the WTO's own Services Database, library and archives services are limited to "the maintenance, sequencing and storage of publications, documents, etc for record and future reference and related consulting services."

In describing each of the threatened services, the following elements are included:

- definition of the service;
- rationale for the service;
- history of its evolution (when it began to be offered, whether it is growing in relative importance);
- resources required to provide the service, expressed as a percentage of the library's budget; and
- government measures that assist financially or in some other way with the provision of the service.

1. DIGITAL PUBLICATION OF SCHOLARLY RESEARCH

Definition of service: In Canada, as elsewhere, university-based scholars have an important, though not exclusive, role as researchers and producers of knowledge. Academic scholars are expected or required to publish their findings to ensure wide dissemination of information, to allow the replication of results, and to encourage further exploration and experimentation. This is perceived as an essential public good. The most common method of dissemination of research is through peer-reviewed scholarly journals that are acquired and made available for consultation and study in academic libraries. Academic libraries are the principle [*sic*] source of revenue for publishers of academic journals and monographs. New strategies are being developed in the academic sector internationally to alter this pattern of dissemination of research.

History: In some cases scholarly publishers are learned societies or universities, but predominantly they are specialist commercial publishers. Over the last decade, there has been a significant concentration in the ownership of scholarly journals and, at the same time, dramatic increases in subscription costs, which have exceeded general annual inflation levels by factors of 5 or even more. Commercial publishers do not pay researchers for the articles published; moreover, a common practice is to for the publisher to assume ownership of the copyright for articles published and to benefit from free editorial services from academics. Therefore, it can be argued that both directly and indirectly, commercial scholarly publishers are benefiting from a public subsidy (in the form of the publicly funded scholars and higher education infrastructure).

Rationale for changes in scholarly publishing: Academic libraries and scholars themselves have now developed initiatives designed to limit or offer competition to the controlling position that major international commercial publishers now enjoy in the scholarly publication sphere. Commercial publishers are seeking to extend their control through their lobbying for restrictive copyright provisions in the digital environment. These combined strategies threaten to undermine the traditional balance between the creators' interests and public access to information. In this context, academic institutions and societies, as well as academic libraries, are offering financial support to seed the launch of journals that deliberately compete with prestigious but excessively expensive commercial publications. Secondly, there is a growing movement towards establishing scholar-controlled or university-controlled open archives of digital publications, through which free and open access to new research will be provided, independent of the established publication channels. Notable examples include the Public Library of Science (www.publiclibraryofscience.org/) and the recent Budapest Open Access Initiative (BOAI) (www.soros.org/openaccess/). These recent initiatives are designed to ensure sustainable public access to new research and to undermine the near-monopolies developed by some notable publishers.

Resources: The resources used by academic libraries and their universities to support these archiving and publishing initiatives form a minimal part of their overall budget when contrasted to the cost of the infrastructure supporting the original research on which publication is based. At present the alternative approaches to publication are supported largely on an individual voluntary basis or through consortium initiatives. As the movement grows however, the costs of creating, storing and organizing these archives will increase and, as a direct result of their size and scope, begin to threaten the profitability of commercial publishing in a significant way. The costs of the research that underpins scholarly publication are high, and are borne directly by universities and research institutes (which are publicly funded) and also by government at the federal and provincial level. For the academic year 1999-2000, Statistics Canada estimates the total direct and indirect government expenditure to support research in the higher education field amounted to $1,562.9 million.

Government measures: Direct government support for higher education and research, as well as support for Canadian publishing including learned societies, underpins the academic publishing and research enterprise. In so far as new initiatives within academia threaten publishers' revenues by moving towards alternatives to the established commercial publishing practice, CLA believes that academic libraries and universities are vulnerable to a GATS challenge.

2. VIDEO SERVICES

Definition of service: Since the mid 1980's most Canadian public libraries have incorporated pre-recorded videotapes into their collections.

Rationale: As library users acquired equipment to view videos, they were as interested in borrowing these as they were in borrowing reading material for leisure and entertainment.

History: When these collections were first introduced, a number of private video rental operators raised objections to what they perceived as unfair competition. While CLA is not aware of any library that got out of lending videotapes as a result of such challenges, it does appear that libraries were careful to diffuse such criticism by not competing with the video rental outlet's core business—recent Hollywood feature films. In the early years it was common for library video collections not to contain any feature films. Since the early days of these collections, the prohibition on current Hollywood features has relaxed considerably in most libraries. While libraries do apply critical standards to the acquisition of video, there has been an increasing overlap between library holdings and the collections offered by commercial rental outlets.

Resources: Video (and subsequently DVD) collections now constitute an estimated 6% of public library holdings and contribute a considerably higher portion of circulation, over 15% in some instances. In 2000, 73 Canadian public libraries serving communities of over 50,000 in population reported a combined audio-visual materials expenditure of $7,195,000, the bulk of which would have been videos and DVDs.

Government measures: Provincial legislation in most jurisdictions prohibits libraries from charging for the lending of items whether they be books or such items as video tapes. Given the legislated free provision of tax funded video and DVD collections in direct competition with commercial entities, this service appears to CLA to be a candidate for a GATS challenge.

3. PROVISION OF INTERNET ACCESS

Definition & rationale: Internet access is central to the responsibility of libraries as stated in the Canadian Library Association Statement on Intellectual Freedom: "to acquire and make available the widest variety of materials in order to guarantee and facilitate access to all expressions of knowledge and intellectual activity". The Internet enables libraries and library users free access to resources that might otherwise be inaccessible. With the emergence of the Internet as a fundamental tool for learning, it is critically important that technology be available to everyone, regardless of race, gender, income or age.

History: In 1994, the Government of Canada established the private sector Information Highway Advisory Council (IHAC) to provide advice on the best way to develop Canada's Information Highway. Public, school, academic and special libraries figured prominently in the plans to prevent the development of an "information divide" between "haves" and "have-nots".

The Government of Canada has made a commitment to make sure all Canadians have access to the Internet, regardless of where they live or the size of their income. Since the launch of "Connecting Canadians" in 1998, significant progress has been made to connect Canadians to each other and the world, with the aim of making Canada a global leader in information and communications technologies. The Government has been delivering on this commitment through programs that develop the infrastructure required and are tailored to address the various needs of Canadians. SchoolNet and LibraryNet provide Internet resources to Canada's public schools, libraries and First Nations schools. The Community Access Program (CAP) has been establishing free or affordable public Internet access in urban, rural and remote communities across Canada. CAP has helped to establish more than 4,200 sites; in all, some 10,000 sites were operating by March 31, 2001.

Currently, there are over 6,200 public Internet workstations in public libraries with catchment populations of 50,000 people or more. By early 2001, more than one in two Canadians was using the Internet. Today many adults and children have their first hands-on experience with computers at their public library.

Resources: In addition to these and other government driven programs to expand public access to the Internet, Canadian libraries have benefited from the Gates Library Initiative. Its Canadian partnership was launched in October of 1998 and, through Statistics Canada, provincial and territorial governments, the eligibility of libraries is being established. The Foundation partners with libraries in low-income communities in Canada to provide computers, technical training and Internet access. Approximately half of Canada's 3,300 public libraries are eligible for grants from the Gates Library Initiative. Canadian libraries of all types are leveraging their investment in technology to generate programs and services that support an information literate populace.

Government Measures: There is no direct government measure that legislates free public access to the Internet. Direct and indirect government involvement in developing the infrastructure to facilitate broad access to the Internet has been outlined above, but exploitation of the infrastructure is available to public sector and private sector organizations alike. As public use and interest increases, so will commercial Internet service providers see opportunities for the expansion of fee-based services. In this environment, the access provided free of charge to the public by libraries, may well be seen as subsidized competition.

4. DOCUMENT DELIVERY SERVICES

Definition: Some university, public and specialized research libraries offer document delivery services to local small businesses or specialized professional communities (such as health professionals), nominally on a cost-recovery basis. The services deliver published documents using the library's own collections, augmented by commercial document delivery services or the collections of other libraries. (The most sophisticated document delivery services offered to private and public sector institutions by a publicly funded library are those offered by the Canadian Institute of Scientific and Technical Information, (CISTI). Unlike all other library service providers, CISTI was established specifically by the Government of Canada to support the scientific research needs of government and other research institutions nationally.)

History & rationale: From the 1980s onwards, a few major university and public libraries have developed document delivery services for local business and other institutions in their area. These institutions would normally be free to consult the collections and information resources at the libraries concerned. The document delivery services provide greater convenience, by undertaking to retrieve or locate the publication needed and sending it to the company or private research institution. An example is IBIS at the University of Waterloo (/www.lib.uwaterloo.ca/IBIS).

Resources: Typically, the business model on which these services are based is the recovery of mainly direct costs (staffing, telecommunications and delivery costs) but not recovery of the full indirect costs, which would include a proportion of the costs of acquiring, processing and maintaining collections, general administrative costs, the physical building infrastructure and so on. The principle underlying these services is that only the 'added value' of retrieval and delivery to the workplace or desktop of the researcher/enquirer should be fee-based, since the mandate of publicly funded libraries is to provide access to information resources to support the needs of their community freely. Proportionally the indirect costs far exceed the direct costs, and therefore these services are heavily subsidized.

Government Measures: These services form a natural extension of making materials and information resources available to the public or a specific community (in the case of academic libraries). To that degree therefore they operate under delegated authority. In addition, such services support the longstanding Government policy, recently under discussion in the context of Canada's Innovation Strategy, that 'recognizes the need to consider knowledge as a strategic national asset. It focuses on how to strengthen our science and research capacity and on how to ensure that this knowledge contributes to building an innovative economy that benefits all Canadians . . ." However, to a greater or lesser degree, these services are subsidized, and compete with commercial ventures and are therefore potentially exposed to a challenge under the provisions of GATS.

5. VIRTUAL REFERENCE & INFORMATION SERVICES

Definition of service: Virtual reference can be defined as "the provision of reference services, involving collaboration between a library user and a librarian, in a computer-based medium." To date, virtual reference services include email reference and real-time chat reference. Typically, public library users can find the public library's website and click on a link entitled "Ask a question". Public and academic libraries in Canada today are customarily offering email service, and are gradually introducing real-time chat services. Libraries often rely on their existing partnerships and consortial agreements in order to successfully provide virtual reference services. Examples of these combined efforts include the Saskatchewan Provincial Libraries' "Ask Us!" service (www.lib.sk.ca/askus), and the Vancouver Public Library's "Quick Information Service", which serves all BC residents (www.vpl.ca/branches/LibrarySquare/qis/emailref/eRefIntro.html). "Virtual Reference Canada" is a project that is developing under the leadership of the National Library of Canada. It is a free e-reference service that includes participating libraries from all sectors across the country. Future service models include the possibility of partnering with institutions in other time zones in order to provide longer hours of service. As users become more and more computer literate, and as more and more library resources become available online, the importance of these services will grow.

Rationale: Virtual reference is seen as an extension of traditional reference service, which for years has been offered to members of the public or a specific community in person and by phone. The information and assistance offered provides factual answers to specific questions and supports the discovery and use of a range of information resources for research or leisure. The services support an academic community of students, researchers and teachers, or the general public and public library users, but also remote users and those who cannot physically go to the library. The rationale for this service, as for traditional library services, is that making information available, irrespective of the ability to pay, is a social good in a free and democratic society.

History: Libraries began to offer email reference services in the mid-to-late 1990s, when email and internet use became part of everyday life for many Canadians at work and at home. This introduction roughly coincides with the development of the Web, and of Web-based information services such as 'Ask Jeeves", which are offered to the public free of charge but are financed through advertising, and Internet services offered on a subscription basis, such as AOL.

Resources: The principal resources required to provide virtual reference services are staff time and expertise. These services are usually seamlessly interwoven with established reference and information service delivery. The provision of real-time chat reference is more demanding, and may lead to higher service costs, but still a very small impact on the overall budget of the library.

Government measures: Government support is involved in the provision of virtual reference services, since the institutions offering the services are public sector institutions. There have also been specific federal and provincial government grants awarded to virtual reference projects in academic libraries. The development of the Web and ubiquitous use of the Internet have lead to commercial ventures and the perception that there are significant opportunities in the sphere of information mediation and distribution and research services. As a result, a challenge to publicly funded institutions that offer virtual reference services is possible under the GATS discipline.

CONCLUSION

In conclusion, CLA believes that, for trade negotiations in the services area to progress, signatories to the Agreement must recognize the independence and legitimacy of the not-for-profit sector, a sector that is the result of neither competitive market forces, nor government decree. Canada has an opportunity to demonstrate leadership in this regard by addressing the issues that are of concern to the library community and by proposing that clarifying language be added to Part I, Scope and Definition, of the Agreement.

At a time when the Government and Canadians are embarked upon a broad-based initiative to define a national innovation strategy, nothing should be done to undermine the critical role played by the not-for-profit sector in marshalling, preserving, and making easily and freely available information resources in this country.

CLA hopes that after reviewing our concerns you might be in a position to meet with us to discuss the appropriate next steps.

Yours truly,
Wendy Newman
President
cc. The Honourable Pierre Pettigrew Minister of International Trade

Available at Canadian Library Association, Correspondence, http://www.cla.ca/issues/robertson.htm (accessed 16 October, 2005).

GATS Glossary

Appellate Body The standing seven-member panel that considers appeals in WTO disputes. When any party to a dispute appeals a decision from the WTO Panel, three of the members of Appellate Body review the findings and issue reports that uphold, modify, or reverse the findings of the panels. Members serve four-year terms.

Bretton Woods Institutions Includes the World Bank and the International Monetary Fund, which were set up at a meeting at Bretton Woods, New Hampshire, in 1943. The third institution planned at these meetings, the International Trade Organisation (ITO), never materialized.

Council for Trade in Services The ongoing body that oversees the functioning of the General Agreement on Trade in Services and reports to the General Council.

Dispute Settlement Body The permanent WTO body that is empowered to set up panels, to adopt panel and appellate body reports, and to implement the results of the decisions. The General Council of the WTO also sits as the Dispute Settlement Body.

Dispute Settlement Understanding (DSU) The WTO Agreement (Annex 2) that covers dispute settlement. The full title is "*Understanding on Rules and Procedures Governing the Settlement of Disputes*."

Doha Declaration The November 2001 declaration of the Fourth Ministerial Conference in Doha, Qatar, which set forth the continuing mandate for negotiations on various subjects and which addresses issues concerning the further implementation of the WTO Agreements.

General Agreement on Trade in Services (GATS) The WTO Agreement (Annex 1B) that lays down the rules under which international trade in services may take place among WTO Members. GATS is a framework agreement; that is, the agreement sets forth only general provisions. The actual substance of the agreements—that is, the details of each member's commitments—is determined through an ongoing process of negotiation in successive rounds.

GATT The General Agreement on Tariffs and Trade, which has been superseded as an international organization by the WTO. The updated GATT is now the WTO agreement governing trade in goods.

GATT 1947 The official term for the pre-1994 version of the GATT.

GATT 1994 The official term for new version of the General Agreement, which is included in the WTO Agreement and which incorporates GATT 1947. GATT 1994 is one of several agreements referred to as Multilateral Agreements on Trade in Goods that are included in the WTO Agreement as Annex 1A.

General Council The body located in Geneva that manages the day-to-day operations of the WTO between Ministerial Conferences. Each member country has a representative on the council. The Council for Trade in Goods, the Council for Trade in Services, and the Intellectual Property Council all report to the General Council.

horizontal commitments GATS disciplines that apply across the board. They are termed "horizontal" or "top-down" provisions because the rules are applicable unless a country claims an exemption for an entire, or aspect of, a service. Most Favoured Nation is an example of a horizontal commitment. In contrast, bottom-up commitments (such as National Treatment) apply only to those sectors for which a commitment was made on the country's schedule.

market access The ability of firms from one country to conduct business in another country. Market access also refers to the extent to which a country permits imported goods and services to enter its territory and be sold or consumed in competition with domestic products.

measures Actions taken by central, regional, or local governments of members as well as governmental authorities and even certain nongovernmental bodies that exercise delegated powers. The term *measure* is defined very broadly and can be in the form of a law, regulation, rule, procedure, administrative action, or other form. The GATS rules apply to all measures by members affecting trade in services.

Ministerial Conference The highest-level decision-making body of the WTO, consisting of the trade ministers of the WTO members. The Ministerial Conference meets every two years and is referred to by the location of the meeting:

1st Ministerial Conference held in Singapore, December 1996
2nd Ministerial Conference held in Geneva, May 1998

3rd Ministerial Conference held in Seattle, November–December 1999
4th Ministerial Conference held in Doha, 2001
5th Ministerial Conference held in Cancun, September 2003
6th Ministerial Conference held in Hong Kong, December 2005

modes of supply The manner in which trade in services are supplied and consumed (also referred to as modes of delivery). There are four distinct modes of supply:

1. cross-border supply, whereby only the service crosses a border;
2. consumption abroad, usually involving the consumer traveling to the supplying country;
3. foreign commercial presence—that is, having an office, branch, or subsidiary in a foreign country; and
4. movement of natural persons across borders—that is, a national of one country physically present and providing services in another country.

Most-Favoured Nation (MFN) The principle of not discriminating between one's trading partners. GATS requires that each Member shall accord immediately and unconditionally to services and service suppliers of any other Member such treatment that is no less favorable than it accords to like services and service suppliers of any other country. The goal of MFN is to avoid situations in which countries provide preferential treatment to some countries without affording that same treatment to all WTO members. MFN is a "top-down" commitment; it applies regardless of whether the sector is listed in the schedule of commitments. However, the requirement of MFN is not absolute; a member can maintain a measure inconsistent with the general MFN requirement if it has established an exception for this inconsistency.

National Treatment The principle of giving foreign nationals the same treatment as one's own nationals. The National Treatment obligation applies only to sectors in which a country has made GATS commitments (known as a "bottom-up" commitment). If the sector is covered, then the member must grant foreign services and service suppliers treatment no less favorable than it grants domestic services and suppliers.

Nontariff Trade Barrier A variety of domestic measures other than direct tariffs that may result in the discouragement of international trade. Nontariff barriers include customs procedures, administrative requirements, as well as a range of domestic regulations pertaining to health, safety, the environment, and labor standards.

rounds A set of multilateral negotiations in which countries exchange commitments to reduce tariffs and agree to extensions of the GATT rules. The rounds from the beginning of GATT 1947 through the present have been as follows:

1947	Geneva Round
1949	Annecy Round
1950–1951	Torquay Round
1955–1956	Geneva Round
1960–1961	Dillon Round
1963–1967	Kennedy Round
1973–1979	Tokyo Round
1986–1994	Uruguay Round
2002–	Doha Round

Schedule of Commitments Listings adopted by each member country that sets forth the commitments accepted by WTO members under the GATS. The Schedule is organized according to the Services Sectoral Classification List, and it outlines the specific commitments each country makes in a given sector and lists any conditions on that commitment.

Services Sectoral Classification List A classification system consisting of twelve sectors into which all services are divided. The twelve sectors are as follows:

1. Business Services
2. Communication Services
3. Construction and Related Engineering Services
4. Distributional Services
5. Educational Services
6. Environmental Services
7. Financial Services
8. Health-Related and Social Services
9. Tourism and Travel-Related Services
10. Recreational, Cultural, and Sporting Services
11. Transport Services
12. Other Services Not Included Elsewhere

Each sector is further subdivided into various subsectors. For example, sector 10 includes subsectors A (entertainment services), B (news agency services), C (libraries, museums, archives, and other cultural services), D (sporting and other recreational services), and E (other). It is important to note that various activities might be included within multiple classifications.

services supplied in the exercise of governmental authority Services that are supplied neither on a commercial basis nor in competition with other suppliers.

subsidies Benefits conferred by the government, including any direct or indirect payments made, or revenues forgone. Export subsidies are such benefits as are contingent on exports. A domestic subsidy is a benefit not so linked to exports.

tariff A duty or tax on goods imposed at the border. Traditionally, international-trade agreements were concerned with limiting the distorting effects of tariffs. The WTO agreements have expanded the scope of the international trade regime to include the regulation of various nontariff barriers.

trade in services The supply of a service by a service supplier to a service consumer, through any of the four modes of supply of a service, across national borders.

trade liberalization The process of reducing tariff and nontariff barriers, in order to encourage international trade in goods and services with the ultimate objective of achieving free trade at a regional or global level.

TRIPS Agreement The Agreement on Trade-Related Aspects of Intellectual Property, contained in Annex 1C to the WTO Agreement.

Uruguay Round The multilateral trade negotiations launched at Punta del Este, Uruguay, in September 1986, concluded in Geneva in December 1993, and signed by the Ministers in Marrakesh, Morocco, in April 1994.

Uruguay Round Agreements The package of trade agreements concluded by at the end of the Uruguay Round. The main agreement is the WTO Agreement, to which are annexed all the other trade agreements, decisions, and understandings agreed to during the Uruguay Round. The annexed trade agreements include the GATT, GATS, TRIPS, the Agreement on Agriculture, and the Dispute Settlement Understanding.

World Trade Organization (WTO) Agreement The main agreement resulting from the Uruguay Round (more formally known as the *Marrakesh Agreement Establishing the World Trade Organization, Apr. 15, 1994*), to which all of the other trade agreements (such as GATT, GATS, TRIPS, and the DSU) are annexed.

Bibliography

BIBLIOGRAPHIC NOTE

We recommend the 20-page guide GATS and Libraries Pathfinder, prepared by Sabina Iseli-Otto (September 2005), found at www.cla.ca/resources/GATS_Pathfinder.pdf. It can also be accessed on the Canadian Library Association website (www.cla.ca) under "Resources~Government Information." It provides introductory information on the WTO and the GATS and numerous links to useful documents and articles.

Abelsnes, Kristine. "Fees for Library Services." *IFLANET Social Responsibilities Discussion Group Paper.* Paris: IFLA, 1998. www.ifla.org/VII/dg/srdg/srdg1.htm (accessed 10 July 2005).

Albanese, Andrew Richard. "Foundations for the Future." *Library Journal* 127, no. 8 (1 May 2002): 40–43.

Alberta, Alberta Community Development. "Library Statistics Year 2004." *Building Strong Communities*. Edmonton: Government of Alberta, 2004. www.cd.gov.ab.ca/building_communities/public_library/statistics/statistics/index.asp (accessed 10 July 2005).

American Association of Law Libraries. "Comments of the American Library Association, Association of Research Libraries, American Association of Law Libraries, Medical Library Association, and Special Libraries Association on the Second Draft Consolidated Texts of the Free Trade Area of the Americas Agreement." *Washington Affairs.* Washington: Georgetown University Law Library, 31 January 2003. www.ll.georgetown.edu/aallwash/lt01312003.html (accessed 8 July 2005).

———. *Library-Related Principles for the International Development Agenda of the World Intellectual Property Organization*. Washington: Georgetown University Law Library, 26 Jan. 2005. www.ll.georgetown.edu/aallwash/Principles012605.pdf (accessed 8 July 2005).

——. "RE: U.S.–Chile and U.S.–Singapore Free Trade Agreements." *Washington Affairs,* 19 June 2003. www.ll.georgetown.edu/aallwash/lt06192003.html (accessed 8 July 2005).

——. "Supplemental Comments of the American Association of Law Libraries, the American Library Association, the Association of Research Libraries and the Special Libraries Association on the Second Draft Consolidated Texts of the Free Trade Area of the Americas Agreement." *Washington Affairs,* 28 February 2003. www.ll.georgetown.edu/aallwash/lt02282003.html (accessed 8 July 2005).

American Library Association. *Access to Electronic Information Services and Networks*. Chicago: ALA, 2004. www.ala.org/alaorg/oif/electacc.html (accessed 10 July 2005).

——. *@ your library®—The Campaign for America's Libraries*. Chicago: ALA, 2005. www.ala.org/ala/development/majorfundraising/campaignforlibraries/campaign-americas.htm (accessed 10 July 2005).

——. "Call for Oversight on GPO Initiatives." *Washington Office Newsline* 14, no. 006 (27 January 2005). www.ala.org/ala/washoff/washnews/2005ab/006jan27.htm (accessed 10 July 2005).

——. *Economic Barriers to Information Access: An Interpretation of the Library Bill of Rights*. Chicago: ALA, 1993. www.ala.org/ala/oif/statementspols/statementsif/interpretations/economicbarriers.pdf (accessed 10 July 2005).

——. *Equity of Access*. Chicago: ALA, 2004. www.ala.org/ala/ourassociation/governingdocs/keyactionareas/equityaction/equitybrochure.htm (accessed 10 July 2005).

——. *FBI in Your Library*. Washington: ALA, 2005. www.ala.org/Template.cfm?Section=Intellectual_Freedom_Issues&Template=/ContentManagement/ContentDisplay.cfm&ContentID=21662 (accessed 10 July 2005).

——. *Less Access to Less Information*. Washington: ALA, 2005. www.ala.org/ala/washoff/WOissues/governmentinfo/lessacc.htm (accessed 10 July 2005).

——. *Libraries: An American Value*. Chicago: ALA, 1999. www.ala.org/ala/oif/statementspols/americanvalue/librariesamerican.htm (accessed 10 July 2005).

——. *Links to Washington Office Issues*. Washington: ALA, 2005. www.ala.org/ala/washoff/WOissues/issues.htm (accessed 8 July 2005).

——. *Outsourcing and Privatization* (website). Chicago: ALA, 2003. www.ala.org/ala/ourassociation/governingdocs/aheadto2010/outsourcing.htm (accessed 10 July 2005).

——. "Privatization of Publicly Funded Libraries (ALA Policy 52.7)." *Outsourcing and Privatization in American Libraries*. Chicago: ALA, 2001. www.ala.org/ala/oif/iftoolkits/outsourcing/alapolicy.htm#privatizationpolicy (accessed 10 July 2005).

——. "PubSCIENCE Is Discontinued." *ALAWON: American Library Association Washington Office Newsline* 11, no. 89 (12 November 2002). www.ala.org/ala/washoff/washnews/20026/89nov12.htm (accessed 9 July 2005).

——. "Recommendation on Privatization of Publicly Funded Libraries. (ALA Policy 52.7)." *Outsourcing and Privatization in Libraries.* Chicago: ALA, 2001. www.ala.org/ala/oif/iftoolkits/outsourcing/recommendation.htm (accessed 10 July 2005).

———. "Resolution on Protecting the Interests of America's Libraries Under the WTO General Agreement on Trade in Services." CD #20.7. Chicago: ALA, 2001–2002. www.libr.org/GATS/GATSresol.pdf (accessed 8 July 2005).

American Library Association Outsourcing Task Force. *Outsourcing & Privatization in American Libraries*. Chicago: ALA, 1999. www.ala.org/ala/oif/iftoolkits/outsourcing/outsourcingamericanlibs.htm (accessed 9 July 2005).

Arlington, Virginia, Dept. of Libraries. *Arlington Public Library: Putting the World within Reach*. Arlington, Va.: City of Arlington, n.d. www.arlingtonva.us/Departments/Libraries/LibrariesMain.aspx (accessed 9 July 2005).

Association for Computing Machinery. *The ACM Digital Library*. (New York: ACM, 2005). http://portal.acm.org/dl.cfm (accessed 9 July 2005).

Association of College and Research Libraries. *Opening Day Collection: A List of 1,776 Books the Editors of CHOICE feel Should Be on the Shelves of Every Academic Library when it Opens its doors.* Chicago: ACRL, 1967.

Association of Research Libraries. *PubSCIENCE: A Unique and Needed Scientific Resource*. Washington: ARL, 2002. www.arl.org/info/frn/nsletter/pubscience02.html (accessed 9 July 2005).

Auld, Hampton, ed. "Patrons, Customers, Users, Clients: Who Are They and What Difference Does It Make What We Call Them?" *Public Libraries* 43, no. 2 (March/April 2004): 81–87.

Australia, Parliament, Senate, Senate Environment, Communications, Information Technology and the Arts Reference Committee. *Libraries in the Online Environment*. Canberra: Australian Senate, 2003. www.aph.gov.au/senate/committee/ecita_ctte/completed_inquiries/2002-04/online_libraries/report/index.htm (accessed 10 July 2005).

Beachcalifornia.com (website). *Leisure World.* Sunset Beach, Calif.: California Travel News, 2004. www.beachcalifornia.com/seal5.html (accessed 10 July 2005).

BDO Dunwoody LLP. "2001 Alberta Budget Report." *BDO Federal and Provincial Budget Reports.* Toronto: BDO, 24 April 2003. www.bdo.ca/en/library/publications/taxpub/budgetreports/al0401.cfm (accessed 10 July 2005).

Bendor-Samuel, Peter. "Is 'Contracting' or 'Contracting Out' Just Different Terminology for 'Outsourcing'?" OutsourcingCenter (website). Dallas, Tex.: Everest Co., 2004. www.outsourcing-faq.com (accessed 10 July 2005).

Bennett, Colin J. "How States Utilize Foreign Evidence." *Journal of Public Policy* 11, no. 1 (1991): 31–54.

Bernan Associates (website). Lanham, Md.: Bernan, 2004. www.bernan.com (accessed 9 July 2005).

Berry, John N. "Don't Let Government off the Hook." *Library Journal* 127, no. 8 (1 May 2002): 43.

Bertot, John Carlo, and Charles R. McClure. "Summary Findings and Data Tables." *Public Libraries and the Internet 2000*. Washington: NCLIS, 2000. www.nclis.gov/statsurv/2000plo.pdf (accessed 10 July 2005).

Bill & Melinda Gates Foundation. *Toward Equality of Access: The Role of Public Libraries in Addressing the Digital Divide*. Seattle, Wash.: Bill & Melinda Gates Foundation, 2004. www.gatesfoundation.org/nr/Downloads/libraries/uslibraries/reports/TowardEqualityofAccess.pdf (accessed 10 July 2005).

Bishoff, Liz, and Sally G. Reed. *ALA Proposal on Outsourcing and Privatization*. Chicago: ALA, 2001. www.ala.org/Template.cfm?Section=outsourcing&Template=/ContentManagement/ContentDisplay.cfm&ContentID=19799 (accessed 9 July 2005).

BitPass (website). Menlo Park, Calif.: BitPass, Inc. 2004. www.bitpass.com (accessed 10 July 2005).

Brady, Mike, Richard McCoy, Stewart McLeod, Ron Patton, and Bill Woodcock. *Introducing Best Value*. 1999 IPWEA Overseas Study Tour Group Report. Sydney, Australia: Institute of Public Works Engineering, 1999. www.ipwea.org.au/upload/best_value.pdf (accessed 10 July 2005).

Braman, Sandra. "Defining Information: An Approach for Policymakers." *Telecommunications Policy* 13, no. 3 (1989): 233–242.

———. "The Unique Characteristics of Information Policy and Their U.S. Consequences." In *Information Literacies for the Twenty-First Century*, edited by Virgil L. P. Blake and Renee Tjoumas, 47–77. Boston: G. K. Hall, 1990.

British Columbia, Ministry of Aboriginal, Community and Women's Services. *Public Library Services. Public Libraries in British Columbia: Policy and Legislation*. Victoria, BC: Government of British Columbia, 2004. www.mcaws.gov.bc.ca/lgd/public_libraries/index.htm#policy (accessed 10 July 2005).

British Columbia. Ministry of Employment and Investment. *GATS and Public Service Systems: The GATS 'Governmental Authority' Exclusion*. Victoria: Government of British Columbia, 2 Apr. 2001. http://members.iinet.net.au/~jenks/GATS_BC2001.html (accessed 8 July 2005).

British Columbia Library Association. *Statement and Guidelines on Public Library User* Fees. Vancouver: BCLA, 1995. www.bcla.bc.ca/default.aspx (accessed 10 July 2005).

British Columbia Library Association, Information Policy Committee. *Globalization, GATS and the WTO*. Vancouver: BCLA, n.d. www.vcn.bc.ca/bcla-ip/globalization (accessed 8 July 2005).

Brodart Books. *McNaughton: Popular Reading*. Williamsport, Pa.: Brodart, 2004. www.books.brodart.com/products/mcnaughton.htm (accessed 17 March 2006).

———. *Opening Day Services*. Williamsport, Pa.: Brodart, 2004. www.books.brodart.com/plibraries/opendayserv.htm (accessed 10 July 2005).

Browne, Mairéad. "The Field of Information Policy: 1. Fundamental Concepts." *Journal of Information Science* 23, no. 4 (1997): 261–275.

Budd, John M. "A Critique of Customer and Commodity." *College and Research Libraries* 58, no. 4 (July 1997): 310–321.

Bunge, Charles A., and Richard E. Bopp. "History and Varieties of Reference Services." In *Reference and Information Services: An Introduction*, edited by Linda C. Smith and Richard E. Bopp, 3–37. Englewood, Colo.: Libraries Unlimited, 2001.

Buschman, John E. *Dismantling the Public Sphere: Situating and sustaining Librarianship in the Age of the New Public Philosophy*. Westport, Conn.: Libraries Unlimited, 2003.

———. "Staying Public: The Real Crisis in Librarianship." *American Libraries* 35, no.7 (August 2004): 40–42.

California Library Association. *Fees for Public Library Services* (Position Statement adopted November 18, 1997). Sacramento, Calif.: CLA, 1997. www.cla-net.org/aboutcla/policies.php (5 July 2005).

Canada Dept. of Canadian Heritage. "New Advertising Services Measure to Promote Canadian Culture." News Release, 29 July 1998. www.canadianheritage.gc.ca/newsroom/news_e.cfm?Action=Display&code=8NR064E (accessed 10 July 2005).

Canada Europa Mundi. Canada–EU Joint Statement on the World Trade Organization (WTO), June 2001. Ottawa: Dept. of Foreign Affairs and International Trade, 2001. Related Documents. Statements. www.dfait-maeci.gc.ca/canada-europa/mundi/canada-eu-c-1-en.asp (accessed 17 March 2006).

Canada Language Council (website). Ottawa: CLC, 2004. www.c-l-c.ca (accessed 9 July 2005).

Canadian Association of Private Language Schools (website). Surrey, B.C.: CAPLS, 2004. www.capls.com (accessed 9 July 2005).

Canadian Federation of Students. "How the GATS Threatens Post-Secondary Education." *Fact Sheet* 7, no. 4 (February 2001). www.cfs-fcee.ca/html/english/research/factsheets/fs-7(4)-gats.pdf (accessed 8 July 2005).

Canadian Library Association. *Canadian Guidelines on Library and Information Services for People with Disabilities*. Ottawa: CLA, 1997. www.cla.ca/about/disabils.htm (accessed 9 July 2005).

———. *Canadian Library Association Perspective on the World Trade Organization Meetings*. Ottawa: CLA, 1999. www.cla.ca/about/wto.htm (accessed 8 July 2005).

———. *Library Issues—CLA Briefs*. Ottawa: CLA, 2005. www.cla.ca/issues/clabrief.htm (accessed 8 July 2005).

———. *Corporate Sponsorship Agreement in Libraries: Position Statement*. Ottawa: CLA, 1997. www.cla.ca/about/sponsor.htm (accessed 10 July 2005).

———. *Information and Telecommunication Access Principles*. Ottawa: CLA, 1994. www.cla.ca/about/access.htm (accessed 10 July 2005).

———. *Statement on Intellectual Freedom*. Ottawa: CLA, 1974, amended 1985. www.cla.ca/about/intfreed.htm (accessed 10 July 2005).

———. *Statement on Internet Access*. Ottawa: CLA, 1997, revised 2000. www.cla.ca/about/internet.htm (accessed 10 July 2005).

Canadian Library Association WTO/GATS Working Group. "*WTO/GATS/FTAA Related Resource*." Ottawa: CLA, 2001. www.cla.ca/resources/gats_resources.htm (accessed 8 July 2005)

Charles, John A. "Check Out Library Fees." *Cascade Commentaries* No. 2002-13. Portland, Ore.: Cascade Policy Institute, 2002. www.cascadepolicy.org/pdf/fiscal/2002_13.pdf (accessed 10 July 2005).

Chelton, Mary K. "Three in Five Public Library Users Are Youth; Implications of Survey Results from the National Center for Education Statistics." *Public Libraries* 36, no. 2 (March/April, 1997): 104–108. Abstract available at www.ifla.org/VII/s10/irayls/users.htm (accessed 9 July 2005).

Choi, Won-Mog. *"Like Products" in International Trade Law: Towards a Consistent GATT/WTO Jurisprudence*. Oxford: Oxford University Press, 2003.

Chun, Janean. "Franchise Frenzy." *Entrepreneur Magazine* 25, no. 1 (January 1997): 160, 162–163. www.entrepreneur.com/mag/article/0,1539,226846,00.html (accessed 9 July 2005).

Chute, Adrienne, P. Elaine Kroe, Patricia Garner, Marcia Polcari, and Cynthia Jo Ramsey. "Public Libraries in the United States Fiscal Year 2000." *Education Statistics Quarterly* 4, no. 3 (2003). http://nces.ed.gov/programs/quarterly/vol_4/4_3/5_1.asp (accessed 9 July 2005).

Cleveland Public Library. "Interlibrary Loan." Cleveland: CPL, 2004. www.cpl.org/Locations.asp?FormMode=IL (accessed 9 July 2005).

Coffman, Steve. "Saving Ourselves: Plural Funding for Public Libraries." *Library Journal* 127, no. 8 (February 2004): 39.

Coffman, Steve, and Linda Arret. "To Chat or Not to Chat—Taking Another Look at Virtual Reference, Part 1." *Searcher* 12, no. 7 (July/August 2004). www.infotoday.com/searcher/jul04/arret_coffman.shtml (accessed 10 July 2005);

———. "To Chat or Not to Chat—Taking Another Look at Virtual Reference, Part 2." *Searcher* 12, no. 8 (September 2004). www.infotoday.com/searcher/sep04/arret_coffman.shtml (accessed 10 July 2005).

Corson-Finnerty, Adam, and Ann Blanchard. *Fundraising and Friend-Raising on the Web: A Handbook for Libraries and Other Non-Profit Organizations*. Chicago: ALA Editions, 1998.

Council of Europe. *Directive Concerning the Processing of Personal Data and the Protection of Privacy* (97/66/EC). Brussels: European Union, 1997.

———. *Directive on the Protection of Individuals with Regard to the Processing of Personal Data and on the Free Movement of Such Data*, (95/46/EC). Brussels: European Union, 1995.

County of Los Angeles Public Library. *Homework Centers*. Downey, Calif.: COLA, 2004. www.colapublib.org/children/parents/hmwork.html (accessed 9 July 2005).

Crane, Gregory. "Commercial Digital Libraries and the Academic Community." *D-Lib Magazine* 7, no. 1 (January 2001). www.dlib.org/dlib/january01/crane/01crane.html (accessed 1 July 2005).

Crocker, Steve. "The Siren Song of Internet Micropayments." *IMP Magazine on Information Impacts* (April 1999): 22. www.merchantseek.com/article9.htm (accessed 10 July 2005).

Digital Denmark—Conversion to the Networked Society. Copenhagen: Forskningsministeriet [Ministry of Science, Technology and Innovation], 2000. www.detdigitaledanmark.dk/english (accessed 10 July 2005).

Dolan, Elizabeth, and Liwen Vaughan. *Electronic Access to Canadian Federal Government Information: How Prepared Are the Depository Libraries? (Report to Depository Services Program, Canadian Government Publishing, Public Works and Government Services Canada*). Ottawa: Depository Services Program, 1997. http://dsp-psd.communication.gc.ca/Rapports/DV/rep1-e.html (accessed 10 July 2005).

Donlan, Jeffrey. "We Must Protect State Library Funding." *Library Journal* 128, no. 12 (July 2003): 50.

Dorman, David. "Ebrary at Bat." *American Libraries* 33, no. 1 (January 2002): 96–97.

ebrary (website). "ebrary Discover." Palo Alto, Calif.: ebrary, Inc. 2005. http://shop.ebrary.com (accessed 10 July 2005).

Egholm, Charlotte, and Henrick Jochumsen. "Perspectives Concerning User Fees in Pubic Libraries." *Information Management* 21, no. 6 (2000): 298–306.

Entrepreneur.com (website). Irvine, Calif.: Entrepreneur Inc., 2005. www.entrepreneur.com (accessed 9 July 2005).

———. "Kumon Math and Reading Centers." Irvine, Calif.: Entrepreneur Inc., 2005. www.entrepreneur.com/franzone/details/0,5885,12-12-282507-,00.html (accessed 9 July 2005).

Eurolingua Institute (website). Douglas, U.K.: Eurolingua Institute, 2004. www.eurolingua.com (accessed 9 July 2005).

European Bureau of Library, Information and Documentation Associations. *EBLIDA Position Papers*. The Hague: EBLIDA, 2005. www.eblida.org/position/index.htm (accessed 8 July 2005).

European Commission. *The Lomé Convention: Brief History*. Europa (website). Brussels: European Commission, 2004. http://europa.eu.int/comm/development/body/cotonou/lome_history_en.htm (accessed 8 July 2005).

Evans, G. Edward. *Introduction to Library Public Services*. 6th ed. Englewood, Colo.: Libraries Unlimited, 1999.

Factiva (website). New York: Dow Jones & Reuters, 2004. www.factiva.com (accessed 9 July 2005).

Federal Depository Library Program. "Depository Library Public Service Guidelines for Government Information in Electronic Formats." *Administrative Notes* 19, no. 11 (1998). FDLP Desktop. www.access.gpo.gov/su_docs/fdlp/mgt/pseguide.html (accessed 10 July 2005).

———. "FDLP Internet Use Policy Guidelines." *Administrative Notes* 20, no. 2 (15 January 1999). FDLP Desktop. www.access.gpo.gov/su_docs/fdlp/mgt/iupolicy.html (accessed 10 July 2005).

Fitch, Leslie, and Jody Warner. *Dividends: The Value of Public Libraries in Canada*. Toronto: Book and Periodical Council, 1997. www.nald.ca/fulltext/dividend/cover.htm (accessed 10 July 2005).

Foerstel, Herbert N. *Refuge of a Scoundrel: The Patriot Act in Libraries*. Westport, Conn.: Libraries Unlimited, 2004.

Ford, Peter. "Global Pushback against 'Titanic' Culture: A Proposed UN Treaty Would Protect Nations' Arts." *The Christian Science Monitor* (20 October 2003). www.csmonitor.com/2003/1020/p01s03-wogi.html (accessed 10 July 2005).

"France to Develop Google Rival." *BBC News World Edition*. 17 March 2005. http://new.bbc.uk/2/hi/europe/4358871.stm (23 June 2005).

Franchise Solutions. "Children's Franchises." Portsmouth, N.H.: Franchise Solutions, Corp., 2004. www.franchisesolutions.com/childrens-franchises (accessed 9 July 2005).

Franchise Zone (website). "Educational Services." Entrepreneur.Com, 2005. www.entrepreneur.com/franzone/cats/0,6587,12-12-1-EDUC,00.html (accessed 8 July 2005).

Free Trade Area of the Americas. FTAA Web site, 2005. www.ftaa-alca.org/alca_e.asp (accessed 9 July 2005).

———. *FTAA—Free Trade of the Americas Draft Agreement*. FTAA.TNC/w/133/Rev.3. 21 November 2003. www.ftaa-alca.org/FTAADraft03/Index_e.asp (accessed 9 July 2005).

Freides, Thelma. "The Federal Information Controversy from an Economic Perspective." *College and Research Libraries* 47 (1986), 425–437.

Gell, Marilyn Killibrew. "User Fees I: The Economic Argument." In *Key Papers in the Economics of Information*, edited by Donald W. King, Nancy K. Roderer, and Harold A. Olsen, 154–158. White Plains, N.Y.: Knowledge Industry Publications for the American Society for Information Science, 1983.

General Agreement on Tariffs and Trade (GATT): Punta del Este Declaration, 20 September 1986. *SICE Foreign Trade Information System.* Washington: Organization of American States, 2004. www.sice.oas.org/trade/Punta_e.asp (accessed 9 July 2005).

Global Librarian (website). Vaughan, Ont.: Global Librarian, 2004. www.global librarian.info (accessed 10 July 2005).

Goldberg, Beverly. "What Price Partnerships? Public Librarians Linda Mielke and Sanford Berman Draw Their Bottom Lines over Private-Sector Fundraising." *American Libraries* 29, no. 2 (February 1998): 43–46.

Google. "Company Overview." *Corporate Information.* Mountain View, Calif.: Google, 2005. www.google.com/corporate/index.html (accessed 1 July 2005).

Google Press Center. "Google Checks Out Library Books." Press Release. 14 December 2004. www.google.com/press/pressrel/print_library.html (accessed 9 July 2005).

Google Print. *Library Project*. Mountain View, Calif.: Google, 2005. http://print .google.com/googleprint/library.html (accessed 9 July 2005).

Gordon, Margaret T., Elizabeth J. Moore, and Andrew C. Gordon. *Sustainability in First Ten States to Receive Gates Awards: Most Libraries Maintaining Public Access Computing Programs, But 25% Are Still Fragile (A Report to the Bill & Melinda Gates US Library Program).* Seattle: Public Access Computing Project, Evans School of Public Affairs, University of Washington, 2004. www.gatesfoundation.org/NR/Downloads/libraries/eval_docs/word/sustaina-final-2-13.3.doc (accessed 10 July 2005).

GrantsAlert.com. "Foundation Grants: Starbucks Foundation: Power of Literacy." Tallahassee, Fla.: GrantsAlert.com, 2004. http://grantsalert.com/grants.cfm?id=4& gid=718 (accessed 10 July 2005).

Gregory, Martha. "Entrepreneurial Focus: Fee-Based Service. Tulsa City-County Library. Research Wizard." Handout for an Infopeople.org Workshop "Secrets of a Successful Entrepreneurial Library," California State Library, 2002. Tulsa, Okla.: Tulsa City-County Library, 2002. www.infopeople.org/training/past/2002/entrepreneur/handout2_tulsa.pdf (accessed 24 Mar. 2005, no longer available at this site).

Grieshaber-Otto, Jim, and Matthew Sanger. *Perilous Lessons: The Impact of the WTO Services Agreement (GATS) on Canada's Public Education System*. Ottawa: Canadian Centre for Policy Alternatives, 2002.

Gymboree Play and Music. "Franchise Information." San Francisco, Calif.: Gymboree, 2004. www.playandmusic.com/b2c/customer/francisee.jsp (accessed 9 July 2005).

Hannah, Kathryn Covier. "Alternative Funding for Libraries: A Plan for Success." *Bottom Line* 10, no. 4 (1997): 169–175.

Harbro, Ole. "The Development of Public Libraries in Denmark since 1964." *Advances in Librarianship* 25 (2001): 209–219.

Harger, Elaine. "Editorial: Institutionalizing Silence within the ALA?" *Progressive Librarian* 14 (Spring 1998): 1–4. www.libr.org/PL/14_Editorial.html (accessed 10 July 2005).

Haringey Council. "Libraries." Wood Green, U.K.: Haringey Council, 2005. www.haringey.gov.uk/leisure/libraries.htm (accessed 16 February 2005).

———. "Top Award for Haringey Libraries." Press Release. Wood Green, U.K.: Haringey Council, 2005. www.haringey.gov.uk/pressrelease.htm?id=16947 (accessed 10 July 2005).

Harris, Lesley Ellen. "Micropayments for Libraries, Archives, and Museums." *Copyright and New Media Law Newsletter* 2, no. 3 (1998). http://copyrightlaws.com/newsreps/nrvo2is3.html (accessed 10 July 2005).

Harris, Michael H. *History of Libraries in the Western World*. 4th ed. Metuchen, N.J.: Scarecrow, 1995.

Hennen, Thomas J. "Restore Our Destiny: Full—Not Plural—Funding." *American Libraries* 35, no. 7 (August 2004): 43–45.

HighBeam Research (website). Chicago: HighBeam Research, Inc., 2005. www.highbeam.com (accessed 9 July 2005).

Hill, Michael. *National Information Policies: A Review of the Situation in Seventeen Industrialized Countries, with Particular Reference to Scientific and Technical Information*. The Hague: UNESCO, 1989.

Hudec, Robert. "GATT/WTO Constraints on Domestic Regulation: Requiem for an 'Aims and Effects' Test." *International Lawyer* 32 (1998): 619–649.

Hunt, Fiona. "Hunt's Response to the ALA Washington Office Letter, unpublished by *American Libraries*." Libr.org: Supporting Progressive Librarians since 1998 (website). n.d. http://libr.org/GATS/Hunt-Sheketoff.html (accessed 8 July 2005).

———. "The WTO and the Threat to Libraries." *Progressive Librarian* 18 (Summer 2001). www.libr.org/PL/18_Hunt.html (accessed 10 July 2005).

———. "Why the World Trade Organization Is a Threat to Libraries." *American Libraries* 32, no. 8 (September 2001): 32–33.

Hyman, Karen. "Customer Service and the Rule of 1965." *American Libraries* 30, no. 9 (October 1999): 55–58.

Industry Canada (website). "Community Access Program." Ottawa: Industry Canada, 7 August 2003. http://cap.ic.gc.ca/pub/index.html?iin.lang=en (accessed 10 July 2005).

Industry Canada, LibraryNet. *Internet Connectivity in Public Libraries*. Ottawa: Industry Canada, 2003. http://ln-rb.ic.gc.ca/e/connect/table4.asp (accessed 15 July 2004. The LibraryNet program was discontinued in March 2004, and this document has been removed from the Industry Canada website.

Instant Information Systems. *DocDel.net* (website). Germantown, Md.: Instant Information Systems, 2004. www.docdel.net (accessed 9 July 2005).

International Center for Entrepreneurial Development. (website). Cypress, Tex.: ICED, 2004. www.iced.net (accessed 10 July 2005).

International Federation of Library Associations and Institutions. *The IFLA Position on the World Trade Organization*. The Hague: IFLA, 2001 [latest revision 22 December 2002]. www.ifla.org/III/clm/p1/wto-ifla.htm (accessed 8 July 2005).

International Federation of Library Associations and Institutions Committee on Copyright and Other Legal Matters (CLM). *The IFLA Position on the Geneva Declaration on the Future of WIPO*. The Hague: IFLA, 2004. www.ifla.org/III/clm/CLM-GenevaDeclaration2004.html (accessed 8 July 2005).

——. Committee on Copyright and Other Legal Matters (CLM). The Hague: IFLA, 2005. www.ifla.org/III/clm/copyr.htm (accessed 8 July 2005).

International Responsibilities Task Force of the American Library Association's Social International Responsibilities Roundtable. *Libraries and the World Trade Organization* (website, last modified April 28, 2005). www.pitt.edu/~ttwiss/irtf/wto.html (accessed 8 July 2005).

International Trade Canada. *Dispute Settlement NAFTA—Chapter 11—Investment—Frequently Asked Questions. Trade Negotiations and Agreements.* Ottawa: DFAIT, 2001. www.dfait-maeci.gc.ca/tna-nac/Mun-FAQs-en.asp (accessed 9 July 2005).

The Internet Public Library (website). Ann Arbor, Mich.: School of Information, University of Michigan, n.d. www.ipl.org (accessed 9 July 2005).

Jackson, Andrew, and Matthew Sanger. *When Worlds Collide: Implications of International Trade and Investment Agreements for Non-Profit Social Services*. Ottawa: Canadian Centre for Policy Alternatives, 2002. www.policyalternatives.ca/documents/National_Office_Pubs/wwc_tc_intro.pdf (accessed 8 July 2005).

Jackson, John H. *The World Trading System: Law and Policy of International Economic Relations*. 2nd ed. Cambridge, Mass.: MIT Press, 1997.

Jaeger, John. "User Fees, Community Goods, and the Public Library." *Public Library Quarterly* 17, no. 2 (1999): 49–62.

Johnson, Jon R. *International Trade Law*. Toronto: Irwin Law, 1998.

Johnson, Steve. "How Google Will Scan the World, 1 Book at a Time." *Chicago Tribune*, 25 February 2005, www.chicagotribune.com/technology/chi0502250033feb25,1,3962945.column?ctrack=1&cset=true (accessed 9 July 2005).

Keizer, Greg. "The Best and Worst ISPs." *PC World* (November 2000). www.pcworld.com/reviews/article/0,aid,18624,00.asp (accessed 10 July 2005).

Kent, Calvin A. "The Privatizing of Government Information: Economic Considerations." *Government Publications Review* 16 (1989), 113–132.

Kerkham, Andrew. "Outsourcing." Paper presented at Library Information Association of New Zealand Aotearoa Conference, Napier, NZ, October 2003. www.lianza.org.nz/conference/conference03/papers/kerkham.pdf (24 Mar. 2005).

Khor, Martin. "Offsetting IPRs' Adverse Effects on Access to Knowledge." *Choike.Org: A Portal on Southern Civil Societies*. Montevideo, Uruguay: Third World Institute, n.d.), www.choike.org/nuevo_eng/informes/2630.html (accessed 10 July 2005).

Kniffel, Leonard. "Corporate Sponsorship: The New Direction in Fundraising." *American Libraries* 26, no. 10 (November 1995): 1023–1026.

——. "Libraries Aren't Bookstores, and Patrons Aren't Customers." Editorial. *American Libraries* 28, no. 7 (August 1997): 38.

Kumon Math and Reading Centers (website). Teaneck, N.J.: Kumon North America, Inc., 2004. www.kumon.com (accessed 9 July 2005).

Lafayette Public Library. *Rental Charges*. Lafayette, Colo.: LPL, 2004. www.cityoflafayette.com/page.asp?navid=266 (accessed 1 July 2005).

Language Industry Association/Association de l'industrie de la langue. *Mission and Objectives*. Montreal, Que.: AILIA, 2004. www.ailia.ca/tiki-index.php?page=About_en&bl (accessed 9 July 2005).

Lapham, Lewis. "Tentacles of Rage." *Harper's Magazine* 309, no. 1852 (September 2004): 31–41.

Larson, Elizabeth. "Library Renewals: Private Citizens Are Remaking a Public Institution." *Reason* 25, no. 10 (March 1994): 36–40. www.findarticles.com/p/articles/mi_m1568/is_n10_v25/ai_15138944 (accessed 10 July 2005).

Las Vegas–Clark County Library District. "Tax Assistance." *Research: Info Guides*. Las Vegas: Las Vegas–Clark County Library District, 2005). http://www.lvccld.org/library/info_guides/guide.cfm?guideID=36 (accessed 9 July 2005).

Lee, Marc. "Trade Agreements: What the New Alphabet Soup Means for BC." *BC Commentary, A Quarterly Review of Provincial Social and Economic Trends* 4, no. 1 (Winter 2001). www.policyalternatives.ca/documents/BC_Office_Pubs/bc_commentary/bccwinter01.pdf (accessed 8 July 2005).

Leiper, Jeff. "Corporatespeak: Deconstructing the New Language of Business." *Writer's Block* (Winter 2001). www.writersblock.ca/winter2001/essay.htm (accessed 10 July 2005)

Leisure World Seal Beach (website). Seal Beach, Calif.: Golden Rain Foundation, 2004. www.lwsb.com (accessed 10 July 2005).

Libr.org (website). *The GATS and Libraries* (last updated July 2004). www.libr.org/GATS (accessed 8 July 2005).

Library Associates. *Case Studies*. www.libraryassociates.com/index.php4?page=case (accessed 12 July 2005).

———. "Small Business Profile—Shelf Wealth." *Los Angeles Business Journal,* 15 August 2004. www.libraryassociates.com/index.php4?page=busjourn (accessed 12 July 2005).

Library Funding Associates (website). Brentwood, Tenn.: Library Funding Associates, 2005. www.libraryfunding.com (accessed 31 March 2005).

Library Systems & Services (website). Germantown, Md.: LSSI, 2004. www.lssi.com (accessed 10 July 2005).

Lora, Pat. "Public Library Video Collections: Evolving Issues in Media Management." In *Video Collection Development in Multi-Type Libraries: A Handbook*, edited by Gary P. Handman, 17–32. Westport, Conn.: Greenwood, 1994.

Los Angeles Public Library. "Los Angeles Public Library Rental Facilities." Los Angeles: LAPL, 2004. www.lapl.org/facilities (accessed 9 July 2005).

Love, James. "Proposal on Issues Related to the Control of Anticompetitive Practices in Contractual Licenses, 23 January 2005." Washington: Consumer Project on Technology, 2005. www.cptech.org/a2k/anticompetitive.doc (accessed 10 July 2005).

Lundqvist, Lennart. "Privatization: Towards a Concept of Comparative Policy Analysis." *Journal of Public Policy* 8 (1988): 1–19.

Machlup, Fritz. "Uses, Value, and Benefits of Knowledge." In *Key Papers in the Economics of Information*, edited by Donald W. King, Nancy K. Roderer, and Harold K. Olsen, 245–264. White Plains, N.Y.: Knowledge Industry Publications for the American Society for Information Science, 1983.

Mackenzie, Jane. "The Quiet Storm." *Information for Social Change* 16 (Winter 2002/2003). www.libr.org/ISC/articles/16-Mackenzie.html (accessed 10 July 2005).

Mail Boxes Etc. (website). San Diego, Calif.: MBE, 2004. www.mbe.com (accessed 9 July 2005).

Mardiros, Shelley. "Spreading the Word: Banff's Very Public Library." *Alberta Views* 4, no. 1 (January/February 2001): 37–39. www.albertaviews.ab.ca/janfeb01/janfeb01social2.pdf (accessed 9 July 2005).

Martin, Robert S., et al. *The Impact of Outsourcing and Privatization on Library Services and Management.* Denton, Tex.: School of Library and Information Studies, Texas Woman's University, 2000. www.ala.org/ala/oif/iftoolkits/outsourcing/outsourcing_doc.pdf (accessed 10 July 2005).

Maskus, Keith E. *Intellectual Property Rights in the Global Economy*. Washington: Institute for International Economics, 2000. www.iie.com/publications/chapters_preview/99/2iie2822.pdf (accessed 10 July 2005).

Matsushita, Mitsuo, Thomas J. Schoenbaum, and Petros C. Mavroidis. *The World Trade Organization: Law, Practice and Policy*. Oxford: Oxford University Press, 2003.

Mediavilla, Cindy. *Creating the Full-Service Homework Center in Your Library*. Chicago: ALA, 2001.

Medical Library Association, Government Relations. *Information Issues and Policy.* Chicago: MLA, 2005. www.mlanet.org/government (accessed 8 July 2005).

Merriam-Webster Online. Springfield, Mass.: Merriam-Webster Inc., 2005. www.m-w.com/dictionary.htm (accessed 10 July 2005).

Minneapolis Public Library. "INFORM." Minneapolis: MPL, 2005. www.mplib.org/inform.asp (accessed 9 July 2005).

Mintzberg, Henry. "Managing Government: Governing Management." *Harvard Business Review* 74, no. 3 (May–June 1996): 75–83.

Kent, Allan, Harold Lancour, and Jay E. Daily, eds. *Encyclopedia of Library and Information Science.* New York: Marcel Dekker, 1977. S.v. "Non-Print Material: Sound Recordings, Motion Pictures, and Pictures," by Andrew M. Modelski. 106–107.

Montviloff, Victor. *National Information Policies: A Handbook on the Formulation, Approval, Implementation and Operation of a National Policy on Information*. Paris: UNESCO, 1990.

Multnomah County Library. "Starbucks to Enrich Summer Youth Programming at the Library." News Release. Portland, Ore., 13 March 2003. www.multcolib.org/news/2003/sbsummer.html (accessed 10 July 2005).

———. "Library and Starbucks Brew Up Partnership." *Entrepreneurial Libraries: Bright Ideas for Today's Librarians*. Portland, Ore.: Multnomah County Library, 1998. www.multcolib.org/products/entre/espresso.html (accessed 10 July 2005).

Murphy, Cynthia. "Research on Library Patron Privacy Policies with Regard to the USA PATRIOT ACT: An Annotated Bibliography." *Library Patron Privacy and the*

USA Patriot Act (website). n.d. http://xauen.nudio.net/patriot/main.html (accessed 6 July 2005).

Murphy, Shawn. "Campaign for Release of Historic Census Records Finally Over." News Release, 29 June 2005. www.shawnmurphymp.ca/news/142 (accessed 4 July 2005).

Museum Stores Association. "Museum Retailers to Get Profit-Enhancing Ideas in Portland, OR, April 17–20, 2004." Denver, Colo.: MSA, 4 November 2003. www.museumdistrict.com/events/PR_11-4-03MRCE.cfm (accessed 10 July 2005).

Nardi, Bonnie A. "The *Genius Loci* of the Library." PowerPoint presentation, 2003. www.simmons.edu/gslis/alumni/Nardi_2003_Presentation.ppt (accessed 10 July 2005).

National Council for Public–Private Partnerships. *How Partnerships Work*. Washington: NCPPP, n.d. www.ncppp.org/howpart/index.html (accessed 10 July 2005).

New York Public Library. *The Library Shop*. New York: NYPL, 2004. www.thelibraryshop.org (accessed 10 July 2005).

———. *NYPL Express: The Express Link to a World of Information*. New York: NYPL, n.d. www.nypl.org/express/index.html (accessed 9 July 2005).

———. *Teen Link*. http://teenlink.nypl.org/HomeworkHelp.cfm (accessed 9 July 2005).

Newman, Wendy. Wendy Newman to Paul Robertson, 23 October 2001. Canadian Library Association Library Issues (website). www.cla.ca/issues/robertson.htm (accessed 9 July 2004).

Nilsen, Kirsti. "Canadian Government Electronic Information Policy." *Government Information Quarterly* 10, no. 2 (1993): 201–218.

———. *The Impact of Information Policy: Measuring the Effects of the Commercialization of Canadian Government Statistics*. Westport, Conn.: Ablex/Greenwood Publishing Group, 2001.

———. "Information Policy and Global Trade Policy as Forces for Change in Public Educational Institutions and Research Libraries." In *Global Issues in 21st Century Research Librarianship: NORDINFO Publication 48*, edited by Sigrun Klara Hannesdottir, 17–35. Helsinki: NORDINFO, 2002.

North American Free Trade Agreement, 1992. *Legal Texts*. Ottawa, Mexico City, and Washington: NAFTA Secretariat, 1992. www.nafta-sec-alena.org/DefaultSite/index_e.aspx?DetailID=78 (accessed 9 July 2005).

"Northern Ireland Launch £500m PPP Programme." *Industry News*. Hampshire, U.K.: Serco Group PLC, 2004. www.serco.com/media/industrynews/ItemPage.asp?ItemID=2664435 (accessed 12 July 2005).

Oder, Norman. "LSSI in NJ: One Contract Ends, Efforts Continue." *Library Journal* 129, no. 7 (15 April 2004): 16–17. http://print.google.com/print/doc?articleid=mlTFUFdiBLG (accessed 20 July 2005).

———. "More on LSSI." *Library Journal* 129, no. 6 (1 October 2004) [only in online version]. www.libraryjournal.com/article/ca457652.html (accessed 10 July 2005).

———. "When LSSI Comes to Town." *Library Journal* 129, no. 6 (1 October 2004): 36–40. www.libraryjournal.com/article/CA456252 (accessed 10 July 2005).

Ohio State Library. *Homework Now*. (Columbus: State Library of Ohio, 2004). www.homeworknow.net (accessed 9 July 2005).

Ojala, Marydee. "PubScience Joins the Endangered Species List." *Information Today* 19, no. 9 (2002): 22–23. www.infotoday.com/newsbreaks/nb020819-2.htm (accessed 9 July 2005).

Online Computer Library Center. "Collection Management." *NetLibrary*. Dublin, Ohio: OCLC, 2004. www. oclc.org/services/collection/default.htm (accessed 9 July 2005).

———. *QuestionPoint: Cooperative Virtual Reference*. Dublin, Ohio: OCLC, 2004. www.oclc.org/questionpoint/default.htm (accessed 10 July 2005).

———. "Worldwide Education and Library Spending." *2003 Environmental Scan: A Report to the OCLC Membership*. (Dublin, Ohio OCLC, 2004). www.oclc.org/membership/escan/downloads/economic.pdf (accessed 10 July 2005).

Online Dictionary of Library and Information Science (ODLIS). Compiled by Joan M. Reitz. Westpqrt, Conn.: Libraries Unlimited, 2004. lu.com/odlis/odlis_o.cfm (accessed 9 July 2005).

Oppenheim, Charles. "The Value of Library and Information Services: And How to Beat the Economists at Their Own Game." *State Librarian* 34 (July 1986): 24–26.

Organisation for Economic Cooperation and Development. *Guidelines on the Protection of Privacy and Transborder Flows of Personal Data*. Paris: OECD, 1981.

Oxford Learning (website). London, Ont.: Oxford Learning Centres Inc. and Learning Centres of America, 2004. www.oxfodlearning.com (accessed 9 July 2005).

Perseus Digital Library (website). Medford, Mass.: Dept. of the Classics, Tufts University, nd. www.perseus.tufts.edu (accessed 9 July 2005).

Personal Information Protection and Electronic Documents Act, Statutes of Canada 2000. C. 5. Unofficial version available at http://laws.justice.gc.ca/en/p-8.6/text.html (accessed 6 July 2005).

Porat, Marc. *The Information Economy, Definition and Measurement*. Washington: U.S. Dept. of Commerce, 1977.

Post 1901 Census Project (website). Campbellville, Ont.: Global, Everything for the Family Historian, n.d.), http://globalgenealogy.com/Census, 2006. http://globalgenealogy.com/Census (accessed 14 March 2006).

Privatization.org. *Libraries*. Los Angeles: Reason Public Policy Institute, 2004. www.privatization.org/database/policyissues/libraries_local.html (accessed 10 July 2005).

Providence Public Library. "Knight Memorial Branch Gifts." Providence, R.I.: PPL, 2004. www.provlib.org/building/branches/kma/gifts.htm (accessed 10 July 2005).

Public Citizen. "NAFTA Chapter 11: Corporate Cases." *Global Trade Watch*. Washington: Public Citizen, n.d. www.citizen.org/trade/nafta/CH__11/ (accessed 9 July 2005).

Public Library Association. *Outsourcing: A Public Library Checklist*. Chicago: ALA, 2000. www.pla.org/outsourc.pdf (accessed 8 July 2005).

Public Library Catalog. New York: Wilson, 1968–.

Quality English, Ltd. (website). Abindon, U.K.: Quality English, Ltd., 2004. www.quality-english.com (accessed 9 July 2005).

Questia (website). Houston, Tex.: Questia Media America, Ltd., 2004. www.questia .com (accessed 9 July 2005).

Quezada, Shelley. "The Role of Libraries in Providing Services to Adults Learning English." *ERIC Digest*. ED334868. Washington, National Clearinghouse on Literacy Education, 1991. www.ericdigests.org/pre-9220/libraries.htm (accessed 9 July 2005).

The Random House Dictionary of the English Language. Unadbridged Edition. Edited by Jess Stein and Laurence Urdang. New York: Random House, 1966.

Reciprocal Trade Agreements Act of 1934. Public Law 73-316, *United States Code* 19, §§ 1001, 1201, 1351, 1354.

Reference and User Services Association. "Guidelines for Implementing and Maintaining Virtual Reference Services." *RUSA Guidelines*. Chicago: ALA, 2004. www.ala.org/ala/rusa/rusaprotools/referenceguide/virtrefguidelines.htm (accessed 10 July 2005).

Reidenberg, Joel. "Privacy Wrongs in Search of Remedies: Fordham School of Law, Pub-Law Research Paper No. 25." *Hastings Law Journal* 54 (2003). http://papers.ssrn.com/sol3/papers.cfm?abstract_id=434585 (accessed 10 July 2005).

Rice, Robin. "The USA Patriot Act and American Libraries." *Information for Social Change* no. 16 (2002/2003). http://libr.org/ISC/articles/16-Rice.html (accessed 10 July 2005).

Rikowski, Ruth. "The Corporate Takeover of Libraries." *Information for Social Change* 14 (Winter 2001–2002). www.libr.org/ISC/articles/14-Ruth_Rikowski.html (accessed 10 July 2005).

———. *Globalisation, Information and Libraries: The Implications of the World Trade Organisation's GATS and TRIPS Agreements*. Oxford: Chandos Publishing, 2005.

———. "Library Privatisation: Fact or Fiction?" *Information for Social Change* 17 (Summer 2003). www.libr.org/ISC/articles/17-Rikowski-2.html (12 July 2005).

Riverside County Library System (website). Riverside, Calif.: RCPL, 2004. www.riverside.lib.ca.us/default/index.html (24 Mar. 2005).

Roberts, Alasdair. "Less Government, More Secrecy: Reinvention and the Weakening of Freedom of Information Law." *Public Administration Review* 60, no. 4 (2000): 308–320.

Rowlands, Ian. "Understanding Information Policy: Concepts, Frameworks and Research Tools." *Journal of Information Science* 22, no. 1 (1996): 13–25.

Royal Borough of Kensington and Chelsea. "Books for Children." Press Release. London: RBKC, June 2002. www.rbkc.gov.uk/news/pressrelease/n020619c.asp (accessed 10 July 2005).

Sanger, Matthew. *Reckless Abandon: Canada, the GATS and the Future of Health Care*. Ottawa: Canadian Centre for Policy Alternatives, 2001. Executive Summary available online at www.policyalternatives.ca/documents/National_Office_Pubs/reckless_abandon_summary.pdf (accessed 8 July 2005).

Schiller, Herbert. *Information Inequality: The Deepening Social Crisis in America*. New York: Routledge, 1996.

Schuman, Patricia Glass. "The Selling of the Public Library." *Library Journal* 123, no. 13 (1998): 50–52.

Seattle Public Library. *Donors Honored by Named Spaces*. Seattle, Wash.: SPL, 2005, www.spl.org/default.asp?pageID=branch_central_naming&branchID=1 (accessed 10 July 2005).

——. *Fees for Printing, Photocopying, and Faxing.* Seattle: SPL, 2005. www.spl.org/default.asp?pageID=about_policies_printingfees (accessed 24 March 2005).

——. *Mission Statement.* Seattle: SPL, 2005. www.spl.org/default.asp?pageID=about_mission (accessed 10 July 2005).

Seattle Public Library (website). Seattle, Wash.: SPL, 2004. http://www.spl.org (accessed 9 July 2005).

Sheketoff, Emily, Rick Weingarten, and Miriam Nisbet. "Washington Office Responds to WTO Article." *American Libraries.* 32 , no. 11 (December 2001): 12.

Shrybman, Steven. *An Assessment of the Impact of the General Agreement on Trade in Services on Policy, Programs and Law Concerning Public Sector Libraries.* Ottawa: Canadian Library Association, 2001. www.cla.ca/resources/execsummary-gats.pdf (accessed 10 July 2005).

——. "Information, Commodification and the World Trade Organization." Paper presented at IFLA 2000 Conference, Jerusalem, 13–18 August 2000. www.ifla.org/IV/ifla66/papers/176-148e.htm (accessed 8 July 2005).

Sinclair, Scott. *GATS: How the WTO's New "Services" Negotiations Threaten Democracy.* Ottawa: Canadian Centre for Policy Alternatives, 2000.

Sinclair, Scott, and Jim Grieshaber-Otto. *Facing the Facts: A Guide to the GATS Debate.* Ottawa: Canadian Centre for Policy Alternatives, 2002, www.policyalternatives.ca/documents/National_Office_Pubs/facing_facts.pdf (accessed 8 July 2005)

Smith, Devlin. "Back to School: Computer U Franchise Teaches Seniors How to Travel on the World Wide Web." *Entrepreneur Magazine* 28, no. 6 (June 2000): 188G. www.entrepreneur.com/mag/article/0,1539,275124,00.htm (accessed 10 July 2005).

Smith, Ian. "Some Myths about Public Library Use." *Impact, the Journal of the Career Development Group* 2, no. 1 (January 1999): 8–11.

Software & Information Industry Association. *Ensuring a Diversity of Information Sources in the Digital Era.* Washington: SIIA, 2001. www.siia.net/govt/docs/pub/gip_brief_gip_01.pdf (9 July 2005).

Sparanese, Ann C. "Service to the Labor Community: A Public Library Perspective." *Library Trends* 51, no. 1 (Summer 2002): 24–35.

Special Libraries Association, *About Us—Advocacy.* Alexandria Va.: SLA, 2005. www.sla.org/content/SLA/advocacy (accessed 8 July 2005).

Starr, Paul. "The Meaning of Privatization." *Yale Law and Policy Review* 6 (1988): 6–41. www.princeton.edu/~starr/meaning.html (accessed 10 July 2005).

Statistics Canada. "Government Expenditures on Culture 2001/02." *The Daily.* Ottawa: Statistics Canada, 7 January 2004. www.statcan.ca/Daily/English/040107/d040107a.htm (accessed 10 July 2005).

——. "Internet Use Rates by Location of Access and Household Income." *Household Internet Use Survey* (Ottawa: Statistics Canada, 2003). www.statcan.ca/english/Pgdb/arts56e.htm (accessed 10 July 2005).

Swan, James. "Alternate Funding Sources: Grass Roots Fundraising." *Bottom Line* 3, no. 3 (1989): 31–32.

——. *Fundraising for the Small Public Library.* New York: Neal Schuman, 1990.

Swenarchuk, Michelle. *From Global to Local: GATS Impact on Canadian Municipalities.* Ottawa: Canadian Centre for Policy Alternatives, Canadian Environmental Law Association, 2002. www.policyalternatives.ca/documents/National_Office_Pubs/gats_municipalities.pdf) (accessed 8 July 2005).

Sylvan Learning Centers (website). Baltimore, Md.: Educate, Inc., 2004. www.educate.com/homepage.html (accessed 9 July 2005).

Thomas, Jeffrey S., and Michael A. Meyer. *The New Rules of Global Trade: A Guide to the World Trade Organization*. Scarborough, Ont.: Carswell, 1997.

Thorhauge, Jens. "Nordic Public Libraries: Denmark." In *Danish Library Policy: A Selection of Recent Articles and Papers*, edited by Vibeke Cranfield, 4–11. Copenhagen: Danish National Library Authority, 2002. www.ifla.org/VII/s8/annual/cr02-dk.pdf (accessed 9 July 2005).

Tulsa City-County Library. *Research Wizard*. Tulsa, Okla.: Tulsa City-County Library, 2001. www.researchwizard.org (accessed 9 July 2005).

Tupper, Allan G. and Bruce Doern. *Privatization, Public Policy and Public Corporations in Canada*. Halifax, N.S.: Institute for Research on Public Policy, 1988.

Tutor.com. *Live Homework Help*. New York: Tutor.com, 2004. www.tutor.com/products/lhwh.aspx (accessed 24 March 2005).

Tutor.com. *Librarians by Request*. New York: Tutor.com Inc., 2004. www.tutor.com/products/lbr.aspx (accessed 24 March 2005).

Tutor.com (website). New York: Tutor.com, 2004. www.tutor.com (accessed 9 July 2005).

UNESCO. Convention on the Protection and Promotion of the Diversity of Cultural Expressions. Paris: UNESCO, 2005. http://portal.unesco.org/culture/en/ev.php-URL_ID=11281&URL_DO=DO_TOPIC&URL_SECTION=201.html (accessed 17 March 2006).

———. "General Conference Adopts Universal Declaration on Cultural Diversity." News Release No. 2001-120. Paris: UNESCO, 2001. www.unesco.org/bpi/eng/unescopress/2001/01-120e.shtml (accessed 10 July 2005).

———. "Questions and Answers." *Culture, Trade and Globalization* (Paris: UNESCO, n.d.) www.unesco.org/culture/industries/trade (accessed 10 July 2005).

UNESCO and IFLA. *Public Library Manifesto*. Paris: UNESCO, 1994. www.ifla.org/VII/s8/unesco/eng.htm (accessed 10 July 2005).

United Kingdom Audit Commission. "Rating." *Report: Library Service, Haringey London Borough Council*. London: Audit Commission, 2001. www.audit-commission.gov.uk/reports/BVIR.asp?CategoryID=ENGLISH^576^LOCAL-VIEW^AUTHORITIES^103717&ProdID=E22BDF13-071E-4D82-82A0-C5217ABC97BF (accessed 10 July 2005).

U.S. National Commission on Libraries and Information Science. "Highlights of the Year 2002." Washington: NCLIS, 2002. www.nclis.gov/about/highlights/bowker02.html (accessed 10 July 2005).

Van House, Nancy A. *Public Library User Fees: The Use and Finance of Public Libraries*. Westport, Conn.: Greenwood Press, 1983.

Verhoosel, Gaetan. *National Treatment and WTO Dispute Settlement: Adjudicating the Boundaries of Regulatory Autonomy*. Oxford: Hart Publishing, 2002.

Virtual Reference Desk. "Ask-A-Locator." Syracuse, N.Y.: Information Institute of Syracuse, n.d. www.vrd.org/locator (accessed 10 July 2005).

Wasch, Ken. Ken Wasch to Walter Finch, 13 September 2001. In Software & Information Industry Association (website). www.siia.net/sharedcontent/govt/issues/ip/09-13-01.html (accessed 7 May 2004; this document has been removed from website).

Watson, Angela. "Compete." In *Best Returns: Best Value Guidance for Library Authorities in England.* London: The Library Association, 2001. See chap. 5, "Best Value Reviews." www.la-hq.org.uk/directory/prof_issues/br5.html (accessed 10 July 2005).

Weimer, David L., and Aidan R. Vining. *Policy Analysis: Concept and Practice*. 2nd ed. Englewood Cliffs, N.J.: Prentice-Hall, 1991.

Weingand, Darlene E. *Customer Service Excellence*. Chicago: ALA, 1997.

West, Jessamyn. "Information for Sale: My Experience with Google Answers." *Searcher* 10, no. 9 (2002). www.infotoday.com/searcher/oct02/west.htm (accessed 10 July 2005).

Whitney, Paul. "Libraries Up for Grabs." *Now Magazine Online Edition* January 19–25, 2003. www.nowtoronto.com/issues/2003-06-19/news_story2_p.html (accessed 9 July 2005).

Wikipedia: The Free Encyclopedia (website). St. Petersburg, Fla.: Wikimedia Foundation, 2005. http://en.wikipedia.org (accessed 10 July 2005).

Wisconsin Dept. of Public Instruction. "Trustee Essential 24: Library Friends and Library Foundations." In *Trustee Essentials: A Handbook for Wisconsin Public Library Trustees*. Madison, Wis.: Dept. of Public Instruction, 2002. www.dpi.state.wi.us/dltcl/pld/te24.html (accessed 10 July 2005).

World eBook Library (website). Honolulu: World ebook Library Consortia, 2005. www.netlibrary.net (accessed 10 July 2005).

World Trade Organization. "Agreement Establishing the World Trade Organization." *Legal Texts.* Geneva: WTO, 1994. www.wto.org/english/docs_e/legal_e/04-wto.doc (accessed 9 July 2005).

———. Appellate Body. *Canada—Certain Measures Concerning Periodicals: Report of the Appellate Body.*, AB-1997-2, WT/DS31/AB/R, Adopted by Dispute Settlement Body, July 30 1997. Geneva: WTO, 1997. www.worldtradelaw.net/reports/wtoab/canada-periodicals(ab).pdf (accessed 10 July 2005).

———. Appellate Body. *European Community—Regime for the Importation, Distribution and Sale of Bananas: Report of the Appellate Body.* AB-1997-3. WT/DS27/AB/R, 9 September, 1997. Geneva: WTO, 1997. www.worldtradelaw.net/reports/wtoab/ec-bananas(ab).pdf (6 July 2005).

———. *Canada—Certain Measures Affecting the Automotive Industry: Report of the Panel.* WT/DS139/R, WT/DS142/R, 11 February 2000. Geneva: WTO, 2000. www.worldtradelaw.net/reports/wtopanels/canada-autos(panel).pdf (accessed 8 July 2005).

———. *Canada—Certain Measures Concerning Periodicals, Report of the Panel* WT/DS31/R, 14 March 1997. Geneva: WTO, 1997. www.worldtradelaw.net/reports/wtopanels/canada-periodicals(panel).pdf (accessed 10 July 2005).

———. *European Community—Regime for the Importation, Distribution and Sale of Bananas: Complaint by Mexico: Report of the Panel.* WT/DS27/R/MEX. Geneva: WTO, 1997. www.worldtradelaw.net/reports/wtopanels/ec-bananas(panel)(mex).pdf (accessed 8 July 2005).

———. *GATS—Fact and Fiction*. Geneva: WTO, 2001. www.wto.org/english/tratop_e/serv_e/gatsfacts1004_e.pdf (accessed 8 July 2005).

———. "The General Agreement on Tariffs and Trade (GATT 1947)." *Legal Texts*. Geneva: WTO, 1986. www.wto.org/english/docs_e/legal_e/gatt47_01_e.htm (accessed 8 July 2005).

———. "General Agreement on Trade in Services. Uruguay Round Agreements, Annex 1B of the World Trade Agreement." *Legal Texts*. Geneva: WTO, 1994. www.wto.org/english/docs_e/legal_e/26-gats.pdf (accessed 8 July 2005).

———. *Japan—Taxes on Alcoholic Beverages, Report of the Panel*. WT/DS8/R, WT/DS10/R, WT/DS11/R, 11 July 1996. Geneva: WTO, 1996. www.worldtradelaw.net/reports/wtopanelsfull/japan-alcohol(panel)(full).pdf (accessed 8 July 2005).

———. *Legal Texts*. Geneva: WTO, n.d. www.wto.org/english/docs_e/legal_e/legal_e.htm (accessed 9 July 2005).

———. *Services Sectoral Classification List*. MTN.GNS/W/120. 10 July 1991. Geneva: WTO, 1991. www.wto.org/english/tratop_e/serv_e/mtn_gns_w_120_e.doc (accessed 8 July 2005).

———. *Trading into the Future*. 2nd ed. Geneva: WTO, 2001. www.wto.org/english/res_e/doload_e/tif.pdf (accessed 8 July 2005).

———. *TRIPS: Agreement on Trade-Related Aspects of Intellectual Property Rights*. Part II –Standards Concerning the Availability, Scope and Use of Intellectual Property Rights. Geneva: WTO, n.d. www.wto.org/english/tratop_e/trips_e/t_agm3_e.htm#1 (accessed 10 July 2005).

———. *Understanding on Rules and Procedures Governing the Settlement of Disputes*, Annex 2 to the World Trade Organization Agreement. *Legal Texts*. Geneva: WTO, 1994. www.wto.org/english/docs_e/legal_e/28-dsu.pdf (accessed 8 July 2005).

———. "Intellectual Property: Protection and Enforcement." *Understanding the WTO—The Agreement*. Geneva: WTO, n.d. www.wto.org/english/thewto_e/whatis_e/tif_e/agrm7_e.htm (accessed 10 July 2005).

———. Council for Trade in Services, Environmental Services. Background Note by the Secretariat. S/C/W/46/ (6 July 1998, 98-2690). Geneva: WTO, 1998 www.wto.org/english/tratop_e/serv_e/w46.doc (accessed 8 July 2005).

———. Secretariat, Trade in Services Division. *An Introduction to the GATS*. Geneva: WTO, October 1999. www.wto.org/english/tratop_e/serv_e/gsintr_e.doc (accessed 8 July 2005).

Xerox Corporation. "Public Libraries Check Out Xerox Solution to Increase Patron Service, Decrease Costs." [Press Release] *Business Wire*. San Francisco: Business Wire, 25 Feb. 2004. www.businesswire.com/webbox/bw.022504/240565039.htm (accessed 9 July 2005).

Young, Stewart. "Whistleblowing in a Foreign Key: The Consistency of Ethics Regulation under Sarbanes-Oxley with the WTO GATS Provisions." *Denver Journal of International Law and Policy* 32, no. 1 (Winter 2003): 55–85.

Index

About the Authors

Samuel Trosow is an associate professor at The University of Western Ontario, holding a joint appointment with the Faculty of Law and the Faculty of Information & Media Studies (FIMS). In the law school he has taught courses in intellectual property, advanced copyright, information law, and legal theory. Professor Trosow was the recipient of the 2004 Dissertation Award in the field of Library and Information Science from the Association for Library and Information Science Education for his Ph.D. dissertation, entitled "Information for Society: Towards a Critical Theory of Intellectual Property Policy." He frequently speaks on topics related to copyright, privacy, and other information-policy issues.

Kirsti Nilsen retired in June 2004 from The Faculty of Information and Media Studies at the University of Western Ontario. Now an independent scholar, researcher, and teacher, she is currently researching and writing in two areas of interest: information policy and reference services. She is the author of *The Impact of Information Policy* (2001) and coauthor of *Conducting the Reference Interview* (2002). Since retiring, she has continued to teach as an adjunct professor both at The University of Western Ontario and at the Faculty of Information Studies, University of Toronto.